T0374159

THE ONE THAT GOT AWAY

BRIGITTE KNOWLES

THE ONE THAT GOT AWAY

iUniverse books may be ordered through booksellers or by contacting:

iUniverse
1663 Liberty Drive
Bloomington, IN 47403
www.iuniverse.com
1-800-Authors (1-800-288-4677)

Because of the dynamic nature of the Internet, any web addresses or links contained in this book may have changed since publication and may no longer be valid. The views expressed in this work are solely those of the author and do not necessarily reflect the views of the publisher, and the publisher hereby disclaims any responsibility for them.

Any people depicted in stock imagery provided by Thinkstock are models, and such images are being used for illustrative purposes only. Certain stock imagery © Thinkstock.

ISBN: 978-1-4917-3098-0 (sc)
ISBN: 978-1-4917-3099-7 (e)

Library of Congress Control Number: 2014906189

Printed in the United States of America.

iUniverse rev. date: 11/18/2014

This is a story of passion, love, and sexual adventure. It is the story of an intelligent, accomplished, and mature career woman who is torn out of her comfort zone and thrown into a culture of sex, crime, violence, danger, and terror in today's West Palm Beach Florida. When Brigitte falls for Johnny, a gigolo, con artist, felon, and fugitive with a history of attempted murder, identity theft and drug trafficking, her misplaced love puts her into a prison of pain and harm that almost destroys her will to survive.

Brigitte, though, decides to fight back to find justice and restitution for herself and the other victims of a notorious financial predator who hides behind his witness protection identity. Despite the trail of women left destitute by a man they believed and loved, the sheriff's office, the State Attorney General, and the FBI all deny there was any crime.

In their own covert operation, the devastated women work together to trace and document the heartbreaking events that made them sisters. When Brigitte refuses to accept law enforcement's dead-end, she works to find a way to end an era of theft, unlawful appropriation, and deceit.

The One That Got Away is based on a true story. The events described in the book are real. Names were changed. There is no bad intention in this book, just a hope that somewhere a woman will read this and get out of a dangerous relationship before it ruins her.

No one should go through this kind of dangerous life without consenting to the consequences and risks of loving a criminal protected by law enforcement. No one should be above the law. No one should be Untouchable.

ACKNOWLEDGEMENTS

Thank you to my therapist C.N., my daughter, my friends E.Z., S.Z., R.M., R.K., L.A., J.S., C.L., and co-workers, F.M., A.B., who understood the importance of writing this book. Thank you to the Legal Aid and domestic violence professionals in Palm Beach County who never stopped giving their time and knowledge to help me advance and recover from a serious trauma that remains under-recognized by law enforcement. Thank you to the judges who see through masks of deceit and who protect victims from danger. Thank you to the police department who came when I called. Most of all, I thank God for lifting me out of reach of the devil's grasp when I wanted to give up. Thank you to my doctor for prescribing Paxil when I needed it. Thank you to J.J. for showing me the way home. Thank you for reading this book and for sharing it with your daughters, cousins, sisters, mother, aunts, friends and neighbors. You can save a life by letting others know this kind of crime exists. Thank you to all of the people who helped me to get away. You know who you are.

INTRODUCTION

Falling in love is like crossing the street with your eyes closed. If you expect to get across alive, you're only fooling yourself. It is the riskiest sport. Rule number one: you never know all of anyone. Even that one person who professes true love, only love, forever love, together love… All love is deception of some sort and some degree. To let someone photograph from you only one side is an honest right to look your best. To outright disguise every ounce of truth about yourself, all the way down to the bottom of your heart, was Johnny's talent. Johnny, Ronny, James, well whichever one was real. Was he just the devil; bald, old, devious and desperate? Someone so elusive, even his shadow was on the wrong side of him on a sunny day. Little did I know the power he would have over me one day. The trauma set like a permanent tattoo on my mind. One day I would understand that only the full body orgasms were real. The rest of my life with Johnny had been a magnificent piece of fiction.

CHAPTER ONE:
IN THE BEGINNING

Southern Florida in January is heaven on earth. You would have to be pretty miserable not to enjoy the sun, the beach, the joy of youth all around you. Despite its reputation of having the worst drivers in the world, lavender colored hair heads that go there waiting to live happily ever after, I still found my bliss there. Every time I got off the plane in Fort Lauderdale I knew I belonged. Everything seemed perfect; nothing was missing. I would leave Quebec, exhausted and fed up with work, and return after a long weekend feeling re-energized, young, healthy and tanned. I was ready to face the challenges of working in the financial world after the economic Armageddon that the last few years had been for me. The change in atmosphere allowed me to retreat from the battle that I had engaged in back home. I had just found out thieves could win and that I could be right; dead right.

I had spent the last fifteen years working twelve hour days, six days a week, building a practice that was lucrative. It paid for fine jewelry, a beautiful home, the best of restaurants and night clubs, excellent private schools for my daughter and family snorkeling trips in Grand Cayman. I was looking for a condo at the Ritz Carlton one day, and then the next day, a company that my clients loaned monies to was missing over one hundred and eighty million dollars. The president of the company, Thomas Popoulos, his house and office as empty as a discarded bag of chips, had flown the coop. In a sweeping move, he destroyed all of his paper trails and maneuvered his way out of what would become a financial hell on earth. He and his family then disappeared without a trace.

I immediately insisted on exercising the five-day client takeover rights in my contract. A retention bonus check of thirty thousand dollars arrived that sealed the deal. It allowed me to continue the necessary paperwork and transition into a new company's arms. With a comfortable financial incentive that paid for bills, I started attending meeting after endless meeting with forensic accountants, liquidators, law enforcement, regulators and attorney after attorney. I had seen enough to know that no one cared. I watched as they chased the wrong man and spent millions trying to prove that my boss, my significant other, was guilty when Paul was the victim here. Two computer experts that knew that Paul's only Blackberry was his old brown leather wallet with phone numbers written all over it in old fading ink had ripped him off. Someone had paid a lot of people a lot of money to look the wrong way.

I decided to do things my way. I realized that even though I couldn't find the thieves who stole millions from my clients, I could follow the money. I held hope that as the money traveled around the world, transferred from account to account, I would find a mistake somewhere; it was in my nature... I had learned a long time ago that nothing was perfect so a crime couldn't be either.

Mike Light and his partner Thomas Popoulos had been inseparable for years. I knew how these two men thought. I knew their wishes, their dreams, their fears, and their fancies. I worked in an office next to theirs for fifteen years. I heard them talking to each other, thinking out loud, and I probably knew more about their financial habits than the women whose ears they snored into every night. I had absorbed so much over the last decade that I had become somewhat of an expert myself, but I was honest. I had never looked under the bed because I had never hidden there, so when the shit hit the fan, and the money was gone, their timing was perfect, their crime meticulous.

It was August 2007. Financial crime was everywhere. The world economy was beginning to enter an era in which the banking system nearly collapsed because of worthless paper that had snuck into nearly every investor's portfolio. North America's economy was in serious rehab. The first signs of a bursting real estate bubble and accompanying stock market near crash were occupying the front page in everyone's lives.

I worked in a male dominated industry full of handsome men of all ages. Men in expensive suits with impeccable credentials surrounded me. I never thought any of them would ever become criminals. MBA's with initials on their cuffs would present new opportunities over lunch at the Ritz Carleton. We met with the Chinese, the Swiss, the South Americans, and I always had an instinct that helped me avoid investing my client's monies in the wrong fund. I once asked the president of a fund company why I should invest in China when their one child policy had left so many men alone; without wives to care for their parents, cook and clean, or give them their one child. I told him that I had no confidence in their social structure and that in order to sustain current productivity levels and reliable profits, a strong family structure was necessary. Like many experts and economists, I never saw the North American economic collapse coming.

You didn't have to be a genius to steal a fortune, and many not so brilliant financial gurus stole billions from less brilliant clients and got away with it. High-powered executives, bankers, mortgage professionals and financial brokers got stay-out-of-jail-free cards and safely spent their loot without consequence. Only the worker ants suffered with penalties in which they lost their jobs, lost their licenses, and in some cases lost their careers. Financial professionals' greed gave them a bad name and I had to work extra hard to convince people to stay with me, invested in the markets, long after the investment climate turned sour. I had watched how the authorities caught monsters like Bernie Madoff, Vincent Lacroix and Earl Jones, and I fully expected to see two more names in the news added to the list of thieves already caught. Only I was wrong, and it looked like Mike and Thomas were getting away with their crime. I spent the better of the next year conducting a secret investigation into the tangled web of business relationships they had spun.

With the guidance of the best lawyer in Montreal, I successfully obtained enforceable, respectable, solid court judgments with compounding interest at five percent, good for ten years in favor of my clients against the two men I was hunting. I was searching for anything I could seize; whether it be their Bentley, wine collection, yacht, bank accounts, or jets from their private landing strips. I was tracking like I did to find a partridge in the bush with my 410. I searched for sounds, sights, smells, anything that would reveal their hiding places. Although they represented scum from the bottom of the cesspool of earth, I had to follow the rule of law. I had to trust that law enforcement would be on my side... only the longer it took to find them, the longer it took to charge them with a crime... Victims' and witnesses' memories eroded and it became harder for me to trust that regulators and financial authorities knew what they were doing. These men were high tech fraudsters who were accused of money laundering, drug dealing, and arms trafficking. They were fluent in the language of modern day organized computer crime.

In mid-February of 2009, a herd of armed uniformed policemen and idiot provincially employed financial regulators descended on my home in the middle of the dark morning while I was still asleep. It was not only a surprise, it was a clear message. They knew fuck all about who took the money if they were looking for it in my home.

I had just turned fifty-four. I had been celibate for five years, my estrogen was running low and I was lucky I didn't have a gun because it would not have been a pretty sight. I was one of the good guys so all I could think of was how much money they were wasting looking for evidence in my residence when I was the one who collaborated with them from the start.

As one uniformed officer pulled his gun and put his other hand on the doorknob of my twenty-three-year-old daughter's bedroom, I stood still. I stopped breathing and promised myself that if I stayed still long enough, this would be over and I would survive. My mind raced through the details of the scene in front of me as urgently as a flight attendant rehearsing her crash rules.

"Please God don't let Pamela wake up with her black cell phone in her hand. Please don't let her move the wrong way, don't let that cop think she has a weapon in her hand. Please dear God, I'll do anything... just don't let anything go wrong." In one second, I rehearsed what I would do if we survived this, and we did survive.

Pamela did scream in her not so debutante manner, clutching her bed sheets to her young naked body. "What the fuck, who the fucking hell?!? Don't fucking shoot me you stupid motherfucker!!!"

The apple doesn't fall far from the tree because I wanted to say the same thing.

"What are you doing? That is my daughter's bedroom!" I screamed out loud as I watched the door being opened. The cop glanced quickly at me and said: "We don't know who is in there and whether or not they have a gun."

"Well, you didn't do your research because there are no weapons here."

Perhaps they had done their research in part because I did once own a Browning semi-automatic pistol that I had left with Pamela's father, my ex-husband Harry, after he bought it for me when I was seven months pregnant. I had to be able to protect myself because he had made many enemies by working in law enforcement. My mind flashed back to Harry, standing oh so still behind me, folding me in his arms as he showed me how to point and squeeze the trigger. He helped me aim and stay steady as I looked at the target that was in front of me, legs apart, mind focused, aiming to kill and not get myself killed.

"Shoot them in the head first then shoot the ceiling. Tell the cops that you fired a warning shot first and they didn't stop."

He had me training at the rifle range, practicing bull's eye art for hours and I was good, very, very good.

When my daughter Pamela was born nine months after Harry and I first met, eight months after we married, conceived on our first night together, my instincts changed about guns and their place in my home. When Pamela was just a baby, I decided that a child and a gun was a recipe for disaster. I left it with Harry and his girlfriend Lynn with whom he had a secret affair while we were together. Well, it was secret only to me since everyone else knew about it.

I had moved to Sault Ste. Marie, just to be close to his family and his work while I was pregnant, and I soon found out that I did not fit in his life, in his family, or in that town where girls wore ski jackets with everything including formal gowns. When I filed for divorce, Lynn was the one who brought me to my gynecologist and my attorney and then to the Airport, and I left her with instructions.

"He likes his underwear and undershirts ironed and folded like this." I watched her curious seventeen-year-old face as she stated that there was no way she would be doing any of that. I had made lunches for him every day as he claimed to have gone to the airport to pick up this union boss or some cop. In reality, he was spending hours with Lynn every morning in a motel bed telling her that after I had our baby he would leave me, and I would shoot myself with a pistol in a suicidal gesture of grandeur because he would take the baby with him. Lynn did not want a baby at seventeen, big surprise. She cried when she stood with me at the airport as I boarded the plane. I left Harry and all of his troubles and decided that life in the world of the criminal element was not for me.

I seemed unable to avoid it because here I was, years later, in the middle of a major criminal investigation courting attention in a way I could never have imagined. How did I go from being a beautiful young deputy mayor of a major city, having solved public security cases, sent criminals to jail for life, traveled the world with matching hats, gloves, shoes and purses, protected and strong, to being targeted here in my home? I watched as a police officer pointed a gun at the one person I loved more than life. Four hours later Pamela was allowed to take a taxi to her University to write a midterm in economics. As she opened our front door, she asked," Mom… is everything okay?"

I smiled and said, "Darling these men are trying to find a couple of hundred million dollars in the wrong place. Go write your exam and ace it." Pamela smiled and left. She did ace the exam, just as honor students do, even surrounded by chaos and bedlam. For the rest of the day, I sat in one chair in the living room watching the two armed policemen as they sat there bored.

"Do you have the Playboy channel on cable, madam?" They grinned as they looked around. "You have a beautiful daughter." They chuckled and I didn't bat an eyelash. I looked at them and said no, as they stared at the beautiful framed photographs of my daughter in her debutante ceremony and the professional modeling shots of her with her perfect smile and glowing eyes. The photographs of her accepting her gold medals in gymnastics rivaled with those of her in economics class with her classmates standing in front of a chalk board full of complicated equations. Pamela was beautiful, brilliant and classy. A product of breeding and hard work; keeping her busy with activities that helped her excel in life. These two simple minded policemen were out of their league. I watched them as they expressed their ignorant thoughts out loud to each other. They watched me as I used the bathroom with the door open after getting their permission to do what most human beings do in private. I promised myself that day that I would get revenge against the men who brought this horrific energy into my life. I was surrounded by people who were violating my privacy and degrading me all in the name of justice.

My nautical dreams of driving my Maybach to the marina to sail the Mediterranean Riviera in my teak-detailed, silk-carpeted bedrooms with custom 800 thread count linen, crystal and prestige china with the initials BK, polished brassware and glass sliding doors, were now sitting indefinitely in dry dock. I lost all of my motivation to work in the financial industry and wanted nothing more to do with money or banking. I needed some serious R&R; tons of rest and relaxation. I decided then and there to go to Florida to find my bliss, the bliss that I had lost so long ago.

CHAPTER TWO:
FROM THE START

I was born in Manhattan, New York, to a Canadian mother. Alena was a strikingly beautiful, budding actress living in Spanish Harlem in the early fifties. She also had made several demo records singing jazz favorites, and her singing voice would calm many on hot sweltering summer nights. She wanted nothing more than to become a famous singer. My mother's fate changed after a torrid love affair with my father; a handsome, six-foot-tall Hungarian Austrian man whom she loved till her dying day. Raised with Sam Cook's honey-soaked voice playing on the radio, crooning me to sleep at Mama Dale's house on St. Nicholas Place, I was safe and sound while my single mom worked in a Manhattan restaurant. My mother told me many stories about how much my father who died in a car accident loved me when, in fact, he never married her. He married a woman his family insisted he marry, a

good Hungarian lady with a heavy pocketbook and…
he was very much alive.

It wasn't long before my mom left the United States
with a different name, a name that had no affiliation
with her real identity. My name as well was pure fiction
and my entry into Canada was facilitated by my aunt
who told the train conductor that ours was a sad story,
one that was better forgotten. My arrival was never
documented and that omission led me into a struggle
that no young girl should be forced to live through.
It later took me thousands of dollars, a good lawyer
and a decent immigration judge to prove I was Alena's
daughter, entitled to live in Canada after her death
when I was twelve. The attestation of affiliation from
my grandmother saved me from being deported at
seventeen. To this day I know little details about my
mother's reason for leaving the United States, only that
my entire family refused to discuss my father in any
detail whatsoever.

My grandmother raised me with strict values and
no nonsense. Every morning I would walk alone to
school with my sardine sandwich on rye in a brown
paper bag and cats would try to befriend me all the
way. I would sit alone at the lunch table reserved for
sardine sandwich eaters, while the peanut butter and
jam table overflowed, and the Kraft sliced cheese on
white bread with butter table was half full. The Italian
sandwich table where olive oil and grilled pepper juice
dripped by the gallons from sliced white bread was
directly in front of me, and I watched as kids argued

about trading desserts. It didn't help my popularity that I wore hand sewed under slips made from 20 pound Five Roses Flour bags. They were crocheted around the edges but still felt like sandpaper against my young budding body.

I was a sad, lonely kid. Although I was an all A-student, I managed to get in trouble even at that early age. Carole, a pretty blonde blue eyed French girl at school, convinced me to steal licorice from the corner store after our lunch hour one day and I got caught while she ran away. I walked to the school yard with my head hung in shame and wondered what would happen to me. Would I be thrown out of school? Would the principal find out? I was so isolated, an immigrant girl with long dresses and old shoes that everyone laughed at. I looked sixteen at ten, with no fashion sense and no money to buy any.

One day I made a new friend Arlene and she joined me on my walk to and from school. We talked and laughed and were safe together. Arlene was a tall, strong black girl and I was skinny and anemic and couldn't fight my way out of a paper bag. Something about her was different. She was very protective of me and I enjoyed her power and confidence in herself. That friendship lasted until my grandfather refused to let her come into our house to play with me one day after school because he was a racist. I understood how hurt she was and that ended our friendship. Soon everyone at school talked about me and I started to walk alone again. I lived in fear of the girls who went to the French Catholic School, Ecole St. Marie des Petits Enfants Mechants. They would try to beat me up and steal my lunch every day. They laughed at my hand-me-down clothes and babushka scarf that my grandmother forced me to wear to protect my ears from infection by the wind. On most days I would run home from school and only feel safe once I was in the house with the door closed. I would throw off my coat and run to the pantry and lift up a cloth towel off the plate to see what my grandmother had baked for me that day. One day there were donuts, another day apple pie, and on another day raisin bread. She loved me so much that I began to believe that my life had not changed for the worst, when in reality, I had been deprived of a normal childhood. Everyone in my family had known that my grandfather was a pedophile, and I was the orphan that supplied his need to fondle young girls.

My mom had tried her best to raise me well but when she was diagnosed at the age of twenty-four with multiple sclerosis, our lives changed forever. She entered a nursing home within two years and suffered as her muscles deteriorated and she lost all control of her bodily functions. For years I visited her once a week, following her from nursing home to convalescent home until they wouldn't allow me to see her anymore. I did not see her for the last five weeks of her life, and one day I came home from school and was told by my grandmother that my mother had died.

She was only thirty-four and missed out on the best years of her life. Just like that, my world fell apart.

I only had my grandparents left and my life seemed hopeless. I stood in front of the mirror in my bedroom and stared at the pitiful girl who looked back at me. I told her that I would never allow myself to love anyone this much and feel this depth of pain again in my life… never again.

I sat in the dark in my bedroom with my ear to the door and listened to the family talk about my mother at her wake. They said things that were confusing. They warned my grandmother that I would grow up and become just like my mother if my grandmother wasn't careful.

"That marijuana, that's what killed her. Walking to and from work in the winter with no socks or stockings and no hat, letting her hair blow in the wind, that's why she died so young, leaving a child all alone for others to raise. God help her daughter Brigitte, she has a wild streak just like her mother. Watch her carefully…" Every aunt and uncle had their turn to put down my mother in their own way, each feeling smugger than the other.

I ran out of my room into the living room and stood there in my baggy flannel pajamas and shouted with tears dripping like rain down my face.

"I hope I grow up just like my mother. You are horrible to talk about my mother like that when she has only been dead a couple of days. I hate all of you. I hope I grow up like my mother, she was kind and loving, not like you assholes." I ran back into my room, lay on my bed staring at the ceiling, wiping my runny nose with my pajama sleeve and promised myself that one day I would leave and never speak to any of my family again.

They continued to talk into the night. There were the stories about her involvement with Frank Sinatra, who frequented the restaurant where she worked. They told a story about how he would pat my head when I sat in my high chair. They said that Frank was a kind and caring man who took a liking to me and they always thought that his blessing had brought me luck. Bad luck; no doubt, but no one counted on my resilience which grew with every painful memory of my loss. That night I packed a bag with some clothes and put my framed picture of my mom in it and vowed to leave the next day to go to New York to look for my father. I fell asleep and slept in the next day and never left town to find my dad. I never thought about him ever again.

I started to wallpaper my room with pages from Life magazine, Time, Vogue. I saved pictures of beautiful women in beautiful dresses who carried expensive purses, wore impossibly high heels. They were married to rich handsome men who smoked cigars while they sat on their comfortable sofas in their luxurious homes on beautiful streets lined with other homes, each with fabulous cars parked outside. I began to focus on my future and dreamed of success, ignoring the sad facts of my life.

Years later as a young adult woman, I had one meaningful date with Leonard Cohen; the famous singer and poet. He asked me to tell him my life story. I did. He focused on my mother and how she must have suffered so much since she couldn't watch over me and how she must have worried so much about my happiness. His words gave me a totally new perspective on life. I realized I was the lucky one, and she, she had been the truly tragic figure. So I assumed a different point of view; one that changed my life.

In my late twenties I used my hair and makeup budget to undergo psychoanalysis for two years to learn more about myself. I discovered that I was a pawn in a dysfunctional family in which all of the girls had suffered abuse and repressed it. I hardly ever had any contact with my family again.

Our family secret was valuable as gold because no one addressed the issue. I lived in a constant state of imposed denial. No one accepted the responsibility of leaving me in that home and I felt that no one cared what happened to me or what I did. My adolescence was spent rebelling for a childhood spent crying for help to deaf ears.

I had one good memory about my young years. I spent early summers in the Catskills with my Uncle Stash and Aunt Connie who had grown up in West Virginia and had a beautiful voice and pickled everything that fit in a jar. I met so many family members there who taught me the difference between my life in Canada, where everything was conservative and British, and their lives in a country that was active on a global scale; fighting for democracy and freedom for all. There I learned to be a strong American girl. I used to come back to Canada with an American accent

and an associated attitude of "I can do it". It served
me well. I received my first fishing rod that I fished
with every day, sitting on the edge of the river bank. I
remembered the day that I caught my first catfish and
cried when I was told to throw it back. I was thin and
lanky and my aunt Connie would insist I eat twice what
I wanted to eat and one night I heard her tell my uncle,
"That girl is gonna eat us out of house and home." That
was the last time I visited them for the summer.

I spent the latter half of every summer with my
aunt Louisa and her husband Vladimir at their country
home in the Eastern Townships, Quebec. They had six
beautiful, tall, long blonde haired daughters that I grew
close to and played with every day. We would swim at
the beach and look for frogs in the river. There was
only an outhouse so going to the bathroom at night
was second choice after using a bucket that everyone
had to use. If you went out at night to use the outhouse,
it meant that you were possibly going to get kidnapped
by ghosts or bitten by a snake. My cousins and I would
tell ghost stories by the bonfire under the stars and
sing camp songs about wild horses and lost loves. The
summers away from my grandfather, away from the
city heat, gave me a reprieve from his sick mind.

Vladimir longed for a son and so I became the
substitute. He never touched me, and that was a relief.
Instead, he taught me to fish, tie my own flies, clean a
rifle and shoot down cans filled with rocks that held
them still on fences in the cow pastures where we often
had to run from the herds of crowding cows that tried

to stampede us. I had acquired an excellent aim. He taught me how to pick mushrooms, how to plant, weed, water and fertilize a garden.

I shared a bed with two of my six cousins, Pepper and Tye. We had played tickle back late into the night, and I slept in the middle. I slept soundly, dreaming that I was a puppy nestled with her brother and sister puppies when I felt a nudge in my back.

"Brigitta, Brigitta."

It was dark, in the early morning when Vladimir prodded me with his cane, telling me to wake up and come outside to the garden with him. He told me to lie down between the dew-kissed rows of beans, and as I did, he said, "Look up through the beans at the sky, look at the beautiful dew drops on the leaves, sitting waiting for the sun to show. Pick a bean and eat it, taste the sweetness."

I did as I was told. It was not the first time I ate raw beans, and they were sweet but at five a.m.? Then he made me pull out a carrot, and told me to eat it from the sweet root. It was so strong and had forged its way through the earth allowing the carrot to suck the moisture and minerals and vitamins out of the rich soil that he had cultivated for over twenty years.

"May I please wash the carrot in the rain barrel?" I asked.

"You are a real sissy aren't you, go ahead." Vladimir had no patience for girls.

I rinsed it, bit into the long skinny, pale tip and tasted something that was as he said, sweet and fresh, but not that great that I wanted to get up at five a.m. to taste.

"Go back to your bed, you are a sissy girl." He left the garden, and I went back to bed.

I awoke to the sounds of forks and spoons hitting dishes, the sounds of breakfast that I missed because I had slept late, my eyes opening at well past ten in the morning. I walked into the kitchen, and there was Vladimir sitting at the table, leaning on his cane, smiling at me. "There is a bowl of berries that I picked for you," he explained. "They are all for you, you do not have to share with anyone, and you don't give any to anyone, you eat it all by yourself."

I smiled that only child smile that showed how happy I was that he cared enough about me to go and pick the berries I loved so much. How hard it must have been for him as the World War II injuries that crippled him made it nearly impossible for him to bend over. While my cousins glared at me and squirmed in their chairs, I ate each berry right down to the last morsel, and I felt special.

Vladimir was a strong father figure to me, providing some sense of normalcy and even though he was rough on his daughters, he treated me with respect. Because I wanted to have his attention, I did learn to clean his rifle, to tie the right fly, and to fish for trout. When fishing in thunder and lightning, he would stare at me and look for fear. I would tremble when I saw the storm clouds creeping above me, but I would not cry or admit my fear. I needed the attention that he gave me.

One day he brought me up to open the cottage in the spring. He told me we would have to kill the mice that he left there in the fall. They had since had generations of baby mice that also had baby mice. By the spring, they fulfilled their purpose and had prevented rats from entering the cabin over the winter. Vladimir preferred mice to rats because they caused less damage to the wiring and insulation. He made me catch each mouse by the tail, swing them over the iron stove opening, hit their head on the edge of the stove's opening to stun them, and then throw them lifeless into the fire. I did what I was told. I felt that there was something wrong with killing the mice, but soon after I had killed half of them, I felt nothing… Nothing until that last mouse that I couldn't catch.

I asked Vladimir, "Uncle Vlad, could I keep this mouse in a cage as a pet? He is a smart mouse, so hard to catch. We should save him. I will take care of him."

"What do you want with a stupid mouse? You are a stupid girl." He sat there and smoked his cigarettes one after the other, silent, thinking.

I kept the mouse and called him Genius. I watched as he ran along the spinning wheel in the middle of the cage and he ran and ran and went nowhere. I was fascinated by his resolve and how he kept going. Even though he wound up tired, he got exercise and an adrenaline rush so he did it over and over and over. One day I would shiver at the significance of this moment in my life and the emotional coldness that my family taught me.

Years later in my deputy mayor office, I was shocked at the news that when Vladimir was a young 17 year old soldier, he had been on the wrong side of the battle; fighting against the West. He had not declared it at Immigration when he entered Canada and was deported at age seventy to Germany. He died shortly after, found face down in a bowl of hot soup. I failed to help his family defend him. I felt betrayed by a man who was my only true father figure. They thought that because I was a politician, I could fix this family shame. I had no power to do so as he had lied about his war activity, and that was grounds for deportation. I hadn't seen him for many years, and I missed this man that I loved deeply as a child. I felt an immense sorrow that he had been forced into a war when he was only a boy. So many lives had been wasted, so much pain and sorrow had devastated Europe.

However, I was haunted by thoughts of the victims of the war and their fate. I fought the images in my mind. I cared more about the horror, pain and despair suffered by the mothers and children and fathers and sons that had met their death in death camps. I could not reconcile my feelings for Vladimir as a child and my repulsion for him as an adult. I was sick to my stomach at the thought that this was the same man who had given me so much kindness and love. I had loved this uncle who had cared about me enough to allow me to add one more plate at an already full table. Eight mouths already sat and ate meals that were delicious and plentiful prepared by my Aunt Louisa who was one of the best cooks in the world. I became haunted by this memory. It was just another betrayal in a series of life changing betrayals that I had to live with. I swore never to forget how evil men at war could be and the thought of sending my children to war was nightmarish. I spent a long time praying for the souls of those that died because of war. It was a dark time.

My spirit and strength, built up as a child and that had helped me survive, took over. I had always been able to slip into another parallel reality; another reality in which I was going to continue no matter what the obstacle. I was going to be successful, drive a nice car, live in a nice house, marry a nice man, and have nice children, and be a nice lady who wore nice clothes, smelled pretty, and smiled all the time.

The only time I spoke of these matters again was with my campaign attorney years later when I ran for higher office in the provincial elections. I told my legal counsel that I had this involuntary connection to a horrible time in history, a time of war in which man and devil shared an evil that had terrorized mankind. He comforted me and told me that I could still run for office. That man is now a federal judge, a wise man whose advice allowed me to do the good in the world that I was meant to do.

CHAPTER THREE:
BACK TO MY ROOTS

D espite a turbulent adolescence, I managed to get a diploma in Health Sciences in College, then study at and graduate from an Ivy League University in Canada. I obtained my Bachelor of Science in Marine Biology. I paid my way through university with an income property that I inherited mortgage free. In college, I worked in the Children's Hospital Hematology department taking blood samples from newborn premature babies. I would spend time with each baby and soothe it until it fell back asleep. I watched as their tiny hands gripped mine, and my heart would sink when some nights they cried without making a sound. I decided that Medicine was not for me. I could not deal with pain and suffering and wanted nothing to do with surgery even though I had successfully delivered a daphnia during a routine saline experiment. My fellow students were amazed at my dexterity. I would have been a great surgeon, but my emotional failings prevented me from being able to operate and ignore my feelings, so I abandoned my dreams of being a top surgeon. Later, still in university, I worked in nightclubs where I studied my material under the bar counter while serving drinks. With the music roaring, smoke in my eyes and loud laughter in my ears, men flirting with me and all, I studied the massive extinction of giant North American Pleistocene mammals.

I was used to stressful change and was a typical child of alcoholics. I had bouts of hysteria and anxiety, mixed with occasional moments of serenity that masked the complicated mind that made me tick. There were memories of drunken fights, where my grandfather threw chairs at my grandmother while she made the sign of the cross at him. These popped into my mind here and there and I had respect for alcohol and the power it held in any moment of life.

When a client asked for a beer for his date at three a.m., I would make him buy champagne because I resented the cheap date he tried to impose on his girlfriend. I got a small tip, but introduced some class into the dirty, beer soaked bar at closing time. Once, I studied so hard all night before an exam, cramming to get an A, and found myself falling asleep at the exam, my face on the paper, snoring as the professor begged me to wake up. I got an F that day in Oceanography; for failed efforts, not for failure. I rewrote the exam and got an A.

Any medically diagnosed label just slid off me because I was in denial about suffering from any serious disorder… but my drinking and experimental drug taking spoke for itself. I was the ultimate achiever with the death instinct of a suicidal spider. I was a success story that had hidden chapters of my life from everyone. I had something to prove to myself, because inside, I felt that I was nothing. No one loved me and I would never amount to anything.

The facade that I created was strong and became my defense plan that fooled everyone but God. He knew the pain I had lived with and how badly I fought to survive the demons that haunted me. To me, it was inconceivable that I should allow the circumstances of my birth to determine my future. I hadn't chosen these circumstances. I was always climbing the ladder, walking up the waterfall of struggle that my life had become. Hard work, determination, and denial were coping mechanisms that helped me function. I appeared to most people as being a happy and healthy gal, which was not the case at all. I battled serious depression, suicidal ideation, constant insecurity and low self-esteem. I suffered from night terrors and would wake up in the night not knowing where I was.

I would also have repeated identical dreams of waking in a house where there were framed pictures of my family beside me, yet I did not know who they were. They were all strangers. I wandered throughout the home, yet I did not know whose house I was in. Then I would walk up to the front door and open it, and there were hundreds of identical houses; left, right, and front. I could not see a way out of the boring life I was living.

I would wake up unable to breathe, sweating, with my heart beating so fast and hard that I thought I would die. I would have nightmares that I was falling down out of the sky at great speed asleep until I hit the ground, or even worse, falling up into the endless darkness of the sky… I would dream that I was naked in a fetal position in a car and that everyone was looking at me through the panes of the windshield and windows… It was hard to get a good night's sleep and it only added to my inability to live a normal life. I was often tired and would fall asleep in class all of the time.

No matter how hard I tried, a tiny voice inside reminded me that my father had abandoned me. Therefore, I was a bastard. My bond with my mother had suffered over the years, leaving me with the independence that out shouted my co-dependent insides, hiding my weaknesses until someone took the time to get to know me. No wonder any romantic relationship with a man always resulted in heartache, unreciprocated love, and abandonment issues. I seemed to be able to walk into a room and pick the one creep who would hurt me and leave me wondering what I did wrong.

It wasn't long before I gave up on love and instead used sex as a weapon; seducing men and making them want my body so badly that they cried when I didn't give them my heart. It was a mutual tango of deceit and exploitation in which men pretended to love me to get sex, and I pretended to love sex to get love. Ugly images of my grandfather touching me made it impossible for me to perform sexually without acting. I had never had a real orgasm, but I had given men a multitude.

It was no wonder that later, at forty, I found myself functioning well throughout a fifteen-year relationship with Paul who was a willing co-dependent. He was a perfectionist who exploited me and abused me psychologically; withholding affection, emotions, and sex, in order to control me while he taught me everything I knew about the financial business. I gained a lifetime of knowledge, contacts, and experience. The success started to overwhelm me.

For years, I had maintained a good-girl bad-girl dance in my head that wound up exhausting me. I was beautiful, thin, popular, and I dated millionaires, politicians, movie producers, the best looking guy on the swim team, and the handsomest artist in my biology class. There was never a lonely moment where men were concerned. When I wanted to party, I would drink, smoke pot, and take the wrong kind of pill. I would play Russian roulette on the road; watching as cars approached me and thinking that if I just turned my steering wheel a little to the left, I would be dead in a head-on collision in ten seconds. Then, I would remember that someone who loved someone, someone's dad or mom or sister or brother, was driving the oncoming vehicle and even though I had no one, I respected other people's love. So I stopped and continued home, sobered by the thought of the danger I courted. I yearned to belong to someone. To have someone proud of me, to have someone who loved me so much that they couldn't live without me. My grandmother died when I was starting university and without her love I was devastated. I started a slow downward spiral into hell.

I spent summers during university working as a flight attendant flying to London, Paris, Miami and Los Angeles. In my short sexy uniform I always had my pockets stuffed with business cards from men whose advances I fluffed off. I was not interested in anything permanent or steady so I played hard to get. I liked pilots and adventurers; wild men who tolerated my impulsive, non-committal demeanor. Most of the time I saved my expense money and ate nothing… I stayed skinny and managed to buy the clothes and shoes that waited for me in designer boutiques. There were layovers spent on rue du Faubourg Saint-Honoré in Paris, Rodeo Drive in Beverly Hills, or Worth Avenue in Palm Beach. All the store windows with their glamorous mannequins mesmerized me…

I was the closest thing to a jet-setter in my group of friends. Everyone envied me, while I envied them for the loving families they belonged to. My best friends, Evelyn and Lynda kept me grounded enough to survive. Their casa became my casa anytime. One night, I woke up and turned the lights on in my new small campus apartment and dozens of cockroaches scattered everywhere. I cabbed to Lynda's house, was comforted with milk and cookies and slept like a baby. The next day the exterminator swept the apartment with his chemicals and the problem was solved. It was not that easy to solve my mental problems. I was often rescued from night terrors by spending nights at their homes. I made my own family and relied on people who really cared.

I remember my university graduation and how beautiful it was. After the lavish ceremony at Place des Arts, I waited for my aunts to find me to drink champagne together in the hall of the reception area. After what seemed like hours and five glasses of champagne, I stood there weaving left to right, right to left. I watched the other students' family members hugging and kissing them. I was dead drunk. Finally, Aunt Louise and Aunt Nelly appeared telling me that they were sorry; they had been delayed because there were so many people they knew and had not seen for years from the Lithuanian community. They had chatted with them there for hours while I hopelessly waited for their approval. I needed to feel that my studies had gotten me the A's that would certify that I was normal; loved.

I never ate the celebratory lunch they took me to… Instead, I found myself throwing up hugging a toilet in my white graduation gown, cuddling my pristine white cap to my heart as I cried because complete emptiness surrounded my feelings of success. My achievement was void of any real recognition and approval because I was alone. Born alone, I was going to live alone and die alone because nothing made me feel loveable. Every stressful moment was a test of my ability to suppress the pain and sorrow that followed me everywhere and waited for me around every corner of my life. The guilt was just waiting to jump on me and say: "Surprise! You are still a child born under a bad star, and you will never be anything but Alena's orphaned daughter."

For some reason, I had always yearned to return to the United States, the land of my birth. It was where I felt I belonged. As soon as I arrived on US soil, I felt at home; safe and protected by the strong men and women that fought for our culture of freedom, liberty, and hope. I thought and felt American. I loved the flag and the duty that surrounded the world in which my family lived. My cousins were in the military. My female cousins became pen pals with men in the military, and married them to live in trailer parks with the men they loved. They raised their kids, found jobs, worked hard to buy a home, and settle down like their fathers and mothers before them. We had an American flag everywhere. On our graves, our cottage balconies, overlooking the rivers we fished in, and our front porches that announced our devotion to the American symbol of democracy; one for which so many men in my family had fought. When I would see the American flag flying in the wind, strong and proud, I would get goose bumps just thinking about the souls that had gone before me in the fight to protect our ideals, our freedom, and our future.

CHAPTER FOUR:
OUT OF SYNC

January 2010: my life was in serious imbalance. Business and working all day with money were my outlets. I had reached the top of the ladder in my career and worked 15 hour days. I loved money and had out earned many of my colleagues. I was trying to learn to respect money and restore the book of business that I had inherited from Paul. He was completely inconsolable since his business had fallen apart. He became distant and cold, and wanted to be alone. I decided to go where I could be near the ocean. I was going home to the USA. It was the perfect opportunity for me to escape who I was; the stress, a career that was getting far too demanding, too dangerous, and too draining… My mind was made up. I was no longer interested in long days and empty nights. I was done with the bullshit world of finance and needed a well deserved respite from the reality of corruption in my industry.

The plane ride was uneventful. I slept like a baby, and when we landed, I knew I was home; back in the USA, the land of the free and the brave, the land I loved. I had been visiting Florida for years and staying on Ocean Avenue in Delray Beach at a dreamy double-town house right on the beach with a view of the dunes, the rising sun, and playing turtles. It was a sanctuary which was perfect for me as it was entirely decorated in marine décor; from mermaids, to shells, to giant beds that appeared to come from a pirate ship. The house belonged to Cameron, the best friend of my long time significant other.

I remembered the day I met Cameron and the beginning of a long infatuation with him; one that would never become consummated. On New Years' Eve 1999, Paul brought me to a gathering of Cameron's friends and work associates. Cameron was a wealthy publisher and he seemed to have the perfect life.

"Oh, Brigitte, this is my friend Cameron. Cameron, this is Brigitte."

He turned around to say hello… it was as though a thunderclap hit my heart. He was lean and tall and had a full head of brown, curly hair that he obviously battled to flatten down. I still see those bounds of soft hair around his smiling face. His surprised look let me know that he sensed it too; my overwhelming feeling that this would be a turning point in my life. I shook his hand. We smiled at each other and electrical impulses flowed through me. It was love at first sight; the very cliché moment that we wait for all of our lives.

"Sit down next to Cameron," Paul said.

I stepped back, "No, I can't."

I couldn't because I feared that everyone would see that my heart was about to leave my body in free fall. I turned and tried to walk away, but Kate, Cameron's wife, approached me and smiled a warm, sincere look that made me feel like a thief of hearts. How could I be in this position so quickly? What was it about this man that made me feel as though I had to find a place to hide my pounding heart? I walked towards the other room and Paul caught my arm.

"Where are you going so fast?" Paul looked at me with his deep green eyes and made me feel safe because I loved him, he was my best friend. After ten years together I knew this man from head to toe, but Cameron, I couldn't look him in the eyes and he surely knew that something was odd... Suddenly Paul pushed me onto the couch next to Cameron and our bodies touched. I felt powerless and very nervous. I had avoided him all evening, feeling like a fool. I had never felt so vulnerable in my life. I wanted to run in the opposite direction and save my heart from the pain of being so close to someone I couldn't possibly want and who could not possibly want me.

We were staying at Cameron's beach house. Later that night, I lay awake in my bed, hating myself for not having the courage to follow my heart and let things fall where they might. All of my life, I had the looks that brought many men to their knees... yet at this moment I felt differently. I couldn't use my looks to seduce this man. He was different; a good person. Something about him commanded my total respect. It was the beginning of what would become a devastating unrequited love.

Paul and I visited Florida often and we enjoyed the company of Cameron and Kate. Cameron walked with me on one perfect day in the warm surf, blessing me with his sunny smile, and we played like pups in the water. He turned to me and then told me to open my hands. He put a dozen beautiful shells in them. He told me he had just picked them for me and I almost wept. The moment was perfect; just a rare moment of bliss and joy that I would remember forever. We looked into each other's eyes and laughed like children. I felt a rare moment of childlike innocence.

The joy of life on a sunny beach wouldn't last long. Soon, Kate was diagnosed with breast cancer. She was undergoing treatment, losing her hair, and feeling sad. She was the woman who had everything and it could all be taken away. Two beautiful daughters and a husband that loved her dearly, all of it up for grabs by the thief called cancer. How did this happen to someone who ate only healthy foods, did not smoke or drink, and had a daily health regime that surely would guarantee a long life? Like many other women who never took risks, this was unfair and unjust for Kate. I watched as she deteriorated and as Cameron lost his glow.

At one point, it looked as though she would lose the battle. I felt so sad for Cameron whose face began to show his sorrow. His smile changed into a grin that betrayed his secret pain. It betrayed the closeness of death and the certainty that he couldn't do more than hope that the best treatment and medication would bring back his smiling wife. I too was angry with the gods for bringing such sorrow to the heart I loved so secretly. Surely this too would pass. I had already suffered the loss of the woman closest to me from breast cancer that had been treated with the wrong chemo drugs. Now I could lose the woman that I wished I was. It made no sense.

Kate slowly recovered from the breast cancer and reappeared thinner, with curlier hair, but beamed a smile that said, "I am happy to be alive, and I always will be because this life is good and will only get better." And it did. Her daughter married in a ceremony that stood out as the most memorable I had ever attended; full of beautiful people and the happiness was contagious. Cameron, who had it all, had more of it.

Life was nearly perfect for him. There were the usual business problems that any successful man had to live to win. The failing economy affected his wealth, but he was still a soft-spoken, good natured man with a sly sense of humor. Books sold less and less, and the publishing business was heading the way of the virtual book, but he was still ahead.

He had bred horses and owned several winning champions, so he was excited with a new horse farm that kept him busy. Kate had a bigger mansion than that which she had in Palm Beach. She began decorating ten rooms with ten different country themes; one Tuscan, one Lauren, one Ashley. She was very busy with her family life. I had never decorated anything but a Christmas tree and I so admired her taste and her ability to create homes full of harmony.

On one occasion, we flew in Cameron's private jet to a race in Saratoga where one of his horses was making his first appearance. When Cameron's horse lost by an inch, he rested his head on my shoulder and pretended to cry. I just laughed and told him everything would be okay. It wasn't, not for me, because I held myself back, denied wanting to hold him in my arms, and make him feel better.

Earlier that weekend, while I visited the Saratoga stables, I helped move Cameron's favorite horse away from the lock on the inside of the fence that he tried to open with his lips. I raised my head, and it bumped right into the hard bridge of the horse's nose. One of my expensive front capped teeth broke off, leaving a tiny stump. I looked like an idiot for the rest of the weekend. I decided to go with the flow and make everyone laugh and used the moment as a source of joy. Inside I was devastated because it would be two days before I could get the tooth repaired. Paul and I were just on our way to Grand Cayman to buy a condo on the beach at the Ritz. I couldn't believe this happened to me. I thought I looked ridiculous but I couldn't do anything about it, so I grinned at everyone in the jet ride back to Delray showing my missing tooth and I laughed as though nothing had happened. Luckily, Kate's dentist worked on weekends and took me in to make a new cap for my tooth and I came out with the best smile I ever had.

That was the week in August, 2004, before hurricane Ivan destroyed Grand Cayman and destroyed the lucrative referral business our clients had loaned money to for over twenty years; offshore, off book... Seven Mile Beach took quite a hit and the Forum employees wanted out because they had nearly lost their lives in the flood. In Grand Cayman, the waters flowed from the East to the West and the West to the East, separating the North from the South of the island. We feared our clients would lose everything but they didn't. There was only one check lost according to Sara and Bill and we had left the island just in time because all tourists were forced to leave. We thought we were lucky that we hadn't lost anything.

Paul and I flew to Fort Lauderdale and stayed at the Trump Tower. Nothing was normal on the outside. There was chaos everywhere. Trees fell into the swimming pool and sand filled it nearly to the top of the steps leading out of it. Time stood still as we watched the reports coming in on the degree of damage that resulted in governments declaring a state of emergency and asking for Federal help.

In Grand Cayman, there were reports of devastation. Trees looked like they were growing out of the swimming pools where they landed and boats, sailboats, even yachts found new homes out of the water in the oddest positions. Some landed on houses and others had houses land on them. Nothing appeared normal.

Pictures from Grand Cayman showed total losses, and it was months before supplies would start to come in. The Grand Cayman culture of privacy did not allow for anyone from the US or anybody who appeared to have any interest in tax matters to set foot on the island. They refused any help from the countries who sent ships to sit offshore. When we finally sent containers with computers and business supplies to our friends, they sat on the dock for weeks and finally were stolen, so we had to start all over and send more; this time with security.

We returned to Georgetown two months later to follow up on the progress with the Forum company offices and verify if all of our help had reached them. We found Seven Mile Beach had been ravished by salt water delivered by the devil's wrath. Communications had been difficult but we never expected the damage and loss we found. So much had been destroyed. So much tragedy brought out the kindness of strangers and everyone shared whatever they could with neighbors and visitors.

I was told that bodies had been found floating in Grand Cayman near Seven Mile Beach. The graves in Cayman were in traditional sand cemeteries created at the surface of the sandy beach areas. When the slabs were washed away by the rough hurricane waves of heavy ocean water, many grave markers and coffins had been damaged by the waves. The bodies that floated were not from anyone who died in the hurricane. They were the bodies of deceased people that had been interred a long time ago that were released from their peace by the force of the storm. There was a terrible fear that there would be disease spreading. There were no known deaths directly attributed to the storm.

During reconstruction, there had been no choice but to create a dump on the center of the island. Officials hid the horrors, depositing the dead and broken things that no one had claimed. Underinsured hotels took the insurance money they were given and moved away. Damaged buildings stood with gaping holes and missing windows that screamed go away. Many who used to call Grand Cayman home left never to return. Grand Cayman was no longer the Grand Cayman I once knew. Little Cayman and Cayman Brac had been spared but Grand Cayman, not so much.

I thought this was the worst moment we could ever experience with our investment friends who suffered PTSD or post-traumatic stress disorder. Upon arrival at the office complex at Seven Mile Beach, we saw the empty offices on the ground floor, papers floating, and pieces of broken furniture everywhere. No one was there.

I had never seen anything so devastating. Georgetown was empty; a ghost town, abandoned and quiet. No cruise ships, no tourists, just locals walking around talking about their experience. Sara was nowhere to be found and Paul was told that it would be some time until normal operations would resume and that if I wanted it, I could have the job of assistant manager. Sara would be leaving to return to Canada, burnt out after having spent twelve hours in a church with rising waters… so the job was mine for the taking.

I called Sara and told her how sorry I was that she had to live through such a horrifying storm. She told me that they had to cut open the ceiling in the church where she had sought shelter. The waters were flowing higher and higher and in order to stay above the rising ocean levels, Sara was forced to enter the sub-roof area to stop from drowning. She thought she was going to drown as the waters rose up to their necks and then finally she was able to climb into the attic. She was traumatized and was done with the life she began to treasure in Grand Cayman. It was a lifestyle of working till four, then happy hour till seven, watching the sunset and snorkeling with friends. So I accepted the offer and opened my Cayman bank account. Paul deposited the money necessary to activate it for future pay deposits. I waited a week, but nothing came out of it so I went home because Sara had decided after all that she would stay as manager after a two week rest back in Canada. My dream job just faded into reality and we left that week after witnessing the unimaginable. Cayman was a banking center for thousands of companies, yet it was helpless; full of homeless citizens who walked around like zombies wondering how they could survive.

Months later, we visited again. Everything seemed to be returning to normal. Our first clue that we were wrong was that Bill never arrived at our hotel to collect the gifts I brought for his new baby. It was unusual that he failed to meet us for our traditional dinner and drinks. Years later, we would find out that almost one hundred and eighty million dollars went missing and our clients would possibly never see their money, or the Greeks who took it, ever again.

On our way home to Canada, we visited Cameron and Kate at their beach house in Delray Beach again. We ate dinner at Cameron's favorite Italian pizza restaurant on Linton, drinking till they closed. Cameron paid and walked out with a half empty bottle of red wine in his hand. He sat outside on a bench drinking from it and his sad brown eyes looked right through me. I thought he saw for a moment some of the hidden tenderness I felt for him. I looked at him and said with a soft voice, "That bad huh?"

Cameron smiled that certain smile, the one that men use when they wish they could say what they truly feel like saying. I wondered what was on his mind.

We spent the weekend with them and saw that their life had regained serenity only blind faith could deliver. They were happier than they had ever been, and they were thrilled that their younger daughter had found love in New York. She finally did marry the young man and had a son, Simon, who was the handsomest little rascal that played with your heart and made you want to have him all to yourself. It was as though a ray of sunshine had delivered this blonde-haired, blue-eyed, healthy boy into their lives. Everyone was all smiles because God was good. I was the only one that had any sorrow in my heart because I regretted that I never told Cameron how I felt and I knew that I never could. I chose to love him in silence.

I began to withdraw from events he attended. Even Cameron's dinners with Paul were off limits because I did not want to refuel my hopeless desire... So I would just give Cameron a quick polite hug when he appeared in his slick, low Mercedes sports car to pick Paul up and they would disappear for hours. I would stay home at the beach house and stare out to watch the ocean as the turtles would dive and re-dive. I would laugh and ask the turtles to do it again, and I thought that they could hear and understand my marine biologist voice because they kept repeating their dives for me, and I laughed. They performed for me right in front of my bedroom on the balcony where I would drink wine until I passed out trying not to cry too hard because I was too good a girl to try to steal him away from his wife. I did not know how to love; I had never watched a woman truly love a man and a man truly love a woman before. It was a vicarious view into a blessed union that kept me wanting a man just like Cameron.

Kate had everything I ever wanted, and I envied her, but I would never think of doing anything in my life to risk bad karma. I never once tried to flirt with Cameron because I respected him too much. My life became a routine of work, tears, work, sleep, and work...

My daughter Pamela was living and working in Paris and planning to live abroad in Shanghai. She had the adventure bug that she inherited from me. I missed her terribly. She had met a wealthy young man whose wicked mother didn't like her. I imagined Pamela married to this man I hardly knew. I imagined his mother seeing the babies every day while I sat an ocean away working in an office all day and all night long.

Even if I flew to Paris several times every few months to visit Pamela, I still missed our life together. I had memories of her debut at the Austrian Ball. I remembered how she excelled academically and was an excellent tennis player and loved to sail. Like so many mothers whose daughters moved to another continent to work and settled there, I was torn between giving up my life and moving to Europe to be with her or letting go. She had to learn to live on her own. I did what was best and left her to her own devices. She thrived and became more and more independent. Pamela was happy on her own and her job in the French government opened up a new world of responsibilities that made her stronger. Her French accent became exquisite and she learned to cook like a fine chef. Those were the happiest moments of my life; watching her bloom in Paris.

I, however, was not thriving at home in what became a silent dark passage into a one way street of work to sleep and wake to work. I was heading into a deep pit of depression. All I had was an empty four-bedroom, three-bathroom apartment, with the most beautiful view to call home. I suffered very badly from the empty nest syndrome. Despite the fact that I had been with Paul for fifteen years, we had never moved in together because our daughters did not get along and they were our priority. I wanted a family life more than anything.

I had settled for weekends and holidays with a man who gave me three engagement rings, each one carat bigger than the last. Still, Paul claimed that he had never asked me to marry him. He claimed that if he had, the ring would be much more valuable, many carats larger. I felt I had sold my soul to DeBeers.

I would sit on the beach at night sometimes and watch the stars flicker and the moon sway across the sky. I would cry about how many material things I had that meant nothing. I watched the perfect marriage and lived vicariously, hoping that one day I would meet someone who couldn't live without me. I felt I was getting older by the day and time was flying by me; time that made it more and more difficult to believe that I would ever be happily married to someone who would share my life with me. Like so many women my age, I found myself realizing that my life was racing ahead and I could not get off.

Cameron, the man I thought I loved, did not know how I felt about him and I could never tell him. It would be nearly impossible for me to ever meet a man like him. Paul was there beside me at work and on vacation but still I felt that I was alone. It was the worst kind of loneliness. I could be in a crowd of people and still feel that I was alone. I felt that something would happen in my life that would change everything, but I had no idea what it could be. I just knew that I couldn't go on this way or I would just dissipate into nothingness. Solitude and sorrow dragged me down. I needed to escape.

CHAPTER FIVE:
HOME SWEET HOME

R eal estate values in the US had hit rock bottom. I had been looking online for my first condo in Florida for months and finally come across Queen's Way in Delray Beach. One week after I turned fifty-five, I drove onto their grounds and headed straight for the sales office, parking my car in the hot sun. I knocked on the door at Premium Day Realties in Delray Beach. An eighty-year-old real estate agent opened the door, looked at me and said, "We aren't open because there is no business. You'll have to come back another day."

"I have cash," I replied, with a smug Canadian grin on my face.

It felt so refreshing to enter the air-conditioned offices that were empty except for this one real estate devotee, Louise Mello. She showed me listings of two-bedroom, two-bathroom condos, and I said that if she found one that I liked, I would pay cash for it that same day.

"Just a minute while I get my car keys and call my daughter to come take my place on duty," she said. She smiled and let me wait inside. It looked like a funeral parlor for buried files and dusty papers. It was clear that the real estate market couldn't be any deader. I had my inactive real estate license in Florida and wanted to learn to flip condos.

"By the way, I want to see the ugliest, cheapest place you've got," I said.

Louise frowned, but drove me to a condo building that looked like all the other ones in Queen's Way, barrack after barrack. I knew what I wanted. I wanted a shack, a country place, a kind of hole in the wall that would be a safe hiding place to get away from the limelight.

"You sure are strange; I have never had that kind of request in all sixty years of my career." She climbed out of the car and led me to the second floor of a pink building.

As we walked into a dusty, long abandoned, dark and musty, but cozy-looking home, all I saw were an old wall to wall carpet, shag, brown and dirty and the original mustard-brown paint that covered the entire condo. I looked at Louise, and I said, "I'll take it."

"Don't you even want to see the rest of it?" Louise asked.

"Louise, I know that the person who lived here was happy. She wasn't materialistic. She had the same carpet for forty years, so she was the kind of woman I want to be. I want to be happy to be home, so happy that material things don't mean anything." I stood there and smiled at her and said that I was taking it, as is.

"Well then, I should tell you that she will take fifteen thousand for it, so the listing price of twenty six thousand, well, it's flexible." She smiled a wrinkled, sweet-faced smile that made me understand that she knew the place was perfect for me.

I spent the next week paying workmen to rip out everything right down to the concrete floor and paint the walls antique white. I sat there, finally feeling at home and safe, far away from the terror I began to feel in the city in Canada that I used to call home. I decided to start something new, start again where I would forget how I had been exploited and abused over and over, working too hard and loved too little.

It was late in the afternoon after a perfect January day at the beach. This lazy, laid back pace was the way I wanted to live. I was a new resident of Delray Beach, the Rose of Southern Florida. Life was comfortable. Sleep, suntan, eat, suntan, sleep. The sun was setting, and the water was that particular shade of turquoise grey that blended perfectly with the horizon when it started to get a little chilly. I was slightly sunburned, sweaty, full of sand, and my makeup disappeared hours ago. I pulled my hair back into my famous ponytail that no hairdresser, however expensive, was ever able to stop me from making. I had learned to place it low and tight, trying to look like a ballerina and not my cleaning lady.

I looked like Olive in Popeye. I was leaving the beach to go home to my condo when Suzie, my blonde bombshell friend stopped me.

"Brigitte, let's have a drink at this karaoke bar before we leave the ocean side," she said. I groaned about my messy state. "Oh Suzie, I am sweaty and full of sand. I can't possibly been seen in public like this!" She gave me one of those looks. "It's not always about you, and you look fine, let's go for one drink."

I reluctantly followed her and her perfect blonde-haired, blue-eyed, smiling face in the direction of the bar. Atlantic was crowded and noisy. Someone was singing a Frank Sinatra song, "My Way." It was just a little out of the way on a quieter side street. I watched Suzie gracefully move ahead of me, and I watched all eyes follow her as she swayed up to the bar. Leonardo's was full of people our age, fifty plus, and I immediately liked it. We sat at the end, away from the street, and I glanced around at the decor that resembled a Bogart movie set; complete with dark shadows and hidden faces.

"May we have two glasses of white wine, please?" Suzie chimed at the bartender. She never spoke, she sang. Everybody loved Suzie because she was happy go lucky and always in a good mood. She was a smart businesswoman who always negotiated everything to her benefit. I never knew why she chose to work instead of marry again.

I started to feel at ease. We toasted to life in Delray Beach, our new getaway from the snow, hail, and sleet of the northern city we called home. I felt self-conscious in my baggy black velveteen sweatpants and black t-shirt, but it was the way I liked to dress; casual, comfortable, and unassuming. Suzie got up and wandered towards the singer at the mike. She was nearly six feet tall with the legs of a ballerina. She stood out, European in the old non Euro trash way. She had breeding and class.

She stood ten feet away from me surrounded by four men who hung on her every word as though she was sharing insider blue-chip stock tips. Gentlemen sure prefer blondes. Suzie was wealthy and exuded blue blood confidence. She sparkled like the multi carat flawless diamond on her finger. She was the seventy year old widow of a very important lawyer who created Prime Ministers in Canada. She was well loved and respected by him and he left her everything he owned. She would never have to work again for the rest of her life. We were miles apart when it came to our desires. She strictly wanted to date young men for the rest of her life and I wanted traditional matrimony. We made quite the pair.

I'm not sure when exactly I noticed a man at the bar… who was staring at me intensely as though I was a fresh donut. He had several cell phones on the counter next to his drink. He kept walking out and taking his calls and then he would come back in to sit down and look at me again. He was mysterious and he looked around him as though he was waiting for someone to come in or something to happen. I was busy reading the words to the songs projected onto a screen behind him, behind the bar, when he walked over to me. He was dark, heavyset, and masculine beyond belief. I felt an instant disturbing attraction to him.

"I believe you were trying to make eye contact," he said bashfully.

I laughed gently and said, "That's a terrific way to meet women! Stand in front of the words projected on the wall. Then they have to stare around you to read the words. Then it looks as though they are singing to you!"

He smiled and stood oh so close to me. I could feel his knee as it touched mine, and I was suddenly aware of a strange chemistry so strong I began to shake.

"My name is Johnny, what's yours?" he said as he offered his hand.

I looked straight at him and blurted, "You look Italian, are you?"

He had dark curly hair, but was bald with sprouts of old hair implants that were trying their best to stand at attention so he could look good… still it was comical to see them, listing and uneven.

He answered softly, "Yes, I am."

I looked away again but saw out of the corner of my eye a black unbuttoned jacket and well-pressed blinding white shirt opened just enough to pull my eyes back. He stood closer and I saw the full chest of dark curly hair that peeked out of the unbuttoned top three buttons. I saw the strong shoulders and neckline, the kind that football players work hard to build and covet. The testosterone factory standing next to me stepped even closer and out of the blue, my lips moved, and I inappropriately said, "Have you ever done time?"

He flashed a bad boy smile. I rolled my eyes, surprised at myself.

He said, "Yes, many years ago for cocaine, and I will never do time again."

Yet another red flag, a warning sign that I did not heed. I sat there silently bewildered and shocked. "Why do you ask?" He said as he looked away as though he was expecting someone.

I told him that I was neck deep in an unsolved crime. I had been working in conjunction with law enforcement departments as the former deputy mayor of my city. I had put criminals behind bars for twenty-six-to-life and worked to make bunkers illegal within city limits so that organized crime would never again build fortresses in which criminals could hide. Now, I was in the spotlight of the RCMP who wanted to know everything I knew about how millions of dollars could just disappear, poof, just like that.

"You should leave now as I am on law enforcement's radar for financial crimes that others committed at my place of business, and I am watched carefully so if you don't want to share my limelight, you should go now and never come back." I sat up straighter.

He laughed, stood closer and intimately whispered in my ear, "I am afraid of no one and if I am with you, no one will ever hurt you."

I could feel the meticulous surgery of expert seduction by a man who could protect me from all harm. I felt so anesthetized by the wine, by his words, by his smell and his maleness, that I was unable to move as I tried to listen to my mind that was screaming, "RUN!!!" I didn't.

Johnny started to tell me about West Virginia in the eighties and how he spent thirty years in the construction business with his father building houses and remodeling homes. I listened to the story of how he broke his foot falling off a roof and how he reset it himself, and then drove himself to the hospital for medical help. He told me how he supported his family by dealing cocaine and how it helped pay for his younger brother's tuition at military school. I sat there and heard how he was set up by a witness in a drug bust in the eighties. The tax records on a criminal enterprise that he submitted got him a deal; four years instead of fourteen. Okay, too much information... I knew this was my last chance to walk away normal.

I didn't. I was mesmerized by Johnny's story telling abilities. I could listen to his soothing voice and everything else was drowned out. All I heard were his words drawing me deeper into his world.

"I'll have another glass of wine, please." I sat and listened to him recite what was a well-practiced tale of adventure; how he used to be a pilot, a boat captain, a skydiver with over three hundred jumps out of a perfectly good plane, a licensed masseur, a scuba diver... He told me how he owned every fast car ever made. He told me how many beautiful and successful women he had bedded and my mind screamed for me to get away from him. "He is going to fuck your head and break your heart!" My words could not break the sound barrier in my head.

Instead, I smiled at him. "You are soooooo cute," I said.

The wine began to take effect and my resistance melted into thin air. Suzie suddenly reappeared, all flushed after dancing forever. I introduced them.

"This is Johnny, isn't he cute? Just look at this chest of hair. Suzie, Johnny, Johnny, Suzie." They smiled at each other and Johnny quickly turned to me, his back facing Suzie in a gesture of devotion to our conversation. His eyes grasped my vision and held it to his eyes.

Suzie saw what was happening and laughed at me because she knew I had been celibate for five years after Paul's quintuple bypass. It was as though Johnny read her mind, and he grabbed my hand to get me away from her.

"Let's dance," he insisted.

He pulled me as I said, "No, my purse, I cannot leave my purse."

He shook his head from side to side, laughed at me and said, "So bring it, and all three of us will dance."

I put my purse by the wall near us on the dance floor. It held the deed to my new condo and a lot of cash that I couldn't afford to lose. I followed Johnny's aggressive lead and he threw me around like a rag doll. He held me closely... closer than I liked. We were the perfect height for each other, fitting like those little salt and pepper shakers that are shaped to meet from top to bottom with the S curves in the right places. There were several very beautiful women watching us closely and as I was sliding and turning, his arms were around me holding me oh so close. I loved the music that was playing. It was dance music from the nineteen eighties. I experienced a nostalgic joy, an adrenaline rush and excitement that I forgot existed. He spun me over and over, and I was dizzy, laughing in my heart for the first time in years.

We returned to our drinks and I felt happy. He stood so close. I could smell an earthy blend of garlic and old spice caressing the air around him, blending with the love songs. I listened to him tell me more about his life, his family, his hard working elderly parents, married for already forty-five years and who still loved each other, and how he wanted the same thing with a relationship; endless love...

He then asked me about my life which suddenly seemed so long ago and far away. I told him what I did for a living and why I was in Florida. I told him everything; too much, too soon. In the next half hour, he learned that I was in the insurance, investment and financial business and that I spent a lot of my time chasing some of my client's missing millions by obtaining court judgments for them. He asked me how it happened. I explained how two Greek men had absconded with anywhere from one hundred and fifty thousand to four hundred thousand dollars per client for a total nearing one hundred and eighty million dollars. I said that the paper trail was impossible to trace. I told him I worked with forensic accountants, liquidators, and regulatory agencies in Canada to try to find my client's monies, but that it seemed hopeless.

Mike Light, one of the Greek con men, had worked for the biggest government fund in the largest institutional pension fund management firm in Canada. In 2008, it was revealed to the public that there had been a 25 per cent drop in the fund's assets, billions lost in worthless commercial paper. The Greeks were well connected politically and I knew from the court cases at which they testified that they had a big favor coming to them. They were not going to be doing any time to avoid creating guilt by association for their associates and partners.

"Do you know anyone who could get the money for me?" I joked.

Johnny looked away and said, "Yes, I do know some people, and they're not very nice."

He explained that his contacts would buy the judgments from my clients at a discount and collect the money in ways that worked exceptionally well. We laughed and that was the end of the conversation on that subject. Still, in the back of my mind, I calculated how useful this man could be to me because he appeared fearless. I liked fearless. I was familiar with fearless. I had been fearless for what seemed like forever.

I told him I was exhausted and had come to Florida with my friend Suzie to transition into my new real estate career. As an inactive real estate sales agent, I had just bought my first retirement property. We discussed my chance to make some good money if instead of living in it, I would think of flipping it after I renovated it. I told him my target age for retiring from finance and joining the real estate sector was the year I would turn 60. We talked nonstop about how he remodeled many distressed properties and his NCR or Nationally Certified Remodelers designation years. His favorite job was to pave driveways and paths around gardens.

He gave me his card, and I read his name out loud.

"Johnny Sorella, C.R. Zippy's Dry Cleaners and Laundry, LLC."

His card had this image of a tiny man running with dry cleaning in his hand over his shoulder. Busy, hurrying, like the rabbit in Alice in Wonderland. Johnny's business was located in West Palm Beach. I had never been there and it seemed like a thousand miles away. I gave him my card. We paused. He looked down at it in his hands, and as my eyes lowered to look at my card in his hands, he suddenly brought his lips to mine as he said, "Hello there Brigitte Knowles."

He kissed me so softly, his tongue separating my lips ever so slightly, bringing me towards that long forgotten place of passion that screamed like an alarm telling me that this was not supposed to happen so fast. I had a sudden impulse to slap him. I didn't. What on earth was happening to me? Who was this man who suddenly turned on a faucet of emotions and feelings that could not possibly belong to me?

"C.R.? What does that mean?" I nervously asked without making eye contact, pretending that he did not just kiss me. I was thinking of how I could make a getaway and looked for Suzie. She was dancing away with some beach boy looking man.

"Certified Remodeler, national licensed and bonded." He looked at me with the most honest face I have ever seen, a real altar boy look that made me think I had won the lottery. I put the card in my purse and took a deep breath. I began to sweat profusely and my anxiety level spiked up and I felt an urgent need to flee. In my mind, I was already gone.

Suddenly Suzie appeared and said to me in French, in her endearing Belgian accent, "Et, alors on y va? Are you okay? Are you ready to go?"

"Yes, I am ready to go," I said.

Johnny was shocked, and he said, "Brigitte, what are you doing, don't go, stay with me awhile, it's early, we can go and eat. Have some breakfast." I was suddenly uncomfortable with the fast track he was on. Breakfast? That usually means we make love all night naked, sleep together naked, wake up together naked, and then go for breakfast, not naked. It was late, nearly midnight.

Suzie looked at me with a funny face, and she said thoughtfully, "Stay, have fun." She gave me that knowing smile.

I got up and abruptly replied, "No, I have to go."

I was so scared of my feelings; scared of what my body was screaming for, what my head was shouting at me, and I just collected my thing and I left thanking him for the drink and the dance. I saw his face, bitter and angry as he turned his back on me, and he threw my business card on the floor. I walked out feeling glad that I had decided to leave and since he did that so coldly; it quickly hit me that it was the best thing to do. Something about Johnny was wrong. I had never felt this mix of feelings before. Part of me was so excited about meeting him and the other part of me pushed me out the door.

CHAPTER SIX:
WALK ON THE WILD SIDE

A week later, I was flying back to Florida to start renovations and I needed someone to help me with a small remodeling project. I called Mr. Sorella before I left my office in Montreal and apologized if I had in any way offended him. I asked about his availabilities because I wanted quotes on work I needed to be done in my condo in Delray Beach Florida.

"Johnny, I have some tile work to do in my condo and I was looking for several estimates, so if you need the work and are available, then maybe you could make me a quote for the work?"

He sounded surprised at hearing from me and even offered to pick me up at the Fort Lauderdale airport that night. He said he would come to see my condo and gave me a verbal estimate for three thousand dollars, sight unseen.

I walked out of the security zone that night in my professional, tight-fitting grey polyester business suit, and a nun white permanent press shirt buttoned up to my collarbone. I looked hot in a menopausal kind of sweaty way. Thankfully, the airport was air conditioned and cool and I regained my composure. It was snowing in Canada and I had dressed for the northern chill, not the humid, warm air that was Florida even in winter. I had expensive, tasteful gold jewelry that suggested wealth. I wore my hair in my famous bun and had no makeup on my face. In contrast, I wore silk black stockings and stiletto heeled, Italian black leather boots that made me appear taller and slimmer. It was a look I had carefully developed that said, "You want to do business with me because I am good at what I do."

As I descended the escalator to the arrivals level, I saw Johnny starting to walk up the escalator towards me, flashing that million-dollar smile. Wait, why was he wearing a baseball cap that said Zippy's Dry Cleaning and a shirt that also said Zippy's Dry Cleaning on the shirt pocket? He took my hand luggage and finished descending the escalator with me to the arrivals floor where I sat with him and waited for my checked luggage. I felt so mixed up and wondered what I was doing with this man who suddenly appeared so blue collar just like my ex husband. I remembered how he wore a T-shirt with Molson Canadian and a baseball cap with "Labatt 50" on the night I met him. There it was. Another bad omen I would ignore, just like so many other omens.

Johnny carried my luggage to his vehicle, a grey pickup truck filled with junk and clothes hangers and bags and dirty rags and tools. It also had "Zippy's Dry Cleaning" printed on rubber magnetic removable labels stuck on both doors. Red flag again.

I was just as nervous and shaky as he was as he said, "Did you eat?"

"Yes, I flew first class and ate well." Something wasn't right.

"So then you don't want this Italian meatball sandwich or the Sambouca I have?"

"No, but I thank you. You are very thoughtful." I was embarrassed at the way he looked; nothing like his affluent looking getup at the club. He was sweaty and ordinary, hands dirty, shirt hanging out of his pants.

Just before he started the truck's engine, he popped out a paper, shoved it into my hands, and I thought, what's this, a Map Quest printout? No, it was a list of medical blood test results, supporting Johnny's proud pronouncement of perfect sexual health.

"What on earth are you giving me here?" I laughed as I realized that he was genuinely surprised that I had never seen anything like it before.

"It's my medical results, to show you that I am STD free.

"I laughed even harder, almost choking as I thought about the fact that Johnny wanted to assure me that he had no sexually transmitted disease. Here I was. I had not had sex at all for over 5 years. This moment was hysterical, and I wondered whether I was on

Candid Camera. I folded the paper in my hand and said, "Johnny you are not going to need this with me. I mean, it's awfully presumptuous of you to think that I want to have sex with you."

I looked at him and shoved it into his glove compartment. It was such a turn-off when a man so intensely informed you of his immediate intentions.

Okay, so I was at least going to get a ride home from the airport. As we drove onto the I-95, I wondered how fast I could get out of this car and into my comfortable bed. I mean, I hardly knew this guy and here I was in a car alone with him in the middle of the night trusting him to drive me home instead of off onto a dark, dead-ended road near the swamps and alligators.

"What the hell?" Johnny suddenly said as the car started to sputter, slowly deciding where and when it was going to stop. He pulled off to the side of the road on the exit ramp and stopped, and turned to me and said, "We just ran out of gas."

Really? I quickly thought to myself. We did not just run out of gas, you did, you asshole. I took a deep breath and said, "I am sorry. I should have thought of this before, but here, this is a hundred dollars for the ride and gas and all."

As I sat there, scared and shaking, he said as simple as that, "I'll just walk to the gas station and get gas." So I looked at him with wide eyes gaping mouth, with my heart beating faster and faster for what seemed a very long moment and then again, he spoke as though nothing was wrong.

"If you need to use this, it is a machete and very sharp and you can cut someone's hand off with it. It is right here next to you between my seat and the console." He opened his car door and with his left foot out, he turned and smiled at me.

"Are you leaving me here all alone?" I was frightened and ready to go and walk with him. As he quickly walked away, I watched his receding form on the horizon of the dark road ahead. I realized I had no choice. I locked the door behind him, and I thought how the full moon was his friend, guiding him as he hunted for a gas station.

I sat for at least half an hour when suddenly, I saw his figure up ahead. He was walking over on the western direction of the overpass highway, towards the exit onto the southern direction of the I-95, across the overpass to the other side of the I-95. My heart sank, and I thought. He did not find a gas station, so I am going to be here a long time. I sat and resolved to breathe deeply, my hand on the machete and my eyes locked on Johnny until I could no longer see him. I heard the strangest noises and saw things moving in the dark, and I wished I could put the music louder to drown out the thoughts in my head.

Cars passed, some slowing down, and I slouched lower into the seat. I was hoping no one would get out and look to see what Johnny had in the back of the truck. It was forty-five minutes before he reappeared on the horizon. He was walking slowly as he swayed from side to side with an obviously heavy container of gasoline, a grin the size of a pumpkin's on his face. He filled the truck with gas, threw the red container in the back, and got into the driver's seat and smiled as though he had just won a gold medal.

"See now? That wasn't so bad after all now, was it? Thank you so much for offering to pay for the gas. I didn't stop at a bank machine so, thank you for thinking of it." He started the truck and quickly drove up to the overpass.

"No problem, glad I could help and thank you for the ride from the airport, I truly appreciate it." I relaxed just for a moment.

He wanted to return the container to the station that lent it to him, so we drove back to it, and he said we could eat nearby at a local restaurant that was popular. I remember thinking that this was not the way Brigitte would usually react in this situation. She would walk away from this guy and here I was, apologizing, for what?

So it started there: the ability to think one thing about him and do another without any difficulty. I had begun to disconnect from myself in what was a stressful, anxiety-provoking dilemma that he put me into but that he could also get me out of, a self-made hero.

We stopped at a restaurant nearby, but it was closed. We drove to Atlantic Avenue in Delray Beach and had a couple of drinks at the Colony Hotel. Everything seemed normal again as we sat inside on their soft, plush, comfortable couches. I was so tired from the stressful events of the evening. We shared our thoughts about life, the economy, love, and what we agreed on was that we were not terribly suitable for each other. Johnny fell asleep on the couch in public, which I found very unusual. I woke him gently, told him we should leave, and he drove me home and left me at my condo parking lot. I had far too much stress that night and I didn't truly care if I ever saw him again.

"You don't need a man, Brigitte, you are a destroyer." He said with a sarcastic smile on his face. I stepped out of his truck, gave him a dirty look and he laughed.

Wow and thank you and who gives a fuck Johnny, I thought. I walked to my door, tired and stressed out from what was a rather awkward night with a very squirmy, tired, sleepy faced and clumsy guy who didn't even know how to read a gas gauge. Oh? Who was he to tell me that I didn't need a man? It was true, but big deal. Little did I know that he had planted a seed in my mind that maybe that was the problem with me. Maybe I should have acted like I needed a man. I mean, I did want a man. I wasn't a lesbian. So maybe that was the problem.

CHAPTER SEVEN: UNDER COVERS

The following week, I returned to Florida. I shopped online on Craigslist and found some lovely antique furniture in a nearby gated community. A Morgan Fairchild lookalike had some Trésors Cachés, hidden treasures; things that I just had to have. I bought them, and needed help transporting them to my condo… I thought of Johnny and said to myself, I need him to move these pieces for me. I called him and said, "Hi Johnny, I need you. I need you to move the furniture that I just bought into my condo, so can you help me?"

He laughed at how I emphasized the "I need you" part and said he would be glad to help, but that I would have to wait for half an hour. Two hours later, he arrived. For the first time, I saw that Johnny had no concept of time. He had no ability to stop what he was doing and do what was next until he finished what he was doing, even if it meant someone had to wait for him for hours when he had committed himself to a particular time and place.

On many occasions after that, I would wait hours for him at the airport alone, in the dark, while he did whatever he thought was more important than picking me up on time. He was supposed to be there to pick me up shortly after my plane landed in Fort Lauderdale. He arrived and picked me up at the security gate where I sat and waited for him, getting more and more frustrated because he wasn't answering his phone. Later, I would find out he was with Carmen, his girlfriend who was still working for him sometimes on Friday nights.

When he finally arrived, we walked into the lady's charming house. It was full of antique luxury pieces, one nicer than the other, and then he saw the ones I had chosen.

"You have good taste." His said as his eyes lit up.

He dismantled the mission-style dark wood armoire and easily put it into the back of his pickup. Then, he made a big deal out of the second piece, cursing at it because he had not brought the right tools. This one was an antique writing desk with heavy carved legs. He lay there on his side on the floor, potbelly sticking out. He then turned around, plumber's backside facing up to the ceiling! His pants slipped off more and more as he stretched out to reach the far carved curved legs that he had to remove the screws from in order to dismantle the desk.

I looked at his bare skin and wondered if it turned me on or not. Did I like his hairy back and potbellied pig front? Or was this the last time I'd see him in any way at all…? I mean, he was rather fat and bursting out of his shirt and pants. He took the time to carefully undo each screw. Then, he placed the pieces gently into the back of the truck, covering everything with blankets. He brought them to my home, driving ever so slowly in his truck, just talking to me for what seemed like forever in his West Virginia drawl for the fifteen minute ride.

He brought the furniture up, left it in the back room unassembled. He saw my condo, measured the floor space with steps, and said he could do the condo and bathroom floors in tiles for six thousand dollars. I looked at him and sneered.

"What happened to three thousand dollars?"

"The two bathroom cabinets and a new tub with jets," he added.

"That's better." I smiled at him and agreed.

I gave him three thousand dollars in cash and he told me he would be back in two days on Saturday to start the work. He was hungry, so I asked, "Johnny, why don't we talk about this over dinner."

I had no food in the condo and I was hungry too. I offered to buy him dinner at the local sports bar, where he watched a basketball game on the plasma screen behind me, up on the wall. I watched him eat as though he was starving. He didn't stop to swallow, or chew and swallow. Instead, he quickly inhaled everything whole. I felt so sorry for him and the smoky, faraway look in his dark brown eyes made me wonder why he was the way he was. He held his hands out to me for me to place my hands in them on the table, and I looked at him.

"No, Johnny, I am not interested in you. I can introduce you to someone else who I think may like you." I did think of my girlfriend Shirley, who lived on her very own island and had no running water. She could use a handyman, but I did not truly intend to introduce him to anyone because I thought he seemed too desperate. He drove me home and went his way, and I went mine.

He worked for me that week. We drove to Tile Alley in Miami to look in warehouses in their clearance sections to find deals. We bought an end of distribution pallet of two hundred tiles in Sicilian Sand. The color was beautiful and was the base for my décor of the condo. Everything was going to be sand and sea, shades of beige and blue. We drove home and he was so excited that we only paid two hundred dollars for the whole lot. It was exhausting to bring the tiles up to the condo even though I had a lift for handicapped people that we used. We imagined how others managed walking up to the second floor with tiles in their hands. He left late that night and returned five days later.

I asked him why he didn't call to let me know that he was not able to be there as planned and he gave me some lame excuse that I half heard. I told him to get to work and he did. He started the long process of laying out the tiles and began to set them meticulously on the floor. He spent three evenings until midnight and finally had everything planned on paper. It took him four days to level the floor and start cementing the tiles and he was a perfectionist. Then he started the grouting of the tiles. With the pale beach shade I picked, everything looked so much larger and lighter. I was pleased with the outcome. I kept busy with my own work and seldom said anything to him as I was not interested in him at all. He would stare at me as I went by him to get a drink or a snack. He would often pause, turn to me, and look at me with a puzzled look on his face. Then he would say, "You're always alone, and you seem sad. You sit there by yourself and just pass the time here with no friends; you don't go out. Would it hurt you to go out and listen to some music? Maybe dance if you know how to?"

I had shown my lack of dance moves on the night we met, and I laughed at his comments. I could use a few dance lessons. I often thought about how learning to dance could change my life, but dance partners who were five-foot-nine and over were rarer than ducks with three feet. Again, I declined the offer, but I thought that maybe it was time to add some flavor to my dull life. He called me the next night, a Friday, and asked me if I wanted to go out and to see the town. I had never done that yet. I paused if only for a moment, then said the four words that would forever change my life: "That would be great."

Johnny came to get me that evening. He cleaned up nicely and had a bright white shirt on with crisp, clean jeans and dress shoes that made him look like a rogue college boy. We went out drinking and dancing to four clubs in West Palm Beach. Each one was more exciting and more crowded than the last. The music was loud and the club was full of smiling and laughing faces. Some faces looked back at me and stared. I was a newcomer, so I thought it was normal that people stared at us. I had given Johnny four hundred dollars to pay for his gas and his time and to allow him to buy my drinks and watch over me. I asked him not to let anyone touch me. I danced on the dance floor by myself, letting the effects of the shots melt my stress away. I was pretty relaxed. I asked him to help me stay out of trouble if I drank too much, then to drive me home, which he did at five a.m. He left me in the driveway and as he drove away I waved goodbye. I had an exhilarating night and met so many of his friends that maybe he was an okay guy, for a friend, anyhow.

He called me the next day and said, "Do you want some hair of the dog that bit you?"

I laughed and said, "I can drink you under the table, buddy." While other kids got cough syrup when they had a cold, as a child I was given straight shots of vodka anytime I coughed. I coughed a lot because I often had bronchitis as a child, but also because I liked the vodka and lemon that my grandmother concocted with honey and tea. I was no teetotaler so I laughed at the thought of anyone successfully drinking me under the table.

Again that night, I blow dried my hair straight. I redid my nail polish, showered, Chanel'd myself all over, and I felt great; ready to go out on the town. We went out for drinks, enjoying the night life until five a.m. Once again, Johnny took me to various famous drinking establishments, this time in Palm Beach where everybody was very young, very thin, and very rich. I left to freshen up in the ladies room and came back out to see Johnny and a blond woman talking, face to face as though they knew each other forever. I realized how sexy he could look when I saw him chatting her up. She sat there with her legs crossed, speaking to him in a very familiar way that night. Her body language was very inviting and her cleavage totally exposed. I felt a tinge of jealousy and I had no idea why. He also stared nonstop at these young beautiful women all night. I could tell that he loved being around them, and I thought, what else is new? At least he likes women.

I had been with the same man, Paul, for fifteen years, and the last five he spent recuperating from open-heart surgery. He was also under investigation for financial theft and gathering his strength for a long legal battle. Even though he was innocent, the charges against him and the defense legal fees stressed him so intensely that they made him uninterested in anything but clearing his name. I had been faithful and devoted to him even though we became only friends who stopped sleeping together. I believed that I had developed into an asexual since I had forgotten what it felt like to be with a man. Johnny seemed youthful, exciting, attentive, and enthusiastic. He seemed to like everything about me.

I had run a background check on Johnny Sorella on Intellius. I also consulted a friend who worked for

Corrections Florida. All that came out were dozens of parking tickets and the drug charge that he disclosed to me from the eighties, so I felt comfortable about the decision to go out with him again, as a friend. Something made me want to be with him even though I was suspicious about his integrity. I had begun to drink the Johnny Kool-Aid.

On the ride home, Johnny gave me a small bottle of booze and told me to take a sip. Soon, I felt totally uninhibited, so intensely aware of my senses and aware of my body, yet separate from it. Before long, I began to say some pretty inappropriate things. As though in a dream, I mumbled to him with immense effort, "I am going to suck your cock so hard, you won't know what hit you. I will give you the best blowjob you have ever had." This was totally out of character for me. Vulgarity was not my thing and I regretted the words as soon as they left my lips, lips that could barely move.

Johnny laughed and said, "I believe I am gettin' some pussy tonight."

I just remember sitting in the car, feeling as though I was someone else, someone who knew what she wanted and how to get it. Then, without understanding the fatal decision that I was making, I let him into my home. I was stumbling and felt nauseous, and I told Johnny that I was going to the bathroom. I peed and then I took off all my clothes. I jumped into the shower, put on the cold water and tried to wake myself up. I kept wondering where I was. It was dark as I stumbled into my bedroom, and there he was lying naked in my single twin bed, his arms behind his head, with a substantial erection. I tried to focus my eyes on his face but I stumbled forward going straight to the bed and told Johnny to move over. I was passing out, in and out of consciousness, trying hard not to fall asleep. I was afraid. Why was this stranger lying here naked in my bed? I suddenly came to, and realized Johnny was performing cunnilingus on me. When I say performing, it was quite a performance and one whole body orgasm later, my first; I realized there was no quitting now. He entered me and held my hands back, and I gave in, thinking there was no way I could ever explain this. It was too late, and no one would believe me, so it was what it was, sex with this man that I should not be attracted to. There I was, and it was good, and it was way too late. I really believed that I had the best intercourse I had ever had in my life.

Later in the early dawn, I realized that I had not consented, but was ashamed to admit it and ignored it. My anxiety level was hitting the roof and I had a terrible panic attack. What happened here and how did I wind up with this man that I hardly knew in my house, in my bed, beside me, naked? How could I have known that it was only the roofie that made me think I was having thrilling sex with this man? A man I barely knew who had at no time asked me if this was okay? Did I want to have sex with him? Did I want to take that step that would change my life forever? Did we use protection? I cannot explain how I changed that night, however, I did. I went from someone who had principles to someone whose principles either disappeared or became totally inactive; deleted from my mind. I was in a state of denial and it was not a river in Egypt. This was really happening to me.

Johnny awoke then and acted like nothing was wrong. He smiled at me and I felt repulsed. At the same time I looked for the sheets as I needed to cover myself. I had the worst case of buyer's remorse. I was exhausted, nauseous, and had a giant headache. I attributed it all to a rocking hangover. I was sick for the whole day and the next day. I could get over it by thinking this was nothing; it was just a bad dream. I could face the next day for sure. But it wasn't just a bad dream, and Johnny had acted like we were lovers and meant to be together. It didn't seem right at all and yet I did nothing about it. Despite my confusion, I thought it would all disappear like clouds in the sky. I would move on, and my life would be just exactly where it was before.

CHAPTER EIGHT:
QUICKSAND

I had returned to work in Canada and business was thriving. The markets had gotten too risky, so I was busy transferring clients into guaranteed insurance products that protected the initial capital as a segregated fund. I worked fifteen-hour days and I was hardly ever home.

It was the middle of a snowstorm and as I struggled to see the road ahead of me in the dark night, my cell phone rang.

"When are you comin' back down here Brigitte? We've got work to do and I miss you. I love you." I didn't know what to say.

"Johnny, this is a bad time to call. I am in the middle of a raging snow storm. I have convoys of long distance trailer trucks flying by me, blinding me with grey snow shit all over my windshield and I am slightly afraid of dying at this moment so I can't talk right now." I watched as truck after truck nearly veered me off the road and I was going to hang up when I heard it again.

"I love you Brigitte, do you hear me? I love you." I really didn't need this right now and I thought to myself, where is this guy coming from?

"Johnny I am scared to death right now, it is not a good time to start talking but we do need to talk and we will. I will call you as soon as I get to Florida this weekend." I hung up the phone and wondered what kind of mess I got myself into.

I suddenly remembered that only a couple of weeks ago on Valentine's Day, I gave Paul white roses and he never said I love you, not even on Valentine's Day. I came through the door returning from work, and he just stared at them and showed no feelings towards me. I was used to walking into an empty house. It had been months since we shared a bed and I felt so alone, afraid of what my life was becoming. I felt like I was floating on an iceberg with no preset destination. The heat that was developing in my world in Florida would end my life with Paul forever. It was inevitable, and he was showing absolutely zero interest in me.

That very night, I walked into Paul's house and the lights were dimmed. I was late and found him waiting for me. He stood there on the staircase like Hugh Hefner in pajamas and smiled and had a manly stance and invited me into the bedroom. I looked at him both sad and surprised, and said, "It's too late. I cannot even think about sleeping with you anymore. I have a lover."

He stared at me and said, "Is it Johnny?"

"Yes," I murmured. We sat in the living room and had the most intimate conversation in years. I told him everything, about Cameron and my unresolved affection for him, my loneliness and how Johnny had seduced me and how I could never be the girl I used to be for him and that we could only be friends. We both cried and we both understood that we could never be what we used to be. That night we became great friends and roommates.

I returned to Florida that weekend, and as agreed, Johnny picked me up at the airport. He had flowers and candy for me. It was candy in a red box in the shape of a heart. I was totally disarmed and confused and knew this wasn't what I wanted. He drove me to my condo to start the renovation in the bathrooms, take the measurements, and list the necessary tools and supplies. I went to Home Hardware with him to pick everything up in order to start early the next morning.

Johnny asked me if I was okay because I looked pale and sullen. I just told him that things were difficult back home, and I tried to ignore the fear and anxiety building in my heart. He began to tell me that he knew just what I needed and that that there was nothing for me to be afraid of, that I should be afraid of nothing at all. He would make me happy because he also had been alone too long and he really, really, really had a good feeling about us. I resolved to let things go as they may. Then, as though we were old happy weds, we went out for dinner and drinks, and everything appeared to be normal. Johnny explained that he felt something very special for me and wanted to know if I felt the same way.

"Do you think you could ever love a man like me? I know I ain't rich and I don't have much to give you right now but I have my heart and I do love you." He took my hands in his and told me that everything was going to be okay. He told me he would protect me and do his best to make me happy until the day he died. I felt like I was in the middle of another woman's life, not anything like the life I was living. Oddly, I did not feel fear nor worry about him despite what he had done the last time we were together. It was as though nothing was wrong, and we were just happy campers.

Suzie had lent me her condo keys. I couldn't stay in my condo because of the ceramic dust. I went there to watch some TV after dinner. Johnny showed up and brought a cardboard box out of his car. I looked inside. It was full of candles, massage oil and moisturizing lotions, and lots of booze. Johnny took the candlesticks out, placed the candles gently into them and lit them, releasing the sweet scent of jasmine. He lowered the lights and put on a music channel on the TV cable station. He poured some cold white wine in two glasses and I wondered what planet he came from? Before you knew it, out came a paraffin wax-heating machine, and my legs and feet were being massaged for nearly an hour and then he dipped both of my sore swollen feet in paraffin.

I thought who is this guy? I said to him, "I could live like this for the rest of my life."

Johnny smiled. How did I go from no desire to immense desire in one hour? I knew I drank too much again and I reminded myself not to do that ever again.

The night was young; we watched TV and laughed, and I felt romance and passion, laughter and joy... How could we be so happy and yet know so little about each other? I was so happy to spend so much uninterrupted time with him. Johnny was constantly endearing himself to me and I started to feel more comfortable with him. Before long, I was in bed with him and the sex was as he would call it, "On fire." When he would call me baby, I melted and thought that I had never heard such a sweet word. I distinctly remember wanting to hear him call me baby over and over again, forever. My feelings of love for Johnny began to stir up in my heart like a country love song. We stayed overnight at Suzie's. We hardly slept.

It was time to return to reality. The next morning Johnny asked me to go with him to his dry cleaning business in West Palm Beach so that he could check in on his employee, Shaniqua. She had been calling him on his cell phone all morning and he couldn't ignore her anymore.

We drove up to a small strip mall on Congress. It appeared to have a lot of empty units and there in the middle of it was the pride and joy that he operated. The Zippy's Dry Cleaning and Laundry store was open and running. Shaniqua walked up to the front, shuffling her feet as she appeared, her face showing how angry she was. She was a big, tough as nails, six foot tall African

American woman who greeted me with a huge hug even though she was giving Johnny hell because he had taken so much time off and left her alone at the shop.

"Where the hell you bin, leavin' me here all alone for two days? Whatcha think ah am, your slave muthafucka? Doncha ever do that again" She was screaming at Johnny at the top of her lungs, and they almost got into a fist fight.

I could not believe how she treated him so badly and how scared he was of her. They walked to the end of the shop and continued to argue about money and how he took her for granted. I had no idea what to think or what I was doing there because it seemed like a very private argument happening right there in front of me. Were they dating or something? Shaniqua walked in and out three times before she agreed to stay for the rest of the day and I wondered… Who was boss in this place?

Johnny told me that he only hired African-Americans to work for him because he could handle them and their attitude. He had to be sure that they got along with the customers, most of whom were also African American.

"Cmon' in Brigitte. C'mon in n' see how things work around here." Johnny was so proud of himself and his business, excusing himself for the mess, explaining that he had just been living in the shop for a couple of months until he found a new place to live. I walked into a hoarding hell; darkness, dust, disheveled clothing and old shoes, old pictures, and just the most bizarre combination of every possible piece of junk that he had obviously collected over the years. The collection of items seemed so unusual and irrelevant. Hidden in between the old clothes and old furniture were some real gems; a brass bell from a yacht, some valuable oil paintings, jewelry, watches, and cufflinks. There were also dozens of very expensive suits, shirts and ties, in a size slightly too small for Johnny... There was a fridge, a commercial washer and dryer, and a bathroom full of personal hygiene products; men's and women's. There wasn't any bed other than a large reclining chair covered with an old blanket and that was where he slept.

I walked to the exit in the back and saw the canal, some trees, and more junk outside his back door. I stood there one foot out the door, just about to step closer to the canal to see the water. I could feel the warm breeze and the smell of fresh laundry mixed with warm sun rays. I liked it there. The moment was interrupted by Johnny, who came up to me and handed me a statue.

"This is you and me: man and wife." He smiled sweetly as he put it in my hands and clasped his hands around mine. It was a simple, soft, sculpted beige and white wooden statue of a couple with their arms intertwined. It was unusual because they had blank faces, and they just held each other in each other's arms. Yuck, I thought. What was this cheesy, corny feeling I was getting from this cheap but adorable, romantic, loving statue?

I smiled at him. "Thank you, it's lovely and I will cherish it."

Again, I sunk a step deeper into the quicksand that was Johnny. We left the shop to pick up some food. The rest of that day was a light moment in a dark place that was just beginning to show it's dreadful, hopeless, and dead end. We sat in the parking lot facing his shop eating our take out lunches. Everything was so strange to me. Johnny was trying so hard to please me. He was always full of tales of adventure. This time he mesmerized me with his stories about his former business in Indiana where he offered renovation services and loans to help his clients pay for his services. He told me about the kind of work he did; windows, roofs, pavers, and remodeling of kitchens and bathrooms. He explained that when they missed their payments, he would seize their homes. I wondered if it was legal or even ethical and left it at that. Still, it made me wonder if even for a moment, who is this man?

He had this charm and a masterful ability to convince me that this was the first time he had ever loved, had ever wanted to marry, and had ever wanted to spend the rest of his life with someone... and that someone was me.

The next day both Johnny and I fell suddenly ill. We stayed in bed for a couple of days, learning about each other and getting used to the feeling of each other in such an intimate setting; his Kleenex, my Kleenex, our Kleenexes. We shared my earphones and listened to Dusty sing about love, 'Walk On By', 'Anyone Who Had A Heart', and 'The Look Of Love'. We drifted in and out of each other's arms, and slowly into sleep. My wishes came true that night; I thought I found the man of my dreams and I would never let him go. Never. I was in love, lust, and in wonder of what a man's body could make mine feel... What he could do to me, with me, in me, and I was him, and he was me. Nothing else mattered but hearing him breathe and feeling his heart beat next to mine. We were like newborn kittens; snuggling, suckling, purring, loving the feeling of each other's love. He held me in his arms and kissed every curve, every part of my ears, my neck, my eyes and then bingo, the kisses found their way to that special place; the heart of my womanhood, the secret place that hid fireworks and flying stars.

"Again!" I said after each orgasm, wanting just one more.

He smiled and said, "You better let me sleep, or I'll die, and you'll miss me."

The bonding molded ours into one destiny, one future, and one way to eternal happiness in each other's arms. Like many new couples, we spent most of those first few weeks in bed.

Shortly after this period of eternally blissful oneness, the marriage proposals started. He insisted we visit his parents to let them see how happy he was. He began pressuring me for more money, explaining that the job he was doing for me cost more and he needed to buy more tools. He needed to pay for the gas, which was expensive, to come back and forth. And so, I gave him more money. So it began; one thousand dollars cash to buy more supplies, a hundred here for a construction lamp so he could work at night, a couple of hundred here for a professional tile cutter, a couple of thousand there for the balance of the six thousand for work that he hadn't yet completed...

It was all right, I thought, this was a business relationship that had turned into a personal relationship but it would work. We liked the same things and wanted the same things. Soon began the routine flights out of Montreal on Friday night and back to Montreal out of Fort Lauderdale or West Palm Beach airport on Monday morning. I took four hour flights each way just to be with Johnny. The efforts I made to be there at his side far exceeded the efforts he made to be with me. Despite the missing pieces of the puzzle, the picture looked perfect. He left no details undone. Everything was well thought out, and candlelight made it all work smoothly. Dinners, lovemaking, extreme Scrabble, tequila parties for two until three in the morning... I started to wonder how I would survive and I jokingly thought that he used sleep deprivation to wear me down.

My nights were short; I would only sleep from three to six a.m. Johnny would force me to wake up, and I would go back to the dry cleaners to help him with his work all day. There was no pay because I was his girl. There was just nonstop hours spent cleaning the mess, washing the floors, the bathroom, the toilet... I never touched the fridge; it was too filthy. It had leftovers in their containers and half eaten sandwiches stuffed into every corner. Some food had mold on the surface. I spent every weekend this way.

All the while, I was concentrating on ways to throw things out without him noticing. Johnny was a seriously ill hoarder who held on tight to things he felt he needed or would need one day; someone who kept nearly everything he had ever touched for the last forty years.

I learned later that he had already lost five storage units full of his tools, furniture, and clothing because he failed to keep up with the monthly payments. Most of his valuables were long gone. He was holding on to this junk because he developed an inability to let go of anything. I started to box up all the extra hangers and extra items that he would not need immediately. I kept things like old sheets and towels, and household items that he was holding onto for the five bedroom house he wanted to buy to rent out to immigrants and construction workers, on a weekly basis, for a sizeable profit. I bought into his dream, a dream that would one day become my nightmare.

CHAPTER NINE:
KISSING COUSINS

S pring had finally arrived in West Palm Beach with the nights and the days starting to warm up, and I began to notice the birds singing. The sun was strong enough to sunburn and I was adjusting to my new half-life in Florida. I would bring all of my laundry to Johnny's in order to spend time with him. I helped him by doing hand laundry for clients who wanted precious dresses and sweaters washed and dried flat so as to protect the rhinestones or the velvet details, as well as the precious buttons sometimes made of mother of pearl. I devised a system to hang laundry in the back, where the wind flowing from the front to the back door was strong enough to dry them without any damage to the wool or cotton that a dryer would destroy. Many clients gave him fluff and fold and laundry by the pound, and I hung those out to dry as well. I so enjoyed those stress free moments, where the only thing that I could think about or feel was how sweetly the birds sang. Wealthy women would pay him twenty four dollars to hand wash, hang dry outside, and then iron and professionally fold their expensive Egyptian Cotton one thousand thread count bed sheets. I even wrapped them with a white ribbon after for presentation. For that money, you had to treat these clients very well.

I redesigned Johnny's tickets, his hanger system, and his delivery system with executive effort, and things began to run smoothly. I helped Johnny restore his bank accounts and reconciled them for him and obtained thousands of dollars back for him because the bank had charged interest on fines, and fines on interest which I claimed was bad bank business practice. The President's offices of the bank agreed with me. Johnny called me his Nancy Grace. I felt so needed and wanted and appreciated. Johnny was at his best, clean cut, bills paid, food on the table, and it was a time of harmony and relative peace.

I would stand there sometimes, stare out the back exit, and listen to the birds singing and the crickets slowly trilling their mating song. Florida had so many beautiful birds. Sometimes white cranes would sit by the canal, almost still. Sometimes I would drink my Kombucha sitting outside on a chair, and tan while I took mini naps. I would see woodpeckers, hummingbirds, and doves. Sometimes I saw doves in pairs and I thought of them as lovers. Once in a while, a crane would appear out of nowhere and startle me, and once a rare eagle sighting was enough to mesmerize me. The wildlife also included rats in the cleaners that frightened me, but I never slept there so it was okay. I could hear them scurrying, building their nest in the ceiling area above us, and I was afraid of ever running into one. Johnny had even been bit by a brown recluse spider and nearly died. He had guaranteed me that there were none at the cleaners. I was terrified of spiders and they certainly had a million places to hide in the dark corners that were full of dust and out of reach, behind piles of anything and everything Johnny dragged home every day. Still, I was relaxed and happy on those weekends and occasional weeks that I spent being with Johnny; those were the good times.

My favorite cousin Don and his wife Annie had called to say that they were coming down from Ontario later that week. Johnny and I went to buy a large mattress for them to sleep on. We laughed as we tried them all out, one after the other, rolling around, on and off of each other as silly as a bunch of teenagers. The laughter never stopped coming. We had shared my twin bed until that moment.

I remember when he first saw my twin bed, laughed and said, "You sleep in that tiny thing?" There was a moment of silence as I thought about this sorry fact.

"I sleep alone and have for years Johnny, so yeah; I sleep alone in that little thing." I mocked his West Virginia accent while, at the back of my mind, I wanted to say goodbye to that lonely life.

For so many nights, we had hugged, cuddled, and slept together in that tiny bed. I remembered thinking that surely he had to love me to spend nights with me in that ridiculously small bed. Here we were, two adults weighing a total of over four hundred pounds, sharing a bed usually used for a teenager. We would laugh late at night and sometimes fight for space, and he would win, pushing me out of the bed till I fell one night and hurt my hip and it wasn't funny anymore. He never stopped laughing and wanted to do it again. I told him to stop, I had a pain in my hip, and it turned into a moment of confrontation. Pain wasn't funny to me. It shouldn't have been to him either, but he never stopped trying to push me out of bed.

Don and Annie arrived, and I brought them to the dry cleaners to see where Johnny worked and lived. They stood there in disbelief at the crowded mess that surrounded them. They looked at each other and laughed and said that it reminded them of my grandmother's basement that was dark and stuffed with old junk. It was not a happy memory for me, and I told them to stop talking about it. They spent a little time chatting up Johnny, and they liked him. Then, they helped me clean up, and suddenly, they were taking his clothing and possessions and putting them into their van and moving him into my two-bedroom condo… just like that. We were both thrilled, and by the end of the day, we were living together under one roof.

I didn't know how hard it was for him to accept to move in with me. He didn't want to leave the safety of his dry cleaner nest. It was where he worked most of the day. Johnny only slept a couple of hours after ironing shirts till the wee hours of the night. Then, when the moon was handing over the reins to the sun, he would wake up. He had short naps in the daytime. He took every chance he could to lay his head down on my lap. He needed me to drive all of the time, while he took mini siestas on my lap and I sang to every song on the radio. I played with his hair, and he fell asleep to my voice. I was giving him the affection he yearned. Maybe now, he could have a healthy lifestyle.

Don and Annie, and Johnny and I had some terrific moments together until the boys decided to get competitive. Johnny claimed to be an expert pool shark and Don just looked at him and laughed until we watched a couple of games where Johnny wiped him out. The mood got serious and Don glared at him, only to finally concede that Johnny was the champion. Don got over it, and we found ourselves going out in the evenings. We shared laughter and food at some lovely Delray Beach restaurants that Johnny introduced us to. I would sneak Johnny some money every time the bill came, because he didn't have the kind of money Don and Annie had. He could barely afford a burger... never mind the seafood and martinis that they liked to order.

I thought everything was going well until after a couple of days, and too many beers, Don, my cousin, told Johnny to his face at my kitchen table that he thought he was a gigolo. "You listen to me very carefully. Should you ever hurt Brigitte, I will come for you. Mess with my cousin and you will have to face me." I was surprised that Don showed such passion in his attempt to play my big brother. I felt perplexed at the silence that followed, until Annie broke the tension by throwing a small plastic water bottle at Don. As she stomped to the bedroom they were sharing in my small home, she complained that he was paying too much attention to me and that she felt ignored.

"It's always Brigitte! Brigitte this, and Brigitte that, stop fucking paying attention to her all of the time!" I couldn't believe what I heard. Annie was jealous of me? She slammed the bedroom door shut, and we could only wonder what was going on as they started shouting at each other, and the moment diverted to Annie. Suddenly, it was quiet, and it seemed that they settled in the bedroom. Then, we could hear them start up and continue arguing for the next half hour. Johnny was upset but determined to prove he was a solid person and he said nothing to Don when he had come out of the bedroom to say goodnight, he just glared back at him, not moving, just breathing.

Later, he told me that he did not like aggression and that Annie's attack was an act of domestic violence.

"I don't like violence. They are bad news, and this was a bad scene. We are never to see Don or Annie again." For a moment, cold, blue, icy fear flowed through my veins, and I was shaking like a leaf. I realized I had no choice. I wanted Johnny and would agree never to communicate with Don or Annie ever again. Without my realizing it, he began to isolate me from my family and friends. I could only contact my cousin in secret from that day on.

CHAPTER TEN:
FAMILY TIES

Easter was upon us, and Johnny insisted that we drive to West Virginia to visit his parents. Maria and Johnny Sr., a lovely couple, seemed to be perfect for each other. Maria was beautiful, dressed in suits and groomed to the T; her hair done up like a model, her nails and jewelry showing how confident she was in her femininity. Johnny Sr. was handsome and sexy, even for his age. His smile was contagious and he knew how to give a good hug. Everything about them seemed perfect. I had every reason to believe that Johnny and I would be just like them one day, happily married, in love forever in a beautiful home with a garden and lots of family around. Nothing was missing.

Theirs was a large bungalow that had a humongous garden in the backyard. We spent four days out there helping them prepare the terrace for the summer. Hours were spent washing down the patio chairs and tables, grooming plants for summer, and clipping dead branches and leaves. They were in their eighties and still active and happy working in their garden together.

They also worked every day at their bridal boutique, where they had countless ballroom and bridal gowns. It was a joy to look at all of the beautiful colors and shapes. Johnny's mother told me I could have any dress I wanted, anytime. The strapless, backless, lacy, crystal-sequined, poufy, clinging dresses for any size and shape meant that I could wear a different dress to any event we went to. I was thrilled.

Johnny was content, relaxed, and happier than I had ever seen him. He loved his parents so much and seemed to thrive in their presence. I followed Maria everywhere; helping her with the cooking, finding out what Johnny's favorite Italian dishes were, and learning about his childhood and his accomplishments. I asked his mom, "What was Johnny like as a child, as a baby?"

She smiled at me and told me that as young parents working together in a restaurant, she and Johnny Sr. often had to keep Johnny on a blanket in an open drawer, in the back room. I wondered what happened if he cried and she was still working. How did he soothe himself? I thought of how alone Johnny must have felt if his basic need to be comforted and held when he cried as an infant had to postponed, because they were so busy trying to support him. Maria smiled as she recalled one time when he was two, after the birth of his younger brother, when they couldn't find him anywhere. They found him hiding in a closet sucking on a bottle of warm milk that Maria prepared for Harry, his newborn brother.

"That's the baby's milk, darling."

Johnny gave her the saddest look, and he said, "But I'm a baby, too!"

Maria smiled and tried to take it away, and he wouldn't give it to her. This moment gave me insight into Johnny's life that I would not understand until much later. He refused to let go of things. Maybe that's why he became a hoarder. He felt the need to collect and hoard things, and surround himself with endlessly irrelevant items. He would not even notice if anything were gone or taken away. Still, he tried so hard to keep track of every item's significance in his mind. There was only one incident that was so alarming that I had serious second thoughts about my life with Johnny.

We were sitting at the dining table when the subject of local politics came up. Johnny and his father began to discuss small-town politics and the subject of the mayor came up, and I suddenly volunteered that I had been deputy mayor of my hometown.

"We don't talk politics at the dining room table." Everyone turned and glared at me.

"Oh no. Really!?" I laughed and said, "Well since you were talking about the mayor here I just thought it was interesting that I had been deputy mayor."

His mother looked at me and said, "Women don't talk politics at the table."

Johnny stood up and turned around and stomped out of the room.

"You need to go after him," she said.

I looked at his father and said, "I am like a wild horse that you find in the pasture, a horse that you can't break overnight. So if I have done something wrong, I am sorry, but I honestly thought nothing of my joining the conversation."

His mother looked at me and said, "You need to go after your man and apologize."

I said, "No, I will wait until he feels better and he will come apologize to me."

Then, I helped clear the table and watched his father smiling at me as though I was a strange bird.

"You are much too cold for my son," his mother stood and watched me, and I finished clearing the table, washed the dishes and went to our bedroom. Johnny came to the bedroom an hour later and apologized. We were alone, cuddling under the covers, and the door opened.

"Oh my God, excuse me!" It was his mother, opening the door wide, no knock, with a friendly smile on her face that quickly turned upside down when she realized what she walked in on. We started to laugh our heads off and things were better after that. The invasion was over and we returned to the den together and watched movies with his parents. I felt a bit uncomfortable and wondered what kind of marriage they had, and what kind of wife they expected me to be.

His mother entered from the kitchen and asked, "What would everybody like to drink?"

His father looked at her and shouted, "Shut up, I'm watching TV!"

I stared at him and screamed, "You do not talk to your wife and the mother of your children like that!" He glared at me, and I glared right back, and his wife looked at me with a small smile as though she was scared to admit that I was the first woman to talk back to her husband like that.

Johnny and I were cuddling on the couch when his mother said, "You can't be like that, all touchy. You are touching my son far too much. We don't do that in our family. Johnny, you can't bring her to the family reunion."

I looked at Johnny and felt so awkward, and I pulled back and then he said, "I am not going to let you talk to my future wife like that Ma, and I am bringing her to the family reunion!"

I felt so awful and told Johnny in the privacy of our room that there was no way I was attending a family reunion and that we had to respect his mother and father. I was not going to be the center of a family dispute.

Then he told me coldly, "You are comin' to the family reunion with me and you are goin' to be my wife."

I gulped and felt confused. Was I happy? Was I scared? How exactly did these words make me feel? The next morning, I overheard Johnny and his mother arguing about me. Their arguing ended quickly when I walked into the room and smiled.

"Good morning, it is a lovely day for a drive home, Johnny. We have to leave soon and get ready for a long drive back."

It was a beautiful morning, yet I sensed such tension in their goodbye hugs and kisses, like there was a power struggle that had begun, all because of me. I would learn later that Johnny was trying to gain the control he wanted all of his life; he wanted to let his parents know that he was the boss and that they no longer could tell him what to do.

We drove home that day, with Johnny speeding faster than I had ever seen. We stopped to buy sausage rolls, and he was eating with one hand and going over one hundred and ten miles an hour with the other until I finally broke down and asked him to slow down. He ignored me, drove faster and faster, one hundred and twenty miles per hour, and I started to scream.

"Johnny! I'm scared, please stop speeding! I don't want to die!"

He suddenly pulled across three lanes into the right emergency lane and stopped the car abruptly. "Do you want to drive and we'll get home in three days? Or do you want to shut up and let me drive?" His face had that ugly "don't fuck with me" look.

I sat there, suddenly one hundred pounds smaller, shrinking into a small round ball of fear. I said nothing and he started to drive again, and I never said another word for five hundred miles. I fell asleep as if it was my only choice. I thought to myself that if I died, I wanted to die instantly and not suffer and know what happened.

I wanted to be home with Pamela and not in this speeding car with this madman. Something happened that began to make feel so afraid of him that I could not resist his decisions. I could not stand up to him, and I was toast. It was the beginning of the end of me; my person. The girl inside took over, and the woman went into a state of denial. I did not understand how it was that his domination of me had started to build up in our relationship and I did not for the life of me know what to do. All that education and here I was, a stupid girl with nothing to say for myself. I was beginning to have moments in which I would fear for my life.

When I woke up, we had arrived in West Palm Beach. The sun was rising. We were just in time to open the dry cleaners; five in the morning. The birds were singing and I was ready to cry again. There was no way out. I returned to Canada and stayed away for a week, and tried to regroup my thoughts. I concentrated on my work and reflected on my future with Johnny, and had decided that I was going to end my relationship with him because of the fear he instilled in me. I had no idea how difficult it would be.

CHAPTER ELEVEN: CANARY YELLOW

It was early May, after what seemed like a peaceful few weeks with no arguments. A calm comforted me, and I seemed to forget the fear in my heart. Johnny bought my ring after he proposed to me for the hundredth time.

"Baby, why don't you want to spend the rest of your life with me? Don't you want an Italian husband? Why wouldn't you marry a man like me? Don't you think we would be happy together in a house on the beach with a dog and a garden and a barbecue and some paved stonework all around the circular driveway and the entrance, the path all the way around the house, my work, what I love to do?" he said to me. Okay, I told myself. Despite his faults and shortcomings, I thought he loved me and I loved him, and I said yes.

He asked me what kind of ring I wanted, and I told him I wanted a Canary diamond.

"I ain' killin' no canary for you!" he said, and he smiled the Johnny smile, a smile he bought with a loan I gave him. He smiled at me with the beautiful teeth his dentist put into his mouth after his partials were falling out and broken and glued with Liquid Nails one too many times. I felt much better that he was no longer in danger of infection. He pretended not to be afraid of the dentist, yet he wouldn't go. I was amazed at how macho he was when it came to going to the dentist. Was he afraid of the pain?

I made an appointment for him, took him for an examination, and it was just in time. He had started to have an abscess. He was too proud to admit it. I could never figure out how he could sit there in the dentist's chair and not feel the pain, no freezing, and still he did not feel the pain. He sat there for hours while the dentist worked on his raw flesh, and I knew he was the man for me. He suffered so much in his life that this was nothing, and I wanted to make a future for us with no pain, no suffering, and only love.

I lacked the common knowledge that substance abusers felt no pain because they were already sufficiently drugged up, and any Novocain could cause a bad interaction. I did not know that Johnny was an addict. I never saw him stoned so I did not have reason to think that he had addiction problems, but he did. I looked for pills and found none. Johnny was very mean to the street people who hung around the convenience store next to the canal, often chasing them away with a bat. He hated how they got drunk and stoned, and used the outdoors for their bodily functions, and I often feared for their lives. He was intolerant towards drug use and alcoholism. I never saw Johnny drunk or using any kind of drug so it was consistent that he wanted nothing to do with the local vagabonds who would walk in asking for clothes and food. He was fierce and terrorized them by calling the police every time they came near the store. I felt safe when Johnny was near me. He was so strong and everyone was afraid of him, everyone.

The next day, I was at the dry cleaners when the phone rang.

"There's somethin' I wanna to show you, and I am common' to get you so git ready!" he said.

I hopped into the car with him, and we drove to the jewelry store. Well, it wasn't a real jewelry store. It was a pawnshop. I went in with him. It was the first time I had ever stepped into a pawn shop. There were so many things in there that caught my eye. Designer purses, cameras, construction tools, televisions, video and music CD's, and then there was the jewelry and watch counter.

The young man behind the counter showed me a Canary diamond ring. It had a square cut yellow stone, set in white gold and one hundred white diamonds. It appeared to be trying awfully hard on Johnny's behalf to convince me to marry him.

It made me the happiest girl north of Miami.

I tried it on and it was so tight, it wouldn't come off...so Johnny bought it for me. We left there, my finger swelling, all red and angry. I started trying to get it off as I thought it was going to burn through my flesh. Was this another omen?

We went to a real jeweler just around the corner.

He looked at it and said, "I can't do anything, but this one around the corner will."

We ran to the car and drove around the block. This jeweler was sympathetic and helped me get the ring off, agreeing to enlarge it for a small fee. My finger felt normal again. The next day, Johnny put the fitted ring on my finger, and I became another woman. I became someone who forgot anything about Johnny that was wrong for me. I began to love him like I never loved a man. I was the woman who wanted to marry an Italian man like Johnny. I was on cloud nine.

"Baby are you happy now? Will this make you happy forever?" He looked into my eyes with a soft smile on his face and I knew it was meant to be. He looked sincere and nothing mattered but being with him forever as his wife. It was the happiest moment I had ever had with Johnny. I never expected him to spend so much money on a ring. It was money I had loaned him the day before.

We stopped at the flea market next door. He told me that his friend was a jeweler there, and that we should get his ring now. We walked up to this jewelry counter full of amazing hand crafted jewelry. There were black coral pieces that I had never seen crafted into rings, and bracelets with gold and diamonds encrusted with semi-precious stones that curved around your wrist like a cobra. This man was built like a stealth bomber; strong, mysterious, and slick. He was extremely cautious, and looked around as we approached him. Johnny introduced me to Mr. Jamaica and told me how both of them met when they would work all night. They were neighbors at the same strip mall where Johnny's cleaners sat. They respected each other, Jamaican respect, loaded pistol on the counter kind of Jamaican respect. I smiled and said hello, and he agreed to fit Johnny for a ring. By the time he finished, his ring had gone up in price threefold, and my ring was still sitting there on my finger, a pawnshop bargain. But Johnny's ring, well, it was worth far more now than I ever agreed to pay. I was paying for it every week, five hundred at a time, and one week, I was short. Mr. Jamaica came to the shop with his gun, and I watched the two of them talking in low voices as I approached them with the money that I got from the ATM around the corner. I asked for a receipt, and they both looked at me as though I was nuts. They laughed and told me I would get my receipt one day.

I never did get a receipt for the whole price of the ring. I had one receipt for five hundred dollars. I later found out that my pretty canary diamond engagement ring was an insurance job, a ring that was listed as worth five thousand dollars for insurance purposes only, just in case it we lost it and needed the money back. This same man became my friend and supported me when I left Johnny. At the time, I did not know why he hesitated about increasing the diamonds on the ring.

Did he know that Johnny would do this to me, con me into buying such an expensive ring for him?

It was mid-May, and the summer was rushing into West Palm Beach where I was finding the days unbearable. I could not believe the heat and humidity. The worst was yet to come. Johnny was pressuring me to work harder and bring more money down. I was spending more and more time working in Canada, and I was trying harder and harder to find the time to be with Johnny… but he kept pushing for me to go back and make more money. He kept coming up with business deals, then another deal where a foreclosed house was on the market, and we had to put a down payment on it or lose it.

There were so many foreclosures, and I took the courses needed to work for the banks one day and administer the large inventory of unoccupied abandoned homes. I became REO and BPO certified, so I knew there was an opportunity like never before to acquire a number of houses at a good price. I knew I had to make the money to pay for them, so I worked eighteen-hour days to deliver the kind of cash he needed.

Once, at 9 p.m., on a Wednesday, when he called me on my cell phone, I was with Suzie and she watched as I responded to his urgency.

"Yes Johnny, what is it? Yes, of course. I will do that right away, no problem. Don't worry, I know." I was nodding my head and smiling.

"What on earth was that Brigitte?" She asked with her eyes wide open.

I told her that he just called to tell me about another house that just came onto the market, one that he had just found, just before it was foreclosed on, and how it was still available. It had a damaged roof and beautiful kitchen cabinets and the kind of bear claw tub I loved. We had to put a deposit on it immediately, or we would lose it. I told her I was flying there in the morning with the money for him.

"Brigitte, why are you jumping so high and so fast for him? What is going on with you? It is too weird the way you respond to his call as though there is a fire," she said in an angry voice.

I smiled and told her, "Suzie, the real estate market is flying, and we have to be there for opportunities when they present themselves. Johnny has found the house for us to live in, and he says I have to bring the deposit to make the offer." With short sales and foreclosures rising, there were many offers for every house and it made it more and more difficult to purchase one.

I left the next morning at six a.m. I arrived at Johnny's dry cleaners at noon with cash, and he was so happy to see me. He then left me there alone for hours. When he came back, I asked for the documentation of the down payments he had made for real estate deals, and he said it would come in the mail because we were not the only offers put on the table. He explained that the bank drafts would come back to us if and when we did not get the deals, and there was nothing that should worry me. He had done this before; many times before.

That evening he took me for another drive to see another property he wanted us to live in, this one on Lake Mangonia. We snuck in through the back of what was an unfinished shell: with only the electrical and plumbing done. He walked me through it and showed me where we would have our kitchen, our Jacuzzi tub, our master bedroom, and it was perfect. The view of the lake from the living room was through the wall to wall window facing the lake front. You could see the view of the lake from the front window near the entrance all the way to the back window, straight through the dining room. It was ready for us to add our special touch, and I had to have this house.

He said he knew the owner who was struggling financially, and that with a cash deal, we could have it for twenty thousand. I agreed immediately that this was where I wanted to live. I was very happy with the plans we were making. I never for a moment doubted him, his claims or his promises, because I wanted the dream so badly. I did not want to wake up to the possibility that he was not forthright.

After everything, I still fantasized about living together forever as a happy couple. Even though it wasn't on the beach, this house was perfect; it was going to be our new home. I could already visualize myself cooking and looking out onto the pool from the kitchen window, while Johnny barbecued the steaks outside. We drove home that evening, and I told Johnny how much I loved him.

"Johnny, for the first time in my life, I feel that I can trust a man. I love you so much; I am so happy that you were single when we met, but even if you were married, I would be still be with you, investing in houses with you. The love I feel is so real. I have never felt this way before."

There was something so strong in the feelings I had for him. It almost didn't make sense. I would never date a married man and never had, so how could I even talk this way? I wondered what was happening to me; why I was changing so much, so fast.

Looking back, maybe I was responsible for my ability to project the future based so little on reality. Maybe it was my fault for wanting things so badly that I was able to fantasize about anything. I was the perfect catch for Johnny; his sport was weaving dreams for women whose reality lacked substance, whose lives had forsaken them, whose hopes were insatiable.

The more I trusted Johnny, the weaker I got and the more I devoted myself to giving him the love I thought he needed; fixing his life, saving his business, and being the woman who would satisfy him in every way. He sucked the life out of me. I reacted less and less, and I became his puppet. Brigitte as I knew was becoming history. He had studied me carefully, found my vulnerabilities, and acted in the exact way that would make me trust him and want him more despite his shortcomings that were becoming more numerous and more evident every day.

Johnny had a hidden agenda. In spite of his attempts to act as the perfect husband, he left clear clues. His main and only goal appeared to be the appropriation of everything that belonged to me. He began to use sex to reward me when I gave him money, and he withheld sex when I had none to give. He used his penis as a weapon of seduction. His behavior became like that of a pimp. He rejected me when I didn't bring home enough money, and would tell me to go back to Canada to make more money. The harder I worked, the more money I made, the more I would give him, and the more he would ask me to bring him.

It was a Thursday, payday, and I gave him my entire pay of seven thousand dollars. He balked at my request for him to buy my lunch the next day.

"Don't you have any money?" he smirked.

"No, I gave you everything," I gulped.

"Well, if that's all the money you have I feel sorry for you." He looked away and walked to the cash and took out five dollars and left it on the counter and then he left the dry cleaners, leaving me hurt and confused.

I felt hungry and surprised, but most of all, I did not know the man who said these things to me. I saw him standing there, but I did not recognize him. Who was this man, this true Gemini, who hours ago, was so happy to have me hand over all of that cash that he needed so badly to pay his bills? Why was he acting so differently? How could he disregard the fact that my hard-earned cash was bailing him out of his horrible financial situation? Where was his undying gratitude that first flowed freely and generously? He had left quickly, and was gone for hours while I stayed behind alone at the dry cleaners for the whole day, hungry and waiting for him to call or at least let me know he was okay. Finally, at nine in the evening, he showed up and closed shop. We barely spoke on the way home.

The next day was a stinging hot Saturday. Again, Johnny disappeared early in the day and was gone for hours. I was waiting to eat lunch, when my hypoglycemia began to upset my sugar wellness, and I called him over and over and he did not answer. I left message after message.

"Johnny, I am hungry, I need lunch. Can't you call me and tell me when you are coming back?" I had been there alone since seven in the morning.

I was beginning to feel faint as I was trying to work. I had to put each piece of clean clothing that was returned from the plant in separate plastic covers over the caped hangers I had designed. The covers were red, white, and blue. They had a little man running with the dry cleaning over his shoulders. I was pulling the tags off of shirts, pants, and jackets, as I hung them and prepared them in order to put them in the front of the dry cleaners, ready for customers to pick up... and I got so dizzy.

It was hot, steamy hot, and I felt claustrophobic with all of the dry cleaning and plastic bags around me. I sat down and wondered how I got this way. What was I doing here living like a working class wife when I had spent years obtaining degrees and licenses to work in a business that was lucrative and paid me over two hundred thousand dollars a year, sometimes up to eighty thousand dollars a deal. After tax and expenses, I was still well paid and could afford the best meal in town, so begging for food from Johnny was incomprehensible to me.

For a moment, I yearned to be in my air conditioned life in Montreal, where I was the boss, where no one told me what to do, or how to do it. After what seemed like forever, at four p.m., the phone rang, and his voice brought relief to me as he said, "Hey baby, what's up?"

"Johnny, I'm hungry. I need to eat, can't you bring me something?" I felt whiny.

"Yeah baby, sure, I'll be back soon." I could hear the laughter and the music in the background. He was not alone, and he was not working.

He returned hours later holding a container of ribs, only to find me eating a McDonald's hamburger. He looked at me and said, "What the fuck are you doing eating that shit? How did you get it, did you leave the store?"

I swallowed and said, "Johnny, I was so hungry, and you were taking forever and I couldn't wait…"

He threw the ribs at me and said, "Fuck you Brigitte! You make me go out and get your food, and you don't even need it because you already ate that shit?"

I pushed the container away and said, "I don't want your crappy food that you got at some party."

"I was at Moe's daughter's restaurant opening, and I stayed for a while to mingle and give out my business cards, so stop acting like I was doing something wrong!" he mumbled. His shirt was all wrinkled and his hair was totally messed up. His eyes were bloodshot and half shut.

"Johnny, I could not wait, I took five dollars from the till and walked to McDonald's to get something to eat because I was going to faint. Why am I standing here working all day while you go out to parties and mingle with women and socialize without me?" I took a step closer to him to smell him. That was not his perfume wandering all over him.

"Brigitte, you are bipolar and sick in the head, I didn't bring you because it is too dangerous in Riviera Beach. I was the only white person there, and you would not have enjoyed it because there were guns and drugs and dealers and prostitutes, and you would not have fit in," he said as his face came closer to mine.

"And you did?" I walked away crying.

We spent the rest of the day apart, with him coming and going without a word, and me faking a smile for each client that walked in, mostly women. Many of them came in dressed to the nines, asking for him with a sly look on their face. All I could do was take their money, give them their dry cleaning, and stand there like an idiot, wondering what I was doing there in West Palm Beach with my heart aching. Just the thought of him being somewhere else, not with me, not loving me, not wanting me, just wanting to be away from me, hurt like hell. I was so unhappy I cried inside, all the while doing my best to serve customers and continue working so that no one would notice how badly I was hurting. I wanted to be with Johnny in spite of the horrible things he said and did. That was not the way things were supposed to be. He was supposed to love me, to be grateful and to appreciate that I gave him my hard earned cash to invest in a house for us, to make a down payment on our home that we were supposed to live in, happily ever after for the rest of our lives.

It was very late that night when Johnny returned. I thought he was high, speeding, rushing the words out of his mouth. He was almost frothing at the mouth; the mouth I so loved to kiss. Out of the mouth that hadn't kissed me in days came the words that cut like a knife, "I won't marry you to live like this. If you don't buy me a house and a business, then I don't want to marry you anymore. So get your fucking trailer-trash-ass back to Canada."

I was in shock as I stood there and thought this can't be happening. I walked to the front of the store and turned around and stomped back and said to him in hysterics, "Johnny, you fucking asshole, no problem, no problem, right now, right here, just say it, I am gone, say it again, no fucking problem you motherfucking asshole!"

He sat down, continued to iron the police shirt, and didn't even look at me. Then he said, "I'm surprised ain't nobody shot you in the head yet with a mouth like that."

I stood in disbelief and said, "I am gone. I am out of here. You will get legal papers from my attorney within twenty four hours for my money and the houses and good riddance you fucking asshole. If anyone had a bullet with his name on it, it would be you, you lying fuck. You are the one who was in prison dealing with the mob. You deal with drug dealers and whores and prostitutes all the time. That's what you are, a whore."

As quickly as I turned, he followed me. He ran behind me so closely that I almost tripped. He quickly surprised me, pulling my purse, taking it off of my shoulder. He took it, turned it upside down, and threw it to the floor where everything fell out. My Chanel sunglasses, my perfume… my signature scent, Pucci Vivera, spread like wildfire, all over the store. My lipstick, my money, and my credit cards scattered everywhere, coins running away from us as he glared at me. I bent to my knees and bowed my head collecting my stuff, and I saw him, with a look I had never seen before. He came closer, and I thought he was going to kill me.

"You can have it all, you can have the condo and the car, the houses, just let me go, let me out of here. Call a cab for me so I can go home," I said slowly while I stood up and started stepping back.

I thought to myself, Wait, do I even have any money to pay for a cab? I had given him every last cent; not a smart move on my part. He suddenly grabbed my cell phone as I tried to call Cameron, my dear friend that I was hoping would answer. Please God, let him be there, please.

"No, you're not calling anybody, you are not leaving me." I looked at him straight in the eyes, looking for a tear or any sign of emotion other than hate, but I saw only steel-cold darkness in his eyes; nothing that would give me any hope that I could leave safely. I was trapped as he stood between me and the door. I had made the mistake of going behind the counter to pick up some stupid coins that had fallen and rolled there, and he blocked my exit.

"Don't hurt me, I am sorry, please just let me go, I will give you what you want, just let me leave, please Johnny, you're scaring me." I stepped past him, out the door.

Johnny's facial expression changed. "Baby, don't do this. I love you, you love me, and this is just a bad day! You'll see... You don't need to do this. You need to be with me, stay with me, and everything will be okay. You are just working too hard. We'll go to the beach tomorrow, and we'll spend the day together and you'll relax. I'll give you a massage, and everything will be all right. Just let me close up, stay here, I'll be right back. Let me get the back door closed and locked."

I had a moment in which I stood outside, in the darkening sky at night; the strip mall was vacant and silent. No sign of human life... just a couple of parked cars that had been there for weeks. I calculated my chances, and thought of running to Congress Avenue to scream and wait for someone to hear me, but as fast as he disappeared, he was back, sweating and panting.

"Baby, let's go. I'm driving, come on. Don't just stand there, come on! Everything is fine, stop making everything so complicated. You make everything so difficult for us." He stood there, looking like he was giving me directions to the closest washroom.

I looked at him and wondered how he could go from implying that I should already have a bullet in my head, to calling me out for being responsible for the horror show of the last half hour, and to suddenly professing his love for me, for us, for our life together. Maybe he was right; maybe I made everything so complicated. I wanted so much to lie down and sleep. I was shutting down again.

I followed him to the car, and he opened my door like a gentleman. I sat there as he drove holding my hand, saying over and over that we were going to be so happy. We were going to have a house on the beach, and a dog, and a garden, and make love every night, and spend the rest of our lives together as man and wife; lovers forever.

I looked away and said, "Johnny, keep your eyes on the highway please. Everything will be okay. Please just stop looking away from the road. I'm scared. You are going so fast, please slow down."

I closed my eyes and went to that special place where nothing mattered; it was quiet and still, angels were protecting me, and I fell asleep. We arrived home, and we went to bed. He held me and gently made love to me, gentler than ever before. I just knew that I loved him, more than my life. Everything that happened that night had been forgiven and forgotten.

CHAPTER TWELVE:
MOB RULES

S ince late March, Johnny had been explaining to me that he was struggling with his car payments for his truck. I went with him to meet the people at his acquaintance's dealership. Joey appeared to be a nice bad guy and showed us vehicle after vehicle until we came across a 2000 Lincoln Continental that Johnny oohed and aahed over.

"You like that car Johnny? That makes you look like an executive dry cleaning service and it will be more economical than renting on a weekly basis." I said. "Go ahead and get it."

I lent Johnny the two thousand and five hundred dollars to make it the new delivery limousine. He only had small payments to make over time so that he could be the owner one day, rather than continuing to pay hefty leasing fees to Enterprise Car Rental.

As we were leaving, I turned my head towards the rear of the parking lot. I saw a beautiful old 1997

Jaguar sedan. It looked identical to the one driven by the Queen of England. As I approached it and looked inside, I saw that the racing green exterior came with caramel leather seats and a mahogany dashboard, and the interior was in excellent condition. Joey offered to sell it to me for six thousand five hundred dollars cash. I wanted an old Jaguar for myself to drive around West Palm Beach, and I agreed to buy it.

As we sat and signed the paperwork, Johnny explained that I could not buy a car in my name and told me to put it in his name so he could save me four hundred dollars by using one of his old license plates.

"Baby, we can save the money to put towards the house we want to buy. By usin' my old plates for the time being, we can put the Jag in my name. Since we are gettin' married, and things will be ours instead of yours and mine, why not just buy it in my name?"

So I did. I let him put it in his name, and we got temporary plates that would work for two months. I was driving a car that I paid for, but did not own. I justified it with the thought that if he had any accidents or parking or speeding tickets, those would be in his name too. I knew in the back of my mind that I was quick to believe him, and yet I did nothing to verify the information.

The temporary registration expired two months later in early May, and the car had been in front of the dry cleaners for a month. Johnny would still not let me drive it.

"Why can't I drive my car Johnny?" I asked innocently expecting a logical reply.

"The guys at the dealership made a mistake... The guys at the dealership lost the plates... The paperwork is late... The registration got lost..."

He went on and on, lie after lie. I started to wonder what the real problem was, and I decided to do something to find out. One day, I called Joey at the dealership and asked him.

"Joey, why are we not getting permanent plates for the Jag? I can't drive it because the temps have expired." I heard a hesitation.

After what seemed like forever, Joey asked me, "Brigitte, do you want the car in your name?"

There was a long silence, and I answered him, "What do you mean Joey, the car is in Johnny's name."

"I am going to ask you one more time sweetheart, do you want the car in your name or Johnny's name. You need to tell me now." Joey was trying to tell me something and I wasn't hearing him. I was uncomfortable with his insinuation, but I understood that this was important for some reason. What was he trying to tell me?

I got scared, and I said, "Just leave it in Johnny's name, I don't want any trouble."

"Okay, I just wanted to be sure that you knew that it could still be put in your name if you want it to be." It was then that Joey said, "I like you Brigitte, and if you ever leave Johnny, I'll take good care of you."

What? Later it would make sense to me that Johnny could not have been that influential if this friendly car salesman could hit on me. As helpful as Joey was, I saw it as an odd thing to say. I was right; nobody respected Johnny. They regarded him as a low life; a small-time criminal. He was a rat whose health was failing and whose aging body limped and struggled to keep up with his duties. I thanked Joey and understood that this would be the last discussion we would have on the subject.

"Joey, I don't want any favors, and I don't want to owe anyone any favors."

When Johnny walked into the shop later that morning, he charged towards me, fuming and shouting at the top of his lungs.

"You have no business callin' the mob. You are not to deal with them directly. You do not get involved in that business, what do you not understand? You just made a deal with the devil. You have no idea what you are doin.' How dare you call Joey and discuss the Jag? You made me look like a patsy callin' him behind my back. Who do you think you are and how do you think it made me feel knowin' that my future wife was dealin' with the mob behind my back! Are you tryin' to get me killed? Are you tryin' to conspire to get me killed?" When Johnny got angry, his West Virginian 'suthurn' accent would kick in, different from his Florida voice. That's how I knew he was furious. I laughed a little inside as I realized that he probably couldn't even spell conspiracy if his life depended on it, and I waited for him to calm down.

He threw papers everywhere and walked back and forth, towards me and away from me, as though he was trying to decide what to do to me, with me, about me. I began to get scared, I shuddered and was speechless as I sat and regressed into a place inside me I had not visited in decades. Years ago, far ago, long ago, when my grandfather would molest me as a child, I would close my eyes and disappear into a small hole in the ceiling where I was safe in the dark. Where no one could see or hear me. I felt that way again. I was a grown woman who felt that she was in danger and needed to disappear into thin air until he calmed down.

He stormed out the door and did not listen to anything I tried to say, and I did not see him until late that night when he walked into the store right by me, ignoring me, still furious, and for the first time, he did not kiss me. I knew there had been a fateful change in our love, my love, his hate, his game. I would find out later that this was the time that he had gone to Broadway to pick up hookers to play with so that he could feel that he had avenged my disloyalty to him. It was the beginning of a series of events that would lead to a discovery that would shake my world.

The next day, Taneisha was hired. She was an African-American thirty two year old woman, tall and silent. I tried to make small talk with her, but when she opened her mouth, she sounded like a rapper and acted like trash. She was a skinny woman, with bad manners, an ex-prostitute that he claimed he wanted to rehabilitate. He wanted to train her to be his new manager. She was dumb, lazy and buck-toothed, with one single gold tooth in front. Johnny whispered to me that some angry john had smacked her in the mouth when she did the wrong thing at the wrong time. Taneisha ignored me and refused to acknowledge my presence. Johnny would spend hours training her, yelling at her nearly making her cry, and I felt sorry for her at times and wondered how she let him disrespect her like he did. I started to ask myself why she stayed. He assured me she would work out and told me to just ignore her.

Despite his story, I felt that she was more than just a trainee. Taneisha acted disrespectfully, wore provocative clothing, and refused to clean anything. She constantly threw her chicken bones in the garbage can with no bag leaving me to wash the cans with chlorine solution to disinfect them. She basically came and went as she pleased, she would talk on the phone all day to friends and family, barely work, and yet he would give her benefits and leeway that I could not agree with… but I was told to mind my own business. *This* fiasco was my business though: it was my money that supported his failing business.

When he would buy me flowers, Taneisha would also get a small bouquet. When I got lunch, she would get the same lunch. He would call her baby, sweetheart, just like he would call me baby. The sound of the word baby began to hurt me because I knew that I had fallen for endearments that meant nothing to Johnny. They were just words that he used to manipulate everyone into feeling important and loved. I couldn't interfere with his decision to have her as his right-hand woman, his manager, and I hated being there when she was there.

One night when we went to bed, Johnny ignored me and snored like a dying elephant. I wondered what happened to the Rudolph Valentino wannabe that had claimed he loved me and would make passionate love to me every day for the rest of my life. I had time to think about how I felt, and I realized that something was wrong; very wrong. I couldn't pinpoint it, and I hardly slept that night, wondering over and over what it was that my instincts were trying to tell me.

Early the following morning, the sun was barely up. Johnny told me the plates on the Jag were not valid anymore, and we couldn't renew them because there were two trucks that he owned that were towed and impounded for unpaid traffic tickets. I had to give him two times four hundred dollars for a total of eight hundred dollars to pay the company that seized and towed the vehicles. That or we had no renewed plates. He told me that his trucks were about to be auctioned off at ten a.m. and that I had to go and pay the fines, or they would be sold off, and he would lose them. He had tears in his eyes, and his face was puffy as though he was genuinely upset, so I felt I had no choice.

He sent me to pay the tickets at the motor vehicle department and the tow-truck auctioneer office. I started to wonder about why he wanted me out of the dry cleaners. Was there something happening between

Johnny and Taneisha? Suddenly, she began to act very differently around me. One day out of the blue, she smiled at me, tried to befriend me, and asked if I wanted to go party with her. I declined. She gave me a look of hatred that I could feel all the way down my back. Another day, she asked personal questions about our sex life and whether I was happy with Johnny. I ignored them. I told Johnny I was uncomfortable with the way Taneisha was crossing the line and getting personal.

"Johnny, do we need her here? I can do the job she is doing, and we don't have to pay her for doing fuck all around here. She is not pulling her weight." I was serious.

"Taneisha lives with her man that she stole from a woman Teena, who was his wife and who had five kids with him. PJ was a hit man," Johnny told me that about her as though that was an accomplishment.

I was suddenly frightened of those who surrounded me, but again I ignored the warning signs. It was only in August that I found out Taneisha was Johnny's mistress. That was why he paid her one hundred and fifty dollars a week, and why he bought her lunch and delivered it every day she worked.

"Why are you buying her lunch if she comes at one p.m.? Why doesn't she eat at home before she leaves for work here?"

Johnny started to yell at me, "Taneisha is the mother of a kid in prison for life for murder, and she is very tough, and if you don't stop asking questions you'll upset her, and you do not want to do that!"

I repressed all thoughts about her and her strange attitude. Taneisha worked very little while I mopped the floors and emptied garbage cans. I spent hours organizing Johnny's hoards into two warehouses. I did it so that he would not get shut down by the city of West Palm Beach that also complained that he didn't have a business license. The dry cleaners operation was not abiding by the city fire code. I spent hundreds of dollars buying fire extinguishers, exit lights, and emergency lighting. I paid an electrician to fix everything according to code. I then hired additional help to move the things that blocked the access from the front to the back of the dry cleaners.

I was exhausted, and I noticed Johnny did not kiss me anymore and started to refuse to make love. Was it because I told him that there was no more money as we were starting to spend too much on his business, and my cash flow did not allow more? Was it because I said that I had to pay for my income taxes, and for the wedding we were planning? June was coming fast, and the wedding preparations were getting more and more expensive. He would start to scream in anger that I had to go home to Canada to work harder until I had more money for him. So I did leave and stayed away for nearly two weeks.

CHAPTER THIRTEEN: WEDDING BELLE

A couple of weeks before the wedding, Suzie convinced me that I needed to lose weight. I went to see a plastic surgeon with her in Fort Lauderdale. We got estimates for face-lift surgery on a package deal for two. It was ten thousand dollars for my face and neck. When they showed me what I would look like after the surgery, I decided to do it, all to surprise Johnny. I wanted to appear more youthful because I was beginning to have jowls, and since I worked all week in Canada in my financial business and all weekend at Johnny's dry cleaning business, I appeared tired.

When I returned to West Palm Beach, I told Johnny about my plans to sign for the surgery and asked him which day would be best for me to do it since I needed his support to help me heal and rest for a week after the surgery.

He looked at me and said, "Brigitte I can't understand why you think this is so important when we need money to pay bills and fix this place up and buy a new Laundromat and a house."

I looked at him, and I said, "Johnny, how many houses do we need to make offers on? I want to look fabulous and feel fantastic at the wedding."

He pulled me aside and grabbed me by both arms. He acted as though something terrible was about to happen and asked me to lend him twelve thousand dollars, or he would do something illegal.

I looked at him and said, "Are you talking about doing something illegal? Don't I get you money every time you need it to put a down payment here and pay a bill here, and now you want twelve thousand dollars?"

He looked right at me, breathing heavily, and suddenly I was afraid of what he was and what he meant by illegal, and I gave in. I cried and agreed to lend him money. I loaned him ten thousand dollars. He said he would put it down on two houses as a deposit for purchase. He signed an agreement for ten thousand dollars.

Later that same day, he asked me for an additional two thousand five hundred. I gave it to him. He laughed when I asked him to sign an amended loan agreement for twelve thousand dollars. He said, "You will never get any money from me anyways, so why bother?" Shocked at his statement, I made him repeat it. He said we would be married anyhow, so why argue?

By sheer coincidence, that week I found the loan agreement between him and Amy in his documents. This time it made sense, and I realized I might be involved with someone who borrowed money from women, lots of money, too much money...

I waited for him to return from yet another business meeting, and then I gently asked him, "Who's Amy? And what is this paper showing that Amy has lent you forty-five thousand dollars?"

As I showed it to him and asked him if he paid her, he stood silently, his face getting red and his veins bulging in his neck. Then he shouted, standing over me at the desk as though to strike me, "Why are you going through my life? Why are you going through all of my papers and finding out everything about me and my past? Who do you think you are, asking me questions about things that are none of your business? You just won't stop will you?"

He started to terrify me with his angry outbursts. I realized that there was danger, and there were secrets, and something was growing in my heart, and it wasn't love.

"Johnny, you asked me to help you organize your office, remember? And I was just filing everything for you and came across some papers that I didn't know what to do with?" I explained. I was suddenly aware that I was, again, terribly afraid, so I said I would stop looking at his papers and stop filing them.

Early in June 2011, we discussed just eloping, but I started to have second thoughts about marrying Johnny at all. One day I told him so.

"Johnny, I don't know why you are not able to contribute anything to the bills. It just seems that I am footing the bill for everything including the wedding. You seem to feel that there is nothing wrong with this situation."

He gave me one of his 'Johnny can't believe what you just said' looks and quite clearly enunciated, "If you cancel this wedding, my family and I will sue you for damages for making us all go through this emotional turmoil of planning this wedding. Do you understand?"

I stood frozen. I knew what I heard was baloney, and yet it worked. I accepted to go ahead with the wedding, intimidated and afraid of what was to come, but more afraid of what would happen to me if I ran off.

The next day, I reluctantly flew to his mother's to be fitted for a wedding dress. I arrived in Pittsburgh and rented a car, and then drove two hours to Fairmont, West Virginia. I loved this part of the country where people were so warm and friendly and generous.

Maria and Johnny Sr. were at their bridal store working late, and they welcomed me with open arms. They were so happy to see me. I loved the idea of having parents, and they seemed so much like a decent family.

Their home was comfortable and relaxed, yet a full of clothing and too much of everything. I could see now in hindsight where Johnny got his hoarding problem. Every door in the house had hangers on the handle. Dresses and shoes were everywhere. The basement had goodies and candies everywhere, and the coffee table was decked with every snack possible. I was a kid in a candy store, and Maria commented on my addiction to sugar.

"Darlin' you sure love that sugar, don't cha?" She laughed at my weakness and I wondered why there was more candy on the table today than yesterday. I thought for a moment that she was insulting me, but I let it fly by me.

Maria was always busy keeping up her appearance. She always had every hair in place. Johnny Sr. looked as though he just got off the golf course and always had a drink in his hand, a smile on his face. He had sharp wits and a wiry humor that he used to make people like him, and many did.

They took me for dinner at their regular haunt; a family Italian restaurant and introduced me as Johnny's fiancée to their friends. There was no sign of any previous conflict with me, and it was like our past disagreements never happened. I was the golden girl sent to bring their stray prodigal son back home. The meal was good American home cooking and the helpings were very generous. West Virginians knew how to make good food. Homemade rolls were dripping with butter and garlic. Everyone knew everyone, it seemed. I was overwhelmed with the hospitality and warmth. Everyone had this special drawl that sounded just like Johnny.

Later at her bridal shop, Maria made me try on dozens of wedding gowns. The ones that I chose because of their crinolines and puffy skirts, well, most of them made me look ridiculous and enormous. Finally, she picked one. A strapless bustier, A-line champagne dress that was elegant and sultry, and that kept my weight problem somewhat hidden. It was the only one that made me look like a happy bride to be, instead of a nervous turkey the day before Thanksgiving. Maria knew how to dress a bride. She said I looked like I belonged on the cover of Bride Magazine. By the time she was finished with me, I was enchanted. The smile on her face nearly convinced me that I was doing the right thing marrying her son Johnny, making him her married son Johnny.

Then, surprise surprise, she made me pay seven hundred dollars for the entire outfit. I even had a tiara and white gloves, and crystal details spun onto the slim feminine cumber band below my heart. For a short moment, I felt like Cinderella. Then I took out my credit card, and the illusion quickly disappeared.

Maria told me she had to be the one to fit me, as she was the mother in law and had a bridal shop. I had already chosen a vintage dress from the dry cleaners… a beautiful and very original dress that had been unclaimed. I wanted to wear it and not this new beauty queen dress, but I couldn't say no to Maria. I had truly thought she was giving me a dress from her hundreds of dresses at the shop. Still, I said nothing.

Little did I know that Johnny's former girlfriends and wives had their free gowns shipped to them by Johnny's mother with notes begging them to marry him because they were perfect wives for him and vice versa. All the while, Johnny had told me I was the first woman he ever proposed to since his second wife.

I flew home to Canada with my wedding gown and tiara, jewels and shoes, blue garter and colossal headache... Something told me that I was walking into the biggest trap for a bride-to-be. There was so much that I did not understand; such an undercurrent of secrecy and fear. I felt everyone was treating our love story as though it was written in Braille on ice. This wedding was going to be a disaster; I could feel it was not going to go smoothly.

The days flew by so quickly. I worked like a dog for the next few weeks, preparing for the day that I would become Mrs. Sorella, and in my heart I wanted to be happy so badly that I ignored my feelings of fear and anxiety. The daily calls and elusive words of love that Johnny sent my way just added to the pressure that made me think I wasn't at the right place at the right time.

A cloud of stress and determination cohabited in my mind, as I managed to work hard to prepare the Calabrese Italian menu. It had to have Johnny's fried Ziti with parmesan scrapings, and melted garlic butter all over the bread. As well, he ordered excellent Calabrese wine. He told me that no decent Calabrese wedding would ever serve cannoli for dessert, which was served at Sicilian weddings, so we settled on a delicious wedding cake with almond icing. His off-white vintage tux jacket had to match my champagne wedding dress perfectly.

I was sending modern day email invitations to my Big Fat Italian Wedding to my family and friends. Johnny was calling me every day, every night. He told me he was breathing me, living me day and night, while he waited for the day I would become his bride.

The bills started to add up. Only, Johnny was oblivious to the stress I was under and ignored my complaints about money. I paid all the bills and airfare to Las Vegas for us and my family. I paid for the musicians, the preacher, and anything to do with this wedding, while he told me what to do, what to order, how to dress and how to feel.

"Aren't you happy you're marrying an Italian man? Aren't you happy to be an Italian bride with an Italian husband and an Italian family? Baby, you will be the happiest woman in the world. Every woman will wish she had me as a husband. Aren't you lucky that I picked you?"

Why did he pick me? I echoed his emotions and smiled and said that I was the happiest girl in the world. The peak of Mount Everest that my heart was sitting on was starting to make me shaky. Just as quickly as they started, the naive fantasies that took me to the heights of the love I felt for Johnny started to give me vertigo on the way down. Suddenly, the wedding dream that was going to come to life felt like a nightmare. I felt the breath sucked out of me every time I realized that I found myself as tied to Johnny as the little man and woman on the wedding cake, stuck, no way to get off.

I asked him to please contribute to the wedding costs, at least by selling the flatbed trailer that he wasn't using. He blatantly refused. I asked him to please be sure that he bought the wedding band I needed to complement my engagement ring. He told me that his mother was going to give us one of her eternity bands for me to wear as an official wedding ring. I thought that was so thoughtful of her, and then I felt more relaxed. Still, I told him it was important for him to participate, to provide in some way. He threw another Johnny tantrum and told me that if I didn't want to be his wife, I knew where to go.

Once again, I heard him threaten that he and his family would sue me if I left him and canceled the wedding. From that day on I felt sufficiently intimidated to do just as I was told and say what I was told to say and feel how I was told to feel. I became a Johnny doll.

I knew this was going to end in a bad way, and I felt that I had no power to say how I felt or do what I sensed I had to do, which was run in a direction so far away from Johnny that he would never find me. I would wake up sweating and feeling that I was falling into the sky, into the dark, dying, and yet I had to get up, go to work, prepare for the perfect wedding to the perfect man that Johnny kept saying he was. I was being brainwashed so badly that my friends and family began a secret mission to sabotage the wedding before it began. They questioned me and badgered me. The more they resisted, the more I pushed and convinced them that I knew what I was doing and that they should be there for me instead of putting down the man I wanted as my husband. Only, I didn't know what I wanted anymore. I felt so much pressure. I pushed everything to the back of my mind and worked like a dog to make the money that the wedding was costing me.

CHAPTER FOURTEEN:
HERE COMES THE BRIDE

In no time, the moment was near. I flew to Las Vegas two days ahead of time to prepare my bridal suite, and to attend to the details of the wedding and reception. Strangely, Johnny asked me if a friend I cannot name, his homeboy, who carried a loaded concealed weapon, who would be his best man, could sleep in our bridal suite. He would be out all night, and he would sleep in our bed all day while we were out. I was shocked, but again, I said okay because I believed that Johnny was afraid of something in Las Vegas. Although Johnny used a photo of them together as his iPhone screensaver, he denied that he was somehow deeply involved with this man. I asked why his photo was there instead of a photo with me. He just told me he was a close friend. That just didn't make sense.

This kind of illogical thinking and Johnny's lame excuses began to make me think that I was crazy. His friend did not attend our wedding. Johnny flew in, and there was no sex because Johnny said he had a chafed behind from sweating. I was totally confused at this point, and I believed that it was very possible that I was marrying a man that I knew nothing about; a man that was a total stranger to me.

We had attended the family reunion the night before the wedding, and everything changed. I saw a family with so much love, so close, so welcoming. I met his aunts and uncles and cousins, who were so interesting, and loud, and full of laughter. There was so much affection and hugging and kissing, and my daughter and I felt so blessed… so fortunate to be in such a big family that had so many cousins and nieces and nephews. I felt so welcome in Johnny's family; they were so accepting… a family that treated us as though we were a gift from Heaven… and maybe we were.

Only later did I understand why there were so many secret talks behind my back with my daughter and friends; private discussions where Johnny's family reminded them that they were concerned about me. They told them that they should be watching him and that he would have to answer to them if he did anything wrong.

I smiled as though nothing ever could go wrong, and it was probably one of the happiest nights of my life. I had the family and the love I had longed for since I lost my mother. My daughter Pamela seemed comfortable with her new grandmother and grandfather, and aunts, and uncles, and cousins… We were alone for so long. A family of two against the world, and I finally felt I had done something to make her feel included in a family that accepted us with open arms.

For nineteen years Pamela's father had been absent, but her feelings about that were well hidden, and she smiled as though it was the happiest day of her life too.

We married on June 25, 2011.

We arrived at The Viscone Club in Las Vegas, Nevada, in a gigantic black Hummer. Johnny and I looked like the couple you saw on the cover of wedding magazines. I felt as though this moment was meant to be. Everything went smoothly, and the venue was nothing but perfect. The eighty thousand square foot mansion sat on a three acre compound and was a private club for members only, so it was an excellent choice for my very private Italian wedding. Cassidy, Johnny's cousin, was a member and had helped me organize the day from our first conversation on the phone. She made sure the event was an elegant day that no one would ever forget. The family reunions were held there every five years, and our wedding fell on the same weekend, by Cassidy's design. She was more than a sister to me.

The ceremony was short and simple. Since we were both divorced, there was no priest, but a preacher whose words were soothing. When it came to the moment when Johnny was supposed to put my eternity band on my finger, he told me that he didn't have it. His mother was supposed to give it to him to give to me at the ceremony. It was okay; we improvised and I took my engagement ring off and he put it back onto my finger. Not a good omen. Tears swelled in my eyes as

I wondered how he could do that; forget my wedding ring. Then, before we knew it, we were finally man and wife, and we kissed, we cried, we smiled, we hugged, we prayed and it was real.

We were officially a married couple. It was a done deed. Despite the little problems, it was still very romantic. I wanted my marriage to work. I was going to give two hundred percent to make it work. I was marrying for life, and felt that it would work. Despite all of our arguments, I loved Johnny. He was my pit bull, my puppy, the man I would take care of until the day I died.

The family was ecstatic, and they all seemed to sense our happy, loving couple affection and bliss. However, many times in the evening, between magnificent courses of Italian cuisine and Frank Sinatra tunes, there were warnings given to my family and friends and private warnings to Johnny that I almost heard. Something was wrong. I just didn't know what it was… but I was sure that everyone felt it too. No one ever came up to me to say anything but positive wishes for our happiness. I felt that I was attending two different weddings; my wedding and Johnny's wedding. It didn't make sense.

Suzie was elegant and wore a beautiful flowing aquamarine gown that made her blue eyes look like the Caribbean waters on a clear day. She gave the opening speech and told everyone how Johnny and I met. She wished us a happy life together, and asked everyone to take the microphone and give us their best wishes.

Johnny's sister Trudy took it, stood up and toasted, "To you, Johnny, my dear brother who always ruins everything, who always breaks things and ruins lives and manages to get away with it. That's all you are good for."

She wasn't perfectly sober, but very serious, and looked straight at him. Alarmed at the pain in her voice, I thought for a moment that Johnny must have done something terrible to her to make her say these horrible words out loud, in front of all of her family, from all over the United States. Suzie took the microphone away from her.

The music started to play. Johnny and I got up to dance the first dance and I was so proud of him, yet I felt that every nerve in my body was on red alert. Johnny's parents got up to dance with us, and I watched as his mother followed her husband's lead all the way. They danced so well and looked professional. They sat at the head table with us, and smiled as though nothing was said or done to dishonor them. I envied them for the way they lived, so full of love of life, dancing in perfect harmony like nothing was wrong; smiling, laughing, showing the family how much they loved each other.

Suzie got up and approached Johnny's young niece, Miley. She handed her the microphone, kind of putting her on the spot, and Suzie stood up to toast to us. "To Johnny Sorella, Johnny S or Johnny Jr., or Sonny, or James, or whatever your name is. To the jerk that you are, and the mess you leave behind, everywhere you go.

I don't know you well. I just know you are a liar and a thief," she said.

I shot her stare that could freeze the sun. I realized she had too much to drink, and forgot about what she said. I sighed and looked at Johnny. I felt so bad for him. The family he loved, that he said loved him, didn't seem to support him or the marriage that we were celebrating.

My friends and my daughter must have been reeling. I looked for them. They were standing at the open-bar, drinking and chatting, and not paying attention to the toasts by the family... but I heard them. I was about to throw up. I was afraid of the person sitting next to me, smiling as though nothing was wrong. A cacophony of warnings raged in my heart. When I looked into his eyes again, I suddenly felt that I did not recognize the man I just married. In fact, I didn't know my husband of several hours anymore, not at all. I didn't know either that this wedding would turn out to be the biggest farce ever.

We danced the night away, and everyone appeared to be having a marvelous time, but there were whispers and hands hiding lips. I was the only one who did not understand the meaning of this wedding. I was there to legitimize Johnny. To make him look just like a hardworking businessman who became the loyal, loving husband of a seriously legitimate hardworking woman. Johnny was using me to advance himself in the family and look like a good boy, so that his family would give him his due once his parents died. He once told me that he could not wait until they died to inherit his warehouses and the life insurance policies he had taken out on them. I was confused, and never believed he meant it at the time.

There was a total of four hundred dollars in the wedding envelopes, a hand painted beautiful dish showing an Italian village country wedding, and two Rosenthal champagne flutes. Nothing else. All of these people came to our wedding, and Johnny assured me that there was nothing else. No other gifts or envelopes. I was we would receive gifts in the mail, especially since I had paid for travel and accommodations, and this was after all a destination wedding. Maybe they just didn't want me to have to carry all the gifts home to Florida.

Johnny and I never went on a honeymoon. He insisted on returning to work in West Palm the very next day. Although I insisted on taking him to Canada to meet my friends and family, he opposed it with every breath. He just couldn't wait to get back to work in the heat and sweat of the dry cleaners. I accompanied him, and spent my wedding week sorting through dirty laundry, putting tickets on soiled suits.

I had paid a small fortune for the wedding at the Viscone Club; the limo, the band, the open-bar, champagne and liquor… I was saddened and surprised when it filed for bankruptcy a year later. It was a fitting omen, one that pointed to my life with Johnny; a life that would be bankrupt, from beginning to end.

I paid four thousand five hundred dollars for Johnny's diamond studded wedding band. I continued to supply him with cash for this, cash for that, and his demands for money kept increasing. He needed to cover his debts and obligations, reducing my cash flow to zero for my own needs. His pressure and demands overwhelmed me. Johnny had promised me a turnaround of 30 days for the loans. It had been 4 months, and not a single document or deed showing any offers made on properties was handed to me. I figured there were so many offers on each property, it was just a matter of time for one to come through. Then, all of the deposits that did not result in a purchase would come back to me. For a real estate trained person, I was pretty naïve, trusting Johnny to make those offers and deposits…

He wore his ring as proof of my love, and flaunted his new status of husband to all of his clients and business associates. Everyone who knew him and heard about the wedding came by to wish him well. He told everyone how happy I was with him, how happy we would be, how many properties we would buy, and how well we were doing. The wedding pictures were beautiful, and I was so in love; beaming like a lighthouse beacon. I was telling everyone how happy I was. I praised my husband to anyone who would listen.

"Oh Cassidy, you need a Johnny too!", I told his cousin who was broken-hearted and had just ended an eight-year relationship with a man. At eighty-four, he had become more and more distant with her. I felt so sorry for her, and I realized the politics of sex were undeniably age-related. I joked about gay rights advocacy, and shouted to her that it was not about same sex but some sex, and we laughed. Her son was proudly gay, so I touched a tender part of her heart where we could smile at how God gave us children that we loved with all our hearts and minds and soul, no matter who thought they were unlovable. As single mothers, we shared our passion and our pain where our children were concerned, and we made the best of what we had. All the while, we hoped that the world would embrace what we created with the gift God gave us.

One week later, Johnny was upset about money again. I told him that my daughter was going to spend the summer in Paris with her new boyfriend, and I was funding her trip. That meant that we were going to have to be careful about how we invested, and which properties we bought. Already, he claimed we had made several offers on foreclosed properties and short sales.

"I have to help her out, because I promised her long before our wedding that I would give her some money to spend during the summer months. She is summering in Paris, and the south of France."

I looked at him and saw his face. He raged, boiling red, and began to shout at the top of his lungs, "What are you thinking? We are buying properties and fixing them, and this is what you want to do? Waste thousands of dollars on a summer vacation?" His furious gaze fixed on me and I stood still. Torn between my husband and my daughter, I suddenly felt faint and had a pain in my chest. It was the most horrible feeling of fear in my gut, and a fear of something I had never felt before Johnny came into my life.

"Johnny, I explained to her that I lent you some money so I couldn't give her all that I promised immediately. I told her I would send money regularly during the summer months so there wouldn't be a problem." I was aware that he was silently calculating his response, and his voice slowly and quietly spoke to me.

He said as though he was no longer there, "This is grounds for divorce," and he walked away.

I was shaking, and I looked for a place in the ceiling where I could float up and hide and cuddle myself in a fetal position, and I started to cry.

"Wait! Wait, where are you going? Johnny, talk to me and listen to what I have to say, don't walk out like that and leave me alone. Divorce? What? Bon Dieu."

He left the store in a rage and pulled away in my Jag with the speed of lightning, and I was in shock. I prayed he would not hit someone, or something, or a car. The very thought of him dying while we were fighting made me nearly faint.

Standing there, I held on to the counter, lost without him. Lost in my mind, lost in this place that I could not stand without him, lost in time, wondering how I got here, as though I time traveled from somewhere, so long ago, when I was happy and lonely, and no one hurt me, and no one made me cry like this.

I did not know who I was anymore. I did not know why I was shaking and why I couldn't speak because this Brigitte was not the Brigitte I knew. She was not the Brigitte who would fight back and stand up for herself, defending her right to spend her own money, her right to be her own person, her right to keep her promises.

Johnny didn't come home that night. It was the first of many nights that he said he would be staying at the dry cleaners, and that he had lots of work to do. I flew back to Canada to think about my life.

CHAPTER FIFTEEN: JOHNNY'S WAY

It was a slow sunny day that next week when I came back to Delray Beach for the weekend. I arrived at the dry cleaners but Johnny wasn't there. I stayed and waited for his return.

It was late, four in the afternoon when Johnny returned from picking up the dry cleaning at the plant. He was smiling and happy, with a fresh clean shirt on his back. He greeted me with a cold shoulder and acted as though I shouldn't be there.

"What are you doing here? You should be in Canada working. We need more money, and I definitely don't need you here."

I sat down in the back where it was cool, and I started to cry. He left for awhile, and I wondered what I was doing there. I thought of leaving and going straight back to Canada, just for a moment, and then Johnny came back and had a plastic bottle full of cold water that he offered me. By that time, I had dried my tears and felt calmer.

"Here baby, I am happy you are here. I love you very much, and you are so good to me. Baby, drink some cold water, it will make you feel better, and later we will go home and make up for lost time", he said. I was happy. He came back. He was here, he loved me again, and life was worth living.

I opened the bottle, and I took a large swallow. My mouth was full of cold, icy water. So soothing, and then I tasted it… the metal, ugly taste that made me feel sick to my stomach. I looked at the bottle, and I saw something floating around in it. It looked unusually dirty, and not anything like the carbonated Perrier that I was used to drinking. I was shocked, and I spit the water out, running to the front door. I emptied the bottle onto the flowers in the pot holding the door open, and I screamed, "What the fuck did you give me? What's in the water? What are you trying to fucking do? Poison me? Are you crazy?"

I was red-faced, in an enraged stupor, and I stared at him. His face was blank. He was not reacting; he was already calculating his next step. He was trying to understand what I was. I was not his wife; I was not the woman he loved. I was not the woman he wanted to make love to. I was a woman who suddenly figured out that he put something in the water to make me sick, and maybe even kill me.

"Baby, I just thought you were thirsty and wanted to get you some fresh cold water to drink, I won't do it again. No wonder you have no friends and your family ignores you; you are such a bipolar bitch. I will never bring you another bottle of water if that's how you react," he said. His eyes were distant and calm and I couldn't comprehend who he was.

"You are never to give me an opened bottle of water ever again, do you understand?" I yelled. I did not know who I was. I did not know why I was here and why I was speaking in this loud, ugly, shrill voice. I was sickened at what I had become. I had only been married a short time, and already the honeymoon was over.

I thought, I want out, but I have nowhere to go, no one to talk to, and no one who cared. I made my bed, and I thought that I had to sleep in it. In my mind, I had begun to accept and live with the kind of things Johnny did that got on my nerves, and even decided that maybe it was me who was the problem.

It was becoming a quiet summer. Business was slow, and tempers were short. It was hot, so hot you could heat up a frozen dinner on your car hood. No one was out during midday sun unless it was an emergency. On Saturday evening, we were still at the dry cleaners, and I was getting ready to go out with Johnny and some friends. Taneisha stayed late for the first time, and she watched me change into black leggings and a black muscle shirt. I was trying so hard to look sexy for my husband. I was a little overweight, yet I insisted on trying to look hot, just like all the overweight sexy black women did. They still had it going on, even if they were overweight. They still carried themselves like sexy mamas, and I wanted to be one too. I weighed nearly two hundred pounds but I was solid muscle. I didn't believe what I heard next.

"She has bow legs," Taneisha said, as though I wasn't there, laughing. Johnny stood there smugly as they watched me dress. I watched his face to see what he would say, and he smirked with her, and they laughed at me. I looked at him to see his reaction. I waited for him to defend me, to tell her how much he loved the way I looked, but he said nothing. I made a mental note to tell her one day that I did not appreciate her comments, but I was scared to say anything just then. I felt like it was two against one. My emotional blindfold was blocking out so many truths that I should have seen if I only had the guts to face the facts. Why were these two acting so coy together?

That night, Johnny and two of his friends went to an outdoor concert with me. The evening was one event in a series of fabulous, outdoor West Palm Beach activities, "Jazz after Dark." They had Kelly Rowland as the draw, with her new song "Motivation." I heard her beautiful voice and watched everyone around me, just as happy as I was to be there, and I let down my guard and relaxed. I thought that I was the luckiest wife in the world, and my husband appeared even happier. I was surrounded by Johnny's clients and friends, all natives of West Palm Beach. I met so many interesting African-American, middle-class, hard-working, church-going business people that night. They all wanted to get together again and some of them invited us over for dinner one day. They all made me feel as though they wanted to get to know me. I felt the warmth of their friendship. It was the most incredible concert, and Kelly was splendid. There was so much love in her voice, and she made everyone feel peace and joy.

Her songs recalled the music my mother would play for me. It was music she learned to love when we lived with my first nanny, Mama Dale, in Spanish Harlem, Manhattan. Her favorite song was "Harlem Butterfly": "But even though a candle, burned at the ends, can never last out the night, it really makes a lovely light." I still have Mama Dale's letter to me, in which she explained to me as a small child that her black people had their own Santa, and that the gift she sent me was from her black Santa. I tried to find Mama Dale, years later in New York, and I was told she had passed away. I would always remember the songs, the music, the love, and her singing softly, rocking me, as if it were yesterday... I was traumatized when my mother left New York and I never saw Mama Dale again.

That night, we celebrated the reunion of two people who hadn't seen each other in awhile. I sat with Moe and his steady girl Aletha. We smiled, chatted, and all was good with the world. Everyone was kind to me. I made friends with so many women from the community; beautiful, friendly, extraordinary women like Jean. Jean was the most beautiful black woman I had ever seen; even more beautiful than Whitney Houston. The way she moved, it looked like she invented dance. Jean moved like a goddess and when she danced, everyone watched her. This woman treated me as a sister. Every time we met, we hugged, and she asked me how Johnny's new wife was doing and told me how beautiful I was. I became a mini-celebrity in town, and I just felt so much at home. I wasn't treated like this back home. This kind of love didn't exist when I went back to my life of work and stress.

The smell of Mc Raie's magnificent ribs and the side dishes that came with them permeated the air. Even though I could not possibly even spell the names of the dishes, they made my taste buds come alive with delight. There were chitlins and greens, and fried chicken served with beer, and wine that flowed all night long.

That hot summer's night was flowing with reunions, lovers dancing closely, arms intertwined. Warm, glowing bodies, dressed in immaculate white pants and shirts and dresses and jackets were touching and holding each other. It looked like one big wedding, and there I was, in black leggings, a black shirt, and black high heels, looking like the odd girl out. I could smell the bouquet of beautiful cologne and perfumes that permeated the air around me. I danced under the stars and felt like I was happy in my skin. That night, I was happy to be included; accepted, just like all the other women around me. I wasn't black, and it didn't matter to anyone. I was strong and proud, and I wanted to fit into the life I had so gently began to love. Everyone accepted me, and I was at home. Never did I feel anything but friendship and respect.

Even though we read about the daily violence in West Palm, I saw none. I only felt the kindness of those who let me live with them in their separate world, a different world I so enjoyed. It was the calm before the storm.

At one point, I was tired of dancing, so I stood away from the crowd, and I watched Johnny dance around all the beautiful girls. He fit in so well, and I was happy for him. I was not jealous at all. I found this kind of feeling to be a strangely comfortable one. It was one I had waited for all of my life. I found that I finally had the ability to trust and love the man I married. I watched him dance with all of these beautiful women around him, and I was not afraid that he could leave me for one of them.

Johnny's new shoes were shiny as a new penny. His white shirt and white pants by Tommy Bahamas made him look very sexy. The look on his face said, "I stay out of trouble." He acted as attentive as a husband could be, dancing with me here and there all night long, going back and forth to buy me a drink every half-hour, but taking a half-hour to get back to our seat, and I started to wonder. Every time he returned, he was flustered, sweating, and out of breath. I touched his face tenderly with a Kleenex, helping him regain his composure. I was feeling guilty that he was so tired. He was making my night perfect, with every sign of love and adoration he could show.

I didn't know that he was running back to Taneisha, who thought she was Kelly Rowland. I couldn't help but hate her. That woman never did a day's work and yet we paid her every Friday. He was dancing with her; her long witchlike nails painted in ten different colors, with jewels in them, and her nasty feet in slippers because she had poor circulation. He wound up spending half of the night with her. I could only wonder why her cheap Maury lifestyle appealed to him; what trailer-trash ideas were floating in his crooked little mind... Only later would I realize that everyone else knew what he was up to.

It was Johnny's way. Johnny was busy constructing a separate world from ours, and finally it would betray him, and all of his trickery, it would all fall down. All the king's horses and all the king's men would not be able to fix him up again. I didn't know it then, but karma would finally give them the horrible ending they deserved.

Later that month, we attended the Gun and Knife show in West Palm, and it was just another occasion in which I confronted Johnny because he asked me to break the law. Although I had a firearm's acquisition permit and had owned a gun, I had no intention of buying one. He was a convicted felon, and it would be a felony to have a firearm in our home or in his presence.

We argued, and a gun merchant at the show agreed with me. I was winning the argument but losing the war. Johnny convinced me that he needed protection, so I wound up spending a fortune on tasers, mace sprays, batons, and numerous other self-defense devices that he claimed he needed for the business. Johnny had been robbed before; he had to be able to defend himself. I once again began to think that I was the gateway that protected Johnny from being arrested. He pushed the limits on everything.

One beautiful West Palm evening after dining out at one of my favorite places, Crab House, he decided to show me a secret place that no white man was allowed to enter. We drove over to his favorite small haunt. It was on Dixie Avenue, and if you didn't know it was there you would drive right by it. There were Harleys parked outside and a couple of old black men sitting at tables and playing cards in one room. In the other room, wooden stools lined the bar. Through the cigarette smoke, you could see pickled things in jars, and bags of chips, and lots of pictures of singers and actors; all of them black. The bartender was friendly and served us our beers. I was amazed at the music, all signature blues and jazz from before I was born. It was a gem. There was a very sexy black girl dancing by herself, and she was very enticing. Johnny looked at her and invited her over to talk with us. I watched his eyes light up while he asked her if she knew his dry cleaning shop.

"Here's my card. If you want me to pick up your dry cleaning any time, just call me and I will come and get it." His eyes looked like Elvis' when he sang his favorite love song.

Johnny gave her a smile I had never seen before, and I was very uncomfortable... My heart beat so fast, I thought I was going to faint. She was just this tiny, friendly, innocent looking thing, but when she looked at him, he was mesmerized. Then, he asked her to teach me how to dance that way that she did, the way that had the men melting on their chairs. I half heartedly attempted to follow her lead, and she took both hands and tried to show me how to move my body so that I could make Johnny melt too. It was hopeless. I laughed and thought it was funny how she could do the moves she did, so sensual, so tempting. I will never forget how this poor girl with clothes that barely fit her could capture the attention of every man as soon as she stepped onto the dance floor. I wanted to leave. We did.

It was after we left and were walking to the car that Johnny asked me to drive, just like many other times. This night, it felt different though.

After drinking a little too much, he told me he couldn't drive and I needed to take the wheel. It was not unusual for Johnny to drive without a seatbelt and drink a beer while he was at the wheel, especially when we went home in the late hours and there was no one on the road.

I opened the door on the driver's side. Something about the car felt different. I sat down in the driver's seat and tried to put the seatbelt on, but it wouldn't work. Johnny sat in the passenger seat and put on his seatbelt, a rare sight as he was unusually heavy and uncomfortable in one. I had never, ever seen him put a seatbelt on... never. I asked him what was wrong with the driver's seatbelt, and he ignored me.

"Johnny, I can't drive like this. You knew this seatbelt wasn't working, and I don't feel safe," I told him.

He looked at me with one eye open, and said, "Just drink this, and you won't care."

He passed me an open beer can, and I begin to feel anxious.

"I am not driving like this," I repeated, and I didn't start the car.

"If you don't fucking drive the car right now, I am going to get out and get in the driver's seat, and you will fuckin' walk home. Do you understand?" He looked at me with hatred in his eyes.

I was scared, shaking, and I started to cry.

"What is wrong with you and why are you trying to make me drink and drive with a car seat that doesn't have a working seatbelt?"

Suddenly a wave of wisdom came over me, and I was more afraid than ever. I thought, is someone going to follow us and ram us from behind? I was either going to get arrested for drunk driving or die at the wheel, and he would have a seatbelt on for the first time in his life.

I knew there was danger sitting beside me, calling me his wife, and somewhere in the back of his mind he was busy thinking. He was thinking hard about something. I started to count the many ways my husband was thinking of killing me. I began to understand the things that were happening around me; things that isolated, meant nothing, but strung together could make a necklace.

Johnny was angry, gave me a strange look, and I gave in. I pushed the seatbelt clip below the lock and cut myself ever so slightly on the machete that was there, under the seatbelt lock. I raised my hand and looked at the blood on my finger. A small red drop dripped slowly down the edge of my lifeline. It stained my white summer pants right near the crotch. These pants were ruined. I knew I could never get that stain out no matter how hard I tried.

I turned on the engine as though I was a robot.

I drove home crying.

"Johnny, I am not happy. I am scared and I don't know why you are making me do this," I said as I stayed below the speed limit and watched the rearview mirror, while he feigned sleep, and watched me with that one eye he never closed.

I was not able to believe that someone was carefully making me get used to things I usually would never accept. I was beginning to realize that this was discomfort, and it was the way Johnny would make me get used to doing things that scared me, get me used to accepting things that were dangerous, get me used to living life the Johnny way.

I went to bed that night and waited until Johnny fell asleep. He snored for ten minutes and I got out of bed, and just as I pulled the covers over myself in my little twin bed in the spare room, he awoke.

"Brigitte, you get your ass back in this bed right now. This bed is where you sleep. You sleep with your husband and not in another room. What's with you?"

I got out of bed again, I sighed, and took my place next to the person that I was convinced had decided to kill me. I felt I could tell no one. I had to live this way until one of two things would happen; either he would get lucky one day and kill me, or I would find courage and leave him. Which one would come first?

CHAPTER SIXTEEN: VOODOO SPELL

It was a scorching hot, humid, sweating bullets Sunday afternoon in July. One of those Florida payback days; payback for those freezing, snowy, slushy winter days that made you move there in the first place. It was the end of the day; long, hot, sauna-like hours before the sun started to set in the sky, a bright red western sky on fire. It began to cool off, and there was a light breeze, some rain, and it was time for us to go home and work on the condo.

At the condo, I was relaxing on our bed and watching a movie on TV. Something was coming, but what it was, I did not know. Johnny was working on the tiles, trying to finish what he started four months ago. It all seemed so ordinary a day, so normal a marriage; a short respite.

We had another argument. This time it was over a woman who would call Johnny, hang up on him, and who wouldn't leave a message. Johnny would then leave the room to go out on the balcony where I wouldn't hear him call her back. I followed him this time, and he became vicious with me.

I looked at him as he told me to mind my own business; that he was allowed to talk to whoever he wanted to talk to.

"Who the hell do you think you are, my mother?" His face was filling with rage, and slowly I began to feel afraid again.

Who did I think I was? I knew who I was, I was Mrs. Tired. I was tired of the mystery, the calls without messages, being unable to reach him most of the time, and never understanding why.

He came back inside the apartment, and he was laying my dining room tiles down again as though nothing happened. He had almost finished the L-shaped combined living & dining room, and it was finally looking better and better. I watched as my husband worked so hard to cut the tiles, level the floor, and fix them using cement and liquid nails. He was an expert, or so he said. He was sweating, and his back was aching, but he was doing it, here a night, there an evening or morning. At last, he was finishing the last row when another mysterious call came and he left again to answer it and I lost it.

I waited until he returned to the tiles on the floor. He laid his cell phone on the floor, and I took it and walked into the bedroom. I closed the door and pressed on the last incoming call. His phone dialed the number, and a woman's voice was on the recording. I left a message.

"This is Johnny's wife Brigitte. Whoever you are; you need to realize that you are calling a married man. Stop it unless you owe him money and want to pay it back, or want to have your dry cleaning picked up. Thank you." I was proud of myself.

I snuck back into the kitchen and placed Johnny's phone on the ground, and I told him what I did. He stood up, turned to me, and started to turn blue with rage. He yelled at me at the top of his lungs to mind my own business. He said that I was a sick woman, jealous for no reason, and that I was ruining our marriage. I cried.

I finally got it. I finally believed that there was someone else that he was allowing to disturb me and make me sick, and I told him to leave. It was the first time that he knew I meant it. I told him to leave my condo now. I told him that if I was worth nothing to him, he should go to her and fuck her, and live with her, and marry her.

I returned to our bedroom and I shut the door. I was in our bed crying and heard him taking everything; every tool I bought and paid for, every piece of clothing, every toiletry item, and folded his massage table and carried it down the stairs. He put everything into the Lincoln, and he left. He came back again for more stuff, and he filled the Lincoln again, and he left.

That night, at midnight, exhausted and crying, I fell half asleep. I was in that far end zone of solid denial, that space in which reality smacks you in the head and you want to sleep or die, whichever comes first. I was almost completely out when I awoke to the sound of shuffling in my bedroom, and I saw a man standing there naked, staring at me, at the foot of my bed. I rubbed my eyes and couldn't believe what I saw! It was Johnny still as a statue!

"Baby, you left your door open. I am in the construction business and I have been for 30 years, and I can get into any place I want to and you can't keep me out. What do you have to say for yourself?" Johnny had another face, the most innocent face he ever showed me.

I thought to myself, no, this isn't real, I am dreaming. I sat up and I could see him, it was real. It was Johnny, staring at me in the clear full moon lit night. He quickly approached the side of the bed I was lying on. In the dark I could see a weary look on his face that scared me.

"No, Johnny you are in the destruction business," I mumbled and then I thought about how to escape. I realized there was no way out, he was between me and the window and so I couldn't get out that way and I started to cry and I curled into a fetal position. Uninvited, he got into bed next to me.

"Move over baby, I'm very tired and I am sick of your games. You got your way, now I want mine." He lay down beside me and took me in his arms and fell asleep within a minute. I trembled for the longest time before I fell asleep. I was too frightened to move, so scared to get the phone and dial 911. Later that night, he woke me up, held me for hours, and told me how much he loved me. He told me how happy we would be once we got the house on the ocean with the garden and the dog and the…

And I was back asleep.

I awoke the next morning at six and he was there beside me, with his eyes open, smiling at me, and it made me sick. He told me to get dressed and I did. We went to the dry cleaners, and I couldn't get through the front door because all of his things. He stuffed the entire hallway, from front to back, with his clothes and his tools. It was a mess, and I felt hopeless and I cried. I told him to bring everything back to the house, and he looked at me and refused.

"No, I ain't doin' that. My stuff stays here." He walked away, to the front of the store, and started sorting his laundry. He acted as though I wasn't there.

I was in terror at the thought that he had taken the final step of separating his life from mine. I was confused and could not understand what I was feeling. Didn't I tell him to leave? Why would I want him to come back? I stayed there all day, trying to clean up the mess he made, and create some order in the chaos that he had manifested.

Johnny's entire life was chaotic, but I had managed to unravel some of the knots in his mess. Seeing his world all tied up in knots again made me sad. Somehow, I felt this chaos was my fault. I was to blame, so I was determined to fix what I had broken. I worked for hours, trying to put some order into the piles of clothing, hanging up his clothes, when all I wanted was for him to bring all of his mess back to my condo. I caressed the wheat colored barn coat with the corduroy collar. It was a jacket he wore that early spring when I first went out to shop for supplies with him, and it made him look like an LLBean boy. I dreaded going home to my empty condo that night. Johnny acted like it was just another day.

Early that afternoon, a stunning tall Haitian woman had brought in her husband's pants that needed alterations on the hem and waist. Her name was Bronte. She and I spoke French together. So many Haitians were now coming in to bring their dry cleaning to us because I was able to engage in a version of French Patois with them, and talk about their visits to their families in Canada. Some of them brought me home cooked Haitian meals because they wanted to spoil me. Spicy poul was their chicken recipe and came with epis, pepper, garlic, herbs, green onions and parsley, served with rice and raisins, and a smile on their face. They were good, kind customers, who respected me and wanted to help us with our business.

Bronte asked us to have the waist and hem fixed as quickly as possible. The pants were for her husband who was a famous Haitian preacher, so she and I carefully wrote out the specific instructions for his pants. We wanted to be sure that her husband got his things on time for that evenings' Bible event. Later that day, our tailor Vic quickly returned with our orders and brought us the preacher's pants.

Bronte came to pick them up, and took them home after paying.

We were working late. It had been an incredibly busy hot day. We were trying to close up, when she returned, shouting at the top of her lungs. Her husband was furious that the waistband had not been retouched. He couldn't wear them, and he was angry at her.

I looked at her and showed her the ticket that was still stapled to the pants. I showed Johnny that I had written everything properly with her help, so it was the tailor who made the mistake. Johnny accused me, in front of her, of writing the instructions about the waistband just now and said that his tailor never made mistakes.

The preacher's wife stood there, looked at me, and said in broken English, "Your husband is a bad man and you should leave him."

I looked at Johnny, and I told him, "I do not make mistakes and this ticket has not been altered."

Then his tailor, Vic, walked in the door because Johnny had called him, and there were four of us arguing about who made the mistake. Bronte repeated to him that I did not make a mistake. She explained that she was there when I wrote out the instructions. She turned to me again and said that I should leave my husband, who was standing there next to the tailor, insisting it was my mistake.

She was walking out the door when I asked, "Johnny, who do you believe?"

She paused and shouted, "Mais il est fou! You are crazy! Your wife is a good woman and you are calling her a liar!" As though casting a spell, she shouted, "Leave him, leave him, you don't deserve this! No woman does. Give me back my money, this is crazy!"

And I watched Johnny's lips move, and he said, "You're lyin' Brigitte. There was nothing on the ticket about fixing the waist and you just added it now."

Bronte grabbed her husband's pants and left, and thanked me for the refund. I looked at Johnny and told him, "You will never call me a liar again."

I walked out to the Jag and put the key in the ignition, and I left. I was tired. I got home to my condo, and I laid in bed thinking about how far away and how long ago it had been since I was happy, working hard and alone, but happy. There was a time when no one made me so angry and afraid. I was suddenly so sorry that I was in this mess.

I started to yearn for the life that used to be my reality; a life in which I had some self respect. It was early in the evening. I called Paul in Quebec, and he answered. I was crying and sobbing, shaking and scared and lonely, and I told him I made a mistake. In his soft voice that was so kind, he told me everything would be okay. I was rocking myself on my bed, alone, terrified of what I had done with my life, and I fell asleep with the phone in my hand.

I woke up hours later and realized that there was no turning back. I understood that unless I made a permanent decision to leave Johnny, I would cross over into the mind space of women who waited too long to leave, women who disappeared or died at the hands of their husbands.

Johnny was not a loving husband. He made it clear that I would have to live my life his way; a dead end street with no exit.

I waited until the minute Las Vegas clocks rang nine that morning, my noon hour. I had researched online for the fastest annulment attorneys in Nevada, and came up with attorneys James E. Ronaldo and Silvie Rosetta in Las Vegas. I entered the race to initiate immediate annulment proceedings.

I told Ms. Rosetta I believed that I was married to a dangerous man; a mobster, someone who claimed to be Mafia. I was afraid for my life and my sanity. She listened to me as I described the events that had occurred and the money that was disappearing from my accounts. I had no proof of any property purchases in my name. I told her of his failure to disclose his double identity and crimes committed, as well as his law enforcement involvement. I explained his refusal to pay any taxes ever, his substantial unpaid loans from other women, his mental, psychological, economical and physical abuse of me, and how I feared for my safety.

She told me that I had a case for annulment, but it would be difficult, and I would need proof of his false intentions. She instructed me to gather any evidence of what he was, how he treated me, and why this marriage was a fraud. She warned me not to let him know that I was leaving. She reminded me that when a woman decided to leave her husband, this became the most dangerous time in a relationship.

I gave her my contact info, sent her a retainer, and I was sad… sadder than was logical.

I had just missed a train wreck, gotten on a bus, and I didn't know where it was going.

CHAPTER SEVENTEEN:
STEALTH GAMES

L ater that day, my husband appeared at my door.
He said he was sorry.

"I love you Brigitte, but if you don't buy
more properties for me to remodel and a second
Laundromat, I will leave you. I need to work and have
many companies because I am a businessman." He said
as he looked at me with kitten eyes, like all he needed
was a bowl of milk and he would purr.

He stood there and I wondered where his Bible was.
I was emotionally exhausted, and too tired to talk. I
didn't want to let on that I had contacted an attorney.
I began to play along with him because I wanted to see
how far he would go with his lies and his fraud.

He booked time for us to speak to people in the
laundry business about locations available for purchase,
and I went with him to meet them. We had several
meetings with sellers, and each time, I had reservations
about wasting their time. I had already decided to leave.

These meetings just supported my decision to leave. I found out by looking further into his financials that it was true that he had never filed any corporate or personal income tax returns. He did not use his IRS employee number, did not keep records of his business income, did not have a business license, did not have his dry cleaners up to code and he had serious fines for fire-code violations.

As well, I was told how he lost many dry cleaners and Laundromats in the past. The seller refused to make a deal unless I paid cash, all cash. The seller stated that he knew that Johnny was incapable of making a business successful. He never had, and he never would.

I was alarmed at the severity of his criticism, and I decided to look into a number of Johnny's failed businesses. Johnny told the seller that I was the person who would pay for the business and run it, but that it would be in his name… What a fool.

I excused myself to go to the washroom. I washed my face, looked in the mirror, and saw myself. I asked, "What are you doing here girl?"

I went back to the table. I promised to look over the deal and get back to the owner of the business we were looking to buy. Johnny got angry because I didn't want to sign right then and there.

I was shaking. I was cold. It was eighty-nine sweating hot degrees, and I began to shiver with fear. The feeling of sinking into deep dark quicksand was beginning to cause a major panic attack. I realized that I married into a con artist's plot, a plot where the wife became collateral. I slowly withdrew into myself, thinking about how delicate a position I was in and how dangerous a man my husband Johnny was.

I had committed myself to buying a property for us. I would pay for materials, and he would do the renovations. I had loaned him money several times, trusting him put it down as deposits on numerous listings. I could only wait for the signed offers to return. I could be in over my head, or he could be the owner of several nice properties. I knew that my actions could bite me in the butt. I had no one to blame but myself. I allowed a master manipulator to convince me to do business with him, all the while professing his love for me and his devotion to our marriage, in order to cover his true intentions.

The danger was so thick I could feel it in my bones. It chilled me to think that I had to continue to do as my attorney said. She told me to slowly gather the proof I would need for an annulment while keeping myself safe from harm. I started to copy any meaningful papers; anything that could come in handy later. The same thought crossed my mind over and over again. Respect the danger. Respect the danger. Respect the danger.

I once again found hidden copies of loan documents showing that he had done this before. Amy Simpson, forty-five thousand dollars. A judgment against James Delaney Pierce in favor of a client in Boca Raton saying that he did not finish the work he was paid to do. Who was James Delaney Pierce?

In another file, I found evidence of his previous arrests and extraditions... I found receipts in the name of his other identity, photographs of him in his prison uniform, as a member of the witness protection program, with another identity; James Delaney Pierce.

Oh my God, I began to tremble.

There was more and more proof that Johnny had been extradited from Florida and served time in another state, up north, for identity theft. He snuck up on me, with that paper still in my hands, as I searched for more evidence of his con jobs, the games he played to get in the door, the way he played with women's lives...

"What were you doing going through my papers?" he shouted.

"I was trying to file everything, so it makes sense, is that okay?" I answered submissively.

He looked at me with the same steel cold gaze that I had seen many times before. I shook so hard that I slipped as I took a step backwards.

"You have no business going through my life." Johnny said as he moved closer to me.

I held his stare and replied, "Johnny, if you don't want me to organize our lives, just say so."

If he only knew the important document I was holding in my hands.

Then he turned and grabbed the document out of my hands. He screamed at the top of his lungs, "This is none of your business!!!"

I slowly walked backwards and found myself with my back to the wall.

"Stop going through my things! Stop going through my life! You have no right to look at everything I have!" he shouted. He threw the paper at the wall and walked out.

I knew then that this was too dangerous for me to do much longer. I decided that I did not need any more proof of his intentions. I had already given him tens of thousands of dollars that he probably used to buy properties in his name or another woman's name. I knew that I would never see that money again. He was noticing my anxiety and stress, and was surely going to catch on that I was leaving him. I almost fainted at the thought of what he would do if he knew my plans to leave. What would happen to me if he knew I was gathering information against him?

The walk on the wild side that I was taking with Johnny became more dangerous every day. When I hinted, in the way that I looked at him, or in a way I looked away from him, that I was acquiring what would become a safe distance away from him, that I would make my escape, his gaze would become intense. He would demand to know what I was thinking. When I would say nothing, he would grab me and say he knew I was up to something, and I should tell him before he found out. The chill of his trap couldn't get any colder, and I began to feel no love… only fear, regret, and sorrow when I was with him. I felt as though I was heading for inevitable harm. I was feeling, no… I knew he wanted to kill me.

It all made sense. All of the times that he asked to see my businesses and help me run them. I told him at the time that my businesses in Canada were highly specialized. They required licensing and an educational background that he did not have. I told him that as a felon, he could never acquire these licenses. I told him that there was no way I could have him ever deal with any of my clients, or suppliers, or even assist me in any way. I was firm, and he understood. He was not happy, and I could see his mind working on a new, alternative method to get some money for his troubles.

It was the same look I would see over and over again. The cold, calculating gaze, that seemed as though he temporarily left his body to think in some strange place where he could hide his methods, hide his intentions. Only I could read him like a stop sign. It was so obvious and easy to understand. There was only one thing more dangerous than a man who believed he owned a woman; a man who thought he owned her assets. Johnny felt as though he was entitled to everything I had in my name. He was transparent and almost dumb in his continuously visible plans about how to get me out of his life. I began to wonder what my life was worth. I didn't like the odds I was facing. Not many women make it out alive.

CHAPTER EIGHTEEN:
RESPECT THE DANGER

That next week, I was told that Robert, our friend who was an insurance agent, was coming to the cleaners to discuss coverage for our risks such as fire and flood. Over the months, we became close to Melinda and Robert Moses and dined with them in their beautiful home many times. We had watched the fourth of July fireworks from their condo balcony, holding hands while Melinda told us how lucky we were to have found each other. How quickly things had changed.

I remembered Melinda's elderly mother who had the elegance, class, and style that made the Moses family famous. So many times, Melinda invited us over, extending her southern hospitality to us. I remember how I found Johnny sitting next to Melinda's mother one evening, feeding her like a child. Johnny was so tender and attentive that I thought I had the most gentle and caring husband in the world.

Robert entered the dry cleaners that afternoon and told Johnny he was there to discuss the coverage he had requested for the business. He asked Johnny to talk to me. I felt good with Robert there, we worked in the same industry and I enjoyed our talk as we sat outside the front of the cleaners. He explained the policy to me, and after discussing the matter for an hour, we came to a good agreement for an annual premium of a thousand dollars. I asked Johnny to sign a check for that amount to the Aka General Home Insurance Company. His face was shocked and he said, "I don't need insurance for the cleaners, I want insurance on Brigitte's life! Give us a one million dollar policy. I need to be taken care of if something happens to her."

Chills ran down my spine as I realized what I had heard. I saw Robert's face go blank. He was uncomfortable as he knew we hadn't been married for over a month. I attempted to carry on as normally as possible, realizing I was in grave danger. I acted as though nothing was wrong, but everything was wrong and I knew it. I knew there was no going back and no way out. If I made a wrong move, Johnny would be alerted to the fact that I was onto him.

Now, every time he left, I was in the copy store next door photocopying papers that I would need to prove what happened to me. I did so all the while wanting to be somewhere else, anywhere but here, married to anyone but Johnny. I continued to work with him as though nothing was wrong, business as usual. I began to see things as they were instead of what I wished they could be, or what they could become. It was the beginning of the end.

One day he was driving me to the airport, and I realized it was the last time I would be his wife. He asked me for money and I said had none. I told him I would send him what I could in the morning. We didn't even kiss goodbye. He didn't even get out of the car.

I got on the plane, and I was flying home when I realized that the love I felt for him had faded. I held the blue bottle of Chanel cologne that I forgot to give him. It was the smell I loved, on the man I had loved in West Palm Beach, in a world I had loved so much. Something in my heart told me it was finally over. Nothing could ever be the same. Sometimes, clouds mean a storm.

The next morning, despite the reality of our relationship being over, and with my annulment process in gear, I awoke feeling the need to speak with Johnny. I felt guilty that I left him with no money.

I called him from Canada to tell him I had wired three hundred dollars to his bank account. He complained about paying for my meals the weekend before I left, mumbling something to the effect of too little too late, and something about me having to do better.

I was answering him when he just put the new iPhone that I had bought him down without hanging up. I was suddenly able to hear who Johnny really was and what he did while I was away.

"Did your husband suck your pussy last night Taneisha?" he stated jokingly to his manager.

"Naw, ahm on my period," she replied, coyly, giggling.

Johnny was laughing and said, "That don't matter none baby."

I heard him moving the chairs as she laughed, and then he was hugging her, touching her, taking off her clothes as she laughed over and over saying,

"You are such a bad boy Johnny…"

And then I heard her moaning, and I heard him pleasuring her whole body with his mouth. He was making love to her and saying the things he said to me. Then, Taneisha had several orgasms, moaning for what seemed like endless time. It was, in fact, only minutes. Her sounds were identical to mine; sounds of joy, of pleasure, of intense orgasms and moans for more, and I knew it wasn't me. I was here, not there, and I lost my mind again.

I could not move. I could not breathe. I could not hang up. I could not end the pain. I heard them going on and on until they fell asleep in each other's arms, and I finally could move. I held my US iPhone in one hand and called Johnny on his other line from my Canadian phone line.

"Who dat?" I heard a sleepy Taneisha say.

"It's her," Johnny said begrudgingly.

I wondered what he meant. Who was her? I was his wife! She had to be her, not me, and then he answered, and I screamed, "What are you doing, you asked Taneisha if her husband sucked her pussy and then you go down on her and have sex with her when she is on her period? I heard everything! I heard you making love to her! Johnny, you make me sick to my stomach! Oh God, I cannot believe this! What is going on and how can you do this to me?"

There was a silence swollen with meaning. I knew I was right. This time I was very right.

"You don't know what you're talkin' about. You're crazy." His voice was ice cold.

"I heard everything and I just don't believe you did this. Who are you? My God, what have you done? How could you? I am getting an annulment. I want you out of my life. You are disgusting. This can't be happening to me, I…" I couldn't breathe. I was fainting.

His voice was strangely cool and calm as he told me, "You are having a nervous breakdown Brigitte, you are hearing things and imagining things, and I can help you baby. Just come back home and I will take care of you. I am your husband."

"No, Johnny. I am perfectly normal, and I know what I heard! You disgust me and I want an annulment. I will call my attorney immediately. You are never to call me again. I never want to see your face again." There was silence again, a heavy silence.

"There ain' gonna be no annulment Brigitte, not unless you're dead…" He said.

I was frozen in space, floating up in the air above my head, looking down at myself, and I could not recognize the person I saw. I was not that person sitting there in a chair, in my office, surrounded by millions of dollars of paperwork. I saw, in the reflection of the expensive antique mirror on the wall opposite me, a face that was looking at me like a puppy saying, "What's wrong? Why are you frozen like the statue of David and why is your face white with shock?"

I managed to find my voice, and I said, "Johnny, I am calling the police."

"There ain' gonna be no annulment unless one of us is dead!" he repeated. Again he paused, almost holding his breath.

I was speechless, and then I finally said, "Oh and I can just imagine which one of us that is going to be Johnny. After everything is said and done, I know you now. I know what you are, and it all makes sense. Goodbye."

I held the phone in my hand, realized that once again in my life, I was married to a man who wanted me to kill myself. After his attempts to end my life, this was his way of making me so depressed that I would do the job for him.

I heard him speaking, but it was some language that I couldn't understand. I sat there listening like a zombie. I knew that all I had left to do was perform an autopsy on our relationship. It was almost a mercy killing. A relationship that had suffered so much, and so long, that it deserved to die with dignity. So I helped it stop breathing.

No matter what else I was preparing for, nowhere in my plan did I imagine having to deal with infidelity. I knew, or I thought I knew, that I was the best thing that had ever happened to Johnny. I thought he would appreciate that there was no one else like me.

I had told him that I didn't care about his past; he did not have me in his life then. His path had brought him to me, so it was the right one. I told him that now, our path would go in a different direction, one that could not include crimes and constant infidelities. He had promised me to work hard every day to make me proud of him. I met one of Johnny's inner demons that day. It was clear to me there were some things he did not control and could not escape.

It all made sense now. I remembered how I would bathe him, twice a day, like a newborn, because he was sweaty, dirty, and greasy from the hard work at the dry cleaning and laundry business. I remembered on occasion that he would come home smelling like sex, and I thought, that little bugger left without showering this morning. I would tell him he could not go to work smelling like sex. Now, I understood why he smelled like sex. Now, it made sense. It was such a horribly vulgar odor of vagina. I had never smelled it before. I would just scrub him until I thought he was clean. Sometimes, even after that he still smelled, so I would go and get a wet facecloth and scrub his foreskin like he was a crystal knick knack.

My love for him was gone. There would no longer be any reason for me to call him every day, ten times a day, or fly down every weekend. The momentum of our relationship just stopped. I was done, like a cooked lobster. There was no undoing this mess and putting me back in the ocean. I was forever changed. It was over. I could still hear him protesting that I was crazy, he had done nothing wrong, that I needed to come home and be there for him...

Then, my U.S. line rang. It was Taneisha, calling again, crying, and telling me she was sorry. She said Johnny had been molesting her since she started working for us in May.

"You know your husband Brigitte." I listened as a cold chill ran down my body, like a silent snowfall.

"No, I do not know my husband, Taneisha. But I heard everything, and you moaned with pleasure and that is called an affair. It is not sexual harassment because you are having orgasms! You are a whore! I will never forget this and I will never forgive either of you. I never want to see your face again," I said to her with contempt.

"Please Brigitte, do you wam'me to leave, ah will, ah'll leave." Her voice trembled with fear.

I listened, and I thought of how many times I gave her extra money for her kids, even if I didn't like her. She would come back with her nails done. I thought of how many times I should have said something to her, to him, to them, about how odd it seemed that they were close; much too close. I wanted to die right there and then. Just pull the plug and die. I had two phones in my hands, and a third one, my business line, ringing for my attention. I started to laugh, then cry, and I just sat there thinking about how crazy life could be. Not my life, I thought, please, this cannot be my life.

It was at this moment that I decided that I would not lose my mind. I would not feel this pain, and I would not allow what had just happened to define me. I would not let what I just heard make me want to die. I wanted to get up out of my suede black and gold executive chair and walk out of my office into the receptionist area and say to the girls working there, "Have you seen my mind? I think I left it here on the desk somewhere for you to type up in capital letters. CRAZY." I wanted to scream, but my mouth wouldn't open. I felt as though I was going to faint.

It was as though I was 12 again, and my mother had just died. "I will never, ever love this deeply again, and I will never allow anyone to hurt me this much ever again."

Suddenly I looked for God.

"I am my beloveds', and His desire is for me." (7:10 NASB)

"Oh God, where are you, I am falling off the face of the earth into hell. Please save me, hold me close where the devil cannot find me. He is so close, ready to grab me and make me his."

I suddenly felt that strong arms were embracing me and that this too would pass. I got up, and I went to my private washroom. I locked the door, and I sat there for what seemed like hours and I prayed.

I went back into my office, and I said another prayer to God. I knew I would never love this way again. I needed God and would love God. I would trust that it was at this time in my life, when I felt so alone, that He would save me because I felt like I was dying. In fact, the opposite was happening. I was making choices that would save my life.

I was back at my desk making the plane reservations to go back to Florida and take care of my affairs, of Johnny's affair, the affair that ended my marriage. Later, I would understand that Taneisha was sent by an angel to warn me of the demon in my life, and to make me leave him because nothing else was working. How else could the man I loved become such a disgusting stranger? How could he suddenly reveal himself so completely to me and make me feel that I was in the presence of a dark energy, something so strong and so dangerous that it could make me want to throw away my life?

I had survived so many challenges. I became so strong and so full of joy, so trusting that this was a good world and that I was going to have what I finally wanted; a husband who loved me, a home on the beach and a dog, a dream come true. I knew men could have strange ideas and fantasies when it came to sex, and I heard horror stories before. But not like this. How would I ever forget this? It was going to make the next stage of my life easier.

No, I could not love this way again.

I suddenly realized that I was free. This ugly moment was the straw that broke the camel's back. This man was not the Johnny I married; this was a deviant sick man that I did not know. I fell asleep in a fetal position, sitting in my comfortable suede executive chair, with my jacket wrapped around me like a swaddled baby. I awoke to a knock on my office door, the secretary telling me she was leaving for the day, and I realized I had no time to waste. My life was in danger, and it was my own fault if I waited another day to end this God forsaken marriage.

CHAPTER NINETEEN:
DUTY CALLS

I called the Delray Beach police and told them that I needed to file a request for a restraining order. They listened, and then they told me abruptly that I must do this in person at my residence in Delray Beach. I needed to return to the lion's den while he waited for me, where he would be circling, looking for me on the path.

I got into my car and drove to the hospital, entered the emergency department, and asked for my doctor who happened to be on duty. I told her to give me every single possible test for venereal disease, and I lay there during the examination wondering how this could happen to me. I was so afraid of HIV and AIDS and had only slept with two men in twenty years. What if Johnny gave me an infection? Taneisha was very promiscuous and the thought of ever touching anything that touched her vagina made me want to throw up. I tried not to think about whether Johnny had touched me without washing himself after he had touched her. Oh God.

My doctor gave me prescriptions for antibiotics, a Hepatitis vaccination, and told me to come back for a series of checkups and follow-up vaccinations. This battle was a fight for life or death. I couldn't take this lightly as I faced the distinct possibility that my ignorance was going to kick me in the butt this time. How could I close my eyes and ignore what was happening? Why did I get involved with such lowlife? Who was I? What happened to Brigitte, the smart, busy businesswoman?

I was so ashamed that I wanted to kill myself. I thought about the many ways to do it. I remember feeling so lucky not to have been in Florida when this happened because I would have driven over to them at the store and killed them both and gone to jail. Real smart, Brigitte, I thought to myself. Now you've done it.

That evening as I stood in line at US Customs the phone rang. It was Johnny's mom.

"Honey, what is goin' on?" She said, sounding so worried.

I was so happy to hear her voice and wanted to cry and tell her everything, but then I realized that she was over eighty years old and didn't need the stress.

I just said, "Momma, Johnny has been with a black woman that works in our shop, and I can't allow that in my life."

I heard her say gently, "But ah thought you knew that honey?"

There was something in her voice that made me think that she didn't believe that I should leave Johnny over this, and just accept it as part of the package. I thought to myself, yeah right, just like the Sopranos huh? Where wives suffer and enjoy the wealth and profit of organized crime, ignore the mistresses, and just spend hubby's fortune? Only Johnny was spending my money and fooling around on me. It didn't make any difference whether he was rich or poor, I wasn't into emotional pain. I wasn't taking the risk that some idiot mistress would want me out of the way Buttafuoco style. I had to end this bad dream once and for all. It was the last time I ever spoke to my mother in law.

I got on the plane and flew first class to Fort Lauderdale; I drank the soothing burgundy, nibbled on the steak and potatoes, and I passed on the chocolate cake dessert, all mousse and cream. I had the headsets on to watch a movie and to relax, but instead I put the music channel on, and I listened to the words of a beautiful song, 'Every Time You Go Away', and I started to cry. I pulled out my headphones, closed my eyes, and remembered what it was I had to do.

I arrived in Delray Beach in my rental car. It was midnight; too late to see any lights on anywhere in the condo complex, and I was afraid. I dialed 911 and asked for police assistance in order to enter my home, because I was worried that Johnny was waiting for me. They arrived and came to my door, and asked me what was wrong. I told them that I was afraid that my estranged husband was waiting for me in the dark.

I told them what he has said to me, that I would be dead before there would be an annulment. They pulled their weapons out, and they were opening the door and telling me to stand back. Out of my stupid mouth came the words that made no sense, "Please don't shoot him." They looked at me like I was nuts.

"Ma'am stand back and let us do our job," they said.

The two officers opened my door, turned on the lights, and looked through the condo. They came out and told me there was no one there. We sat, and I filed a police report. I was lost in time and did not notice that most of my valuables were missing. My jewelry, Montblanc pen, the flat screen TV from the bedroom, my Rosenthal china; but that was not my focus, my focus was survival. This could not be happening to me. Who called these policemen? Why were they here? I kept trying to forget what had happened and focus on the here and now. I was not the wife who loved Johnny. I was the victim of his death threats and successful robbery, extortion, and larceny attempts.

I was someone else sitting here, telling them everything as they wrote it down. I was told to take the papers to the courthouse, and file them for a temporary restraining order. Then, I would get a court date to obtain a permanent restraining order. That was if the judge felt there was any true danger to my wellbeing. They left, and I was all alone on the longest day of my life.

I called early the next day to speak with a Legal Aid attorney, because Johnny took all of my cash and I had no money to pay an attorney. I was referred to Cynthia Olsen and made an appointment to meet her, so that she could represent me. First, I had to go through procedures to get the application processed.

I arrived at the Palm Beach County Courthouse on Atlantic Avenue. It was a beautiful building that did not appear intimidating. I was wearing high heels that resonated throughout the entry, and then I saw the uniforms. I was told by security to remove any computers, phones, and wires from my purse, and I did. As the police watched, I took out four cell phones, a Verizon MIFI unit, my laptop, a multitude of keys on chains and tangled charging wires for my apparatuses. The security guards looked as though they had never seen the contents of a businesswoman's purse before. Were they looking for rouge and mascara and bubble gum? I walked through the metal-detector and the alarm went off. They looked at my jewelry worth a year of their wages, and they told me to go on through, and I did.

"Do you work in a computer store young lady?" I saw a kind, older man who sensed the sorrow in me. He smiled that million dollar "daddy loves you and you are going to be okay" kind of smile, and I felt better, slightly less afraid. I argued with myself about leaving the chargers loose in my purse because they tangled intentionally, and I hated untangling them.

I looked around. I was definitely not in Kansas anymore, I thought, as I walked through the busy courthouse. I felt a collective tension worse than that in the waiting rooms in any hospital. It was dreary. There were lost souls walking around everywhere. I found the Domestic Violence unit, and I started to tell my story. The lady behind the glass window looked at me with her bifocals like I was ordering a McDonald's trio. She shoved some papers at me with a grin from side to side and said, "Go to that room and fill these out, and bring them back signed and dated."

Okay, so much for the telling of my story part, I thought. They meant business. I looked at the empty rooms and thought that there was not much business in that department. I walked around to find a bathroom, and instead I found the special room with Lonnie Starker's name on the door. Sitting there was a petite, beautiful, smiling woman who asked me to sit down, and I looked around to make sure she was talking to me before I finally sat down. I felt like Alice in Wonderland; in a place I had never been before. I tried to tell her what I was looking for, and she told me to take my coat off and to tell her everything. I had found a woman who was friendly in a courthouse. So I began, and she watched me as though it was the first time she had ever heard this story, and I appreciated her listening to me.

"And that my dear is precisely why I don't date," Lonnie said. She was beautiful. Her lips were perfectly lipsticked, her head perfectly coiffed, and she was dressed to kill. She was sexy, smart, and tough. I felt that I had something to learn from her, and I did. She recited stories about scoundrels who stole everything but plucked eyebrows from women who should have known better. These victims were smart women who worked in important jobs and held high positions in Palm Beach County society. Yet, these women were new to the Florida culture of romance as a tool for economic violence.

The economy was lousy, and there were many desperate people looking for a meal ticket; a way out of poverty.

"There are too many stories like yours, Brigitte". Lonnie began to describe them one by one. Without breaching client confidentiality, she explained that no woman was immune. There was the judge that had to be dragged out of Florida by her kids back to New York because some gigolo robbed her of her last dime, and left her with a thin roll of leftover toilet paper to call her own. Everything was gone, the condo, the car, the money in the bank account. Still, she wanted to stay. Still, she wanted him back.

I sat rigid with shock, listening to her every word, still, not moving anything but my eyes which were growing larger and larger, opening wider and wider to take in every word coming out of her mouth as though I was reading her lips. I felt as though I couldn't hear a word; everything she was saying was as though it was coming from a distant place.

I thought there had to be a Legionnaire love virus that spread throughout the state, and stopped at Georgia and Louisiana's borders. I listened nonstop as I learned that this was a common occurrence, a phenomenon in dating called dating violence. And so, I was lumped in with women of all ages, mostly elderly, who were targeted by men like Johnny. What was it? Was it a crime, or just one lump sum called relational domestic violence? Where did I fit in? I was an intelligent, educated, experienced, worldly, and knowledgeable woman. I certainly didn't belong in the file with the crazy female judge... or did I? I was aware that something had happened to me that I could not and did not want to understand.

I filled the forms out. My brain filled with spilling facts about my life with Johnny, the kind of life I had only seen in TV movies and on the Maury Show. Mr. Rule-Breaker whose self-elevating strategies failed on every count, despite his self-convincing confidence, was coming to his end game; a losing play, a no-win situation. He could not talk his way out of it anymore. It was the beginning of the end for Johnny, the king of the risk takers. For me, it was the start of the rest of my life without Johnny, without the man who professed his love for me, who promised me that I would be the happiest woman in the world, happier than Dolly Parton.

Sometimes he sounded like a robot, a human impersonator as he repeated his stories, recited his bullshit, with his insatiable appetite for self-aggrandizement. No other man north of Miami could possibly be more perfect. According to Johnny, he could solve the problems of the entire world and its leaders if they would just listen to him.

I was done listening to any words that came out of his mouth. If Johnny's lips were moving, he was lying.

I had lost a small fortune in money and most of my self-respect since I first believed his verbal spillage of deceitful phrases, all intended to bring him closer to my money. I was at emotional rock bottom. This could not be happening to me.

I was afraid that I had lost my mind. I was a week away from writing the exams to renew my Florida real estate sales license. I studied day and night. I wrote the three-hour exam in ninety minutes, and I got a mark of ninety-three. At least the intellectual part of my brain was still on duty. As far as emotional intelligence went, I scored zero minus five.

I was only miles away from the scene of the crime. I realized I needed to move on, and I needed to do what was necessary to pick up the pieces of my life. I planned to stay in Florida that week to finish what I started, even if I would be alone, without Johnny, for the rest of my life. The words settled in my mind on a comfortable couch in the mental den in the gray matter of my brain, a place in which I would store all of the details of my life with Johnny. That was a room in my mind, in which I locked the details that I did not want to lose, the details that I needed to make sense of what I was going through. That room would overflow one day with the knowledge of the many women before me and after me that were also victims of his talented way of making them think that they were the only one.

According to Johnny, they were the first, and the last to feel the love of an Italian husband that would make them the happiest women in the world. They had also trusted Johnny and gave him money to do work he never did, and lent him money he would never repay. Worst of all, they suffered the post traumatic shock that came with his hit and run method of leaving them wondering how they could recover from the financial rape they had been subjected to. There was no condom that could have protected them from the mental disease they were left with after Johnny disappeared with their money and their hearts. Call it Stockholm syndrome, call it what you want, it all presented the same way. They suffered from night rage, nightmares, panic attacks, and fear of revealing what had happened to them. They also felt shame that they had believed in Johnny's tales of love, and promises of performance of anything it was that made them fall for his web of lies. Last but not least, they were all out thousands if not hundreds of thousands of dollars that they had counted on for their retirement; for rent, food, travel, health care, car payments, and worst of all, monies they had been entrusted by their late husbands. How terrified they were to tell their children that it was all gone. Their estates would be worthless, maybe even in a deficit. So began the culture of silence.

I was ashamed of myself. I hated myself more than I hated Johnny. I knew I would have to take the punishment that came with the mistake of not having the brains to protect myself. I had allowed some subterranean creature into my life. There was no going back, and there was no stopping me. If I was going to do this, I was going to do it right and win.

I began a two-year process of taking the first step and the next step on my route to justice, even when I was too tired, too depressed, too devastated.

It was on a quiet morning when I sat alone collecting my thoughts and looking at all of the paperwork in my files about the annulment when my cell phone rang. It was Johnny, speaking softly at first and ending up screaming at me at the top of his lungs, demanding that I stop whatever it was that I was doing.

"Baby, I don't know who you are, but you must be real important. The cops stopped me, frisked me, and took my car apart. They went through everything and took away my machete. They came to the dry cleaners and searched it and took my stun gun, my baton, and my mace. How do you expect me to protect myself now? Now somebody can rob me and get away with it! Do you see what you have done? You lied to the police and told them I threatened to kill you? Why would you do that? I am your husband, Brigitte! You need to stop this nonsense and come back to claim your husband. I don't want you to leave me. You need to come home, just be with your man. Do you understand me?" I could feel the dangerous fire of his rage miles away.

I hung up after listening to his rants and tried not to let anything he had to say affect me; I was numb. I became a robot that would continue what I had to do to survive. I could not let him have another chance to harm me again. He was not a person to argue with, not someone to cross. I was the first woman with the balls to make him face the consequences of his crimes.

Johnny began to call me ten times a day, begging for me to come back, crying for me to claim my husband, sounding like an abandoned baby. Although my mind was made up, my heart was weak. How I wanted to hold him close to my breast and rock him, to make it all stop, make it all go away. His pleas haunted me for months.

"I can fix this." He said.

"No, you can't Johnny. You can never fix this. I am not coming back." I held my breath waiting for his reply. He would sit in silence, and I would hear his sniffles and sighs, and I almost believed that he felt some pain. A man who felt no pain appeared to feel some pain for the first time. It wasn't empathy for his victims. It was self pity for his inability to find a woman who would take him as he was. It was all about his childhood feelings of detachment and longing for the affection and attention he never got as an infant. It was a manipulation intended to soften the hearts of those women who he carelessly discarded once they had no money left for him to steal. I had to constantly remind myself that his tears were crocodile tears intended to make women feel sorry for him, sorry for his loss. What about their loss?

"If you ain't comin' back then you need to quitclaim your condo to me and that will fix it." He stated. He waited for my reply. I felt as though we were playing a game of chess. Only this wasn't a game. This was a crime in progress.

"Do you think I am that dumb Johnny? I don't know who you have messed with in the past Johnny but you are messing with the wrong woman today. You are not getting my condo and I want my money and my Jaguar back. That will fix it Johnny. That is what is broken here." I had no doubt that he did not love me. I knew I was never going back.

This could not be fixed. I could not be fixed. I was broken, different, wiser, older, and forever healing.

Then, he told me that he and Taneisha laughed at me all day, and he told me how stupid I was. He told me how happy they were, how profitable the business was, and that I should never have left because things were going so well.

Then he screamed at me at the top of his lungs and said, "This is not over, Brigitte!"

I heard the echo of those words in my soul. My husband was a sick man, a sex addict, dangerous to my mental and physical health. There was so much more that I did not know about him. When he would call, when I would first hear his voice, I would feel myself wanting to be in his arms, and then it always ended with violent words and threats on my life.

I learned to end the call when those words started, and all I could do was hang up the phone and cry all day long. I once thought that Johnny had fulfilled a proverb; 'When one soul with a broken left wing meets another lonely soul with a broken right wing, they join souls to form a stronger whole, a union that allows them flight into a brighter future'. We came so close.

As I lost the man I loved, his words haunted my sleepless nights. I walked the floors of my apartment, I saw the moonlit night sky full of twinkling stars, and I wondered if there was a parallel universe where Johnny worked hard, was faithful, loved to shower, and to make love to me only, and we lived in total bliss…

CHAPTER TWENTY:
STEPS TO RECOVERY

I believe there are angels sent on our path so often, and many times we don't even know it. When you drive too fast and someone in front of you is driving at the speed limit. You can't pass them, and then come across an accident. You may suddenly realize that it could have been you. The car in front of you had slowed your pace, kept you safe. You did not arrive at the intersection at the time you may have, had they not slowed your progress.

I was back at work, doing what I do best, keeping busy making money for my clients, this time with no distractions. That is, without allowing anything but numbers into my head for weeks. The markets were flying again and I had resumed meetings with my high net worth clients to review their accounts. I thought I had everything under control.

I walked into an important client's home to help her review her investments.

Angela had it all, everything but perfect health. She was balanced and brilliant and had all of her responsibilities under control. She was in charge of her family's wealth and had a small family of perfect miniature Yorkies that wrestled with her Hermes bag without her batting a wink.

It wasn't long before Angela looked at me, in a way that caught my attention.

"Brigitte, are you okay?" Angela asked me.

"Yes, I am fine, nothing is wrong, nothing." I kept my head bowed and looked at my papers.

She had her head tilted with a "WTF is wrong with you" look on her face.

I laughed, and looked out the window in an effort to hide my soul. Here I was, with a brilliant woman half my age who had been my client for fifteen years. I helped her family amass a small fortune, and she cared about me and my success. It must have been clear to anyone and everyone who cared about me that something had changed in my demeanor. My normal smiling face was full of pain. I was walking and talking, but I was dead inside. I had been ripped apart from the inside out, my heart and my brain, out from my lips that refused to smile ever again.

"Angela, I…" I started, and I fell apart. I looked at her, and I didn't know what to do. I knew she was a doctor of Psychology and treated patients with post-traumatic stress disorder. Angela specialized in domestic violence, aging brains, and dementia. She was an accomplished author who had written books about dementia and aging. She was young. She lived a beautiful sheltered life with a perfect family and loving parents. She was a millionaire before she was forty. How could she even begin to understand the path that I was lost on?

How could I tell her what I had lived through in the last six months? What if she changed her mind about being my client? What if she changed her mind about respecting me and about what I represented in her life? The manager of her millions who could not see a con artist when he stood naked in front of her?

What do thieves look like?

What do they wear?

How do they speak?

Where are they from?

"I just lost my heart and mind and a small fortune to a man I married after knowing him for only five months. I just lost my place in a world that I wanted to believe was so safe, so beautiful. I blindly believed that by marrying Johnny I would transit into a state of union that would be full of hope. I placed my faith in the wrong man, and thought that if I did everything right and worked hard, good karma would always walk beside me. I truly believed I was helping someone that was going to complete my life. I am finished. I don't know if anyone can ever understand what I have lived through, I..." When I was out of breath, I suddenly stopped and realized how ridiculous I sounded. I was just so ashamed of myself I didn't know what to add.

She looked at me and smiled a shaman's smile, a look of wisdom far beyond her years as she said. "It's okay, sit down. I am here. I will listen, you are safe, and it's okay. Just sit down."

I began to weep, weep for myself, and weep for my future, my past, my dreams, and my fantasies. I cried for that once open mind that believed it was good to trust people and have faith in the world, and mostly, faith in love. It was at least a half hour before I could compose myself enough to look up. Then, I continued to tell her about Johnny, about our sham marriage.

I spoke about the betrayal, how I lost the love of my life. I had thought that Johnny, the man of my dreams, was sent to me here on earth by God. I thought that he was sent here to bless me with affection, companionship, and true love. I had lost that someone who promised the right things about our future, and who reflected everything I wanted in life, right down to the music I loved. I told her how excited I was about making our future the happiest one that any couple ever had.

I was looking forward to a smiling future full of ocean breezes, gardens, and puppies. I believed my husband had a legitimate business in which he was renovating homes. I finally had a family complete with a mother and father-in-law who were happily married for forty-five years, and sisters, and cousins, and aunts for me and my daughter...

And it was all a lie.

I looked up and saw a warm smile, calm eyes, and Angela said to me, "You are now in the right place at the right time Brigitte. Life is a long road and on that road we meet people who are good and sometimes, even when we are good people, we meet dishonest people who harm us. You have been the victim of a financial predator, and you are lucky to be alive. Many women in your situation are dead. They took too long to understand what domestic violence is. You are lucky to be here."

I suddenly sat up and paid attention. She continued to tell me that I would survive this, but I had to listen and do as she said. Angela began to teach me about trauma bonding and psychopaths who use methods to gain your confidence, inject themselves into your life and become indispensable, separating you from those who love you. She described to me the process that begins with romance and sex, and then often ends with the death of a woman after all the money is gone, and no proof of love remains. She said that I could have been killed.

"Imagine how Pamela would feel if he killed you. Imagine your funeral and the people who love you, and their feelings of loss." I realized that I had dodged a bullet that aimed at my very being, my heart and soul.

The next few months were very busy. My calendar was booked solid with client appointments, and I survived by becoming an even worse workaholic than before. I resorted to the long days and excessive work that got me into trouble in the first place, but I had no choice. It was that, or declare bankruptcy. My days were filled with daily visits to Angela, and mixed doses of

Paxil, Avapro, caffeine, and sleep. I held a small rubber lizard in my hand that Angela told me was Johnny; a lizard, a dangerous biting, killing, heart-stealing lizard.

"He is not the frolicking puppy you had imagined him to be, Brigitte. Your description of him as a playful puppy that needs to hump everything is totally dangerous to your recovery. You need to see Johnny for the expert criminal that he is. Only then can you walk down that path of recover and abandon all aspects of denial." I still have that lizard in my wallet. I take it out when I think of Johnny. I hold in my hand and I remember what got me into the biggest mess of my life.

Another way she helped was to tell me that even though the amount of money he stole was large, I should just visualize it as the price of a Hermes bag. It became a goal for me in the future, when I would resume my normal life, my normal earnings. One day I would buy myself a beautiful Hermes bag, yes, but for now it was all about how to get there from here. I had to earn that reward with a lot of hard emotional work on myself.

I was living in a small bachelor apartment that I had rented a block from my office. I worked all day, and on weekends I flew home to Delray Beach to my condo to deal with my messed up life. I began to read about trauma bonding and financial predators. I could not put down the book that I found online about loving psychopaths and it saved my life. I reread and highlighted parts of the book that I felt I needed to understand. I was exactly like the women described in the book. I was an overachiever, one who never gave up on fixing something until it was perfect. I understood.

In trying to make Johnny into an earthly god, when he was really a devil in disguise, I had inflated his ego so much that he mistook my generosity and trust for stupidity. There was so much more to come, but he had gotten enough out of our relationship, or his project named 'How Much Money Can I Get Out Of Brigitte'. There were two distinct Brigittes; one before, and one after Johnny. Everything had changed. I had only begun to understand the trauma I had endured and the long journey home, not back to who I used to be but to where I could accept my new reality.

CHAPTER TWENTY-ONE:
RELAPSE GIRL

I received the date for the courts to issue the restraining order. On the date of the hearing, Johnny appeared in person, alone. He looked his best, ready for a performance, as though this was his stage. He begged the judge to let him speak to his wife. The judge seemed to know him, and spoke to him so as to calm him and maintain control of his court.

"Why can't I speak to my wife, she is right there, and I can see her. She and I need to talk. I need to speak with her, and I just want to have a chance to explain. Why can't I just sit down with her for a minute and let her know and tell her what is wrong, and I can fix it? I love my wife," he repeated.

"Now we're not going to have a problem here today are we, Mr. Sorella? I think I'll let Ms. Knowles' attorney discuss that possibility with her but you need to remember where you are and why you are here."

I told my attorney not to let him near me. I told her that he was like Charles Manson. I told her he could sweet talk the skin off a rattlesnake, before it was ready to do so. He could make women do whatever he wanted, and I could not be near him. I could not look into his eyes, so I stared at the wall beside me. My attorney had spent hours researching Johnny Sorella and his alias, finding more than we needed to shut down his access to me. She presented the judge with evidence and past judgments showing that Johnny was linked to organized crime. She showed his previous court cases, including one for armed assault with intent to murder, and assault and battery by means of a dangerous weapon. Johnny's notebook that they found filled with his handwriting was the best proof of his involvement with crime, but somehow he got off, over and over. The accusations made in these archived charges were the most serious of his life. He blew them off with hundreds of legal maneuvers. There were petitions for postponements, requests for more evidence, and for anything you could pay an attorney to do, short of disrobing in front of a jury. She also showed the judge that he participated in a RICO enterprise, as an unindicted co-conspirator. He was a part of a team that distributed methamphetamine, LSD, cocaine, and marijuana. As well, he was found guilty of a felony for identity theft, credit card fraud, and using a false identity to obtain a driver's license.

I took one breath at a time, each time wondering if it would be my last. I felt Johnny's gaze on my back like a sharp knife turning slowly, as my attorney read each felony record out loud. Johnny was no boy scout. He was a rat, a snitch, and someone who would throw anybody under the bus to save his own neck. There were women who loved him enough to have been accomplices in his crimes, and they had done jail time for him. I understood how they came under his spell.

The judge asked Johnny, "Are you guilty of the crime that is presented to me today?"

There was silence only for a moment, and then Johnny said "Yes, your honor."

Johnny was smarter than he looked. I knew he would plead guilty so as to avoid answering any questions under oath. Johnny was no poker player.

Then, the judge read the conditions to Johnny, and told him that if he went near me at any of my addresses at work or at home, in Canada or the United States, he would have to deal with him again. He said to Johnny, "Do you understand everything I have told you? Don't let me see you again in my court. I think we understand each other right?"

Then the judge asked me to come up and sign the official restraining order documents before him. I looked up and Johnny was standing there, waiting for me as he had on the day we married, and I could not get up. I could not move. I was dead frozen in my seat. I was not there; this was not happening. I slowly got up, and it seemed like hours until I got to the podium and the judge gave me a pen; a pen that Johnny had just held between his fingers to sign the documents. I couldn't help but notice that he wasn't wearing a wedding ring. I still was. I still had my canary diamond on my finger and I couldn't get it off. I still wore a daily reminder of my mistake. I felt that it was not fair; this was so much like when we signed the registry at our wedding, and I wanted to die. The sheriff was escorting me out of the courthouse, and as I walked away, Johnny shouted, "Where are you going?"

It took all of my energy not to look back at him, and his voice reached deep into that place in my heart where I still loved him. I kept walking without even looking at him, but I could feel his gaze. I imagined the desperate feeling that he was holding in his heart because deep down inside of his cold heart, he knew I had gotten away.

I was in and out of the courthouse for amended restraining orders because Johnny kept calling.

"Brigitte, it's me, your husband. I will do anything. I will sell everything I have just to be with you. Even if we're poor and we have nothing to live on, I will work day and night to bring the money in to make it up to you. We belong together. You know that, I love you. I will meet with the counselor to discuss the money." He actually cried on the phone and it hurt me so badly to ignore his pleas. Call after call, he begged and pleaded for me to listen to him. He kept wearing me down, until he finally got me to agree to change the no contact order.

I stupidly spent hours finding a counselor that could deal with a repeat felon con artist who would act like the perfect husband and exemplary citizen. I needed someone who would understand that this was not an ordinary man, but a lizard with a reptilian brain in his head that had thirty years of cocaine damage. I knew that I needed a professional who would once and for all tell me who this guy was and what he was capable of. Finally, I found one.

In order to allow contact, I contacted my attorney and got a no violence order, and it replaced the no contact order. I was waiting for Johnny to go and see the counselor first, and then I would meet him. I needed Johnny to show commitment to the work in progress that was his declaration of love to me. I told him he had a lot of work to do on himself before I could think of taking him back and that, at this point, the meeting was only to discuss the money he took from me. He said he would sign anything I wanted him to. I did not believe that he loved me, and I felt that there was no hope for reconciliation, but he told me we could be a miracle.

There was no miracle and he never went to the appointment. Johnny had already found his next victim. He was already busy with a tough looking, buxom blonde, that you didn't want to run into in a dark alley. He was setting her up to give him her disability money and her house. I wound up paying for the appointment and court costs for changing the order to no violence from no contact for nothing. I doubt that Johnny planned it that way, but it worked in his favor. He was now able to contact me.

I realized that the one major miracle during our relationship happened the day I woke up and decided it was over. That was the day I realized I was the victim of a heartless con man who walked into my life like a dream, and left it a nightmare. I had survived a con by a master con artist, who played with women's hearts and with their minds like they were a deck of cards. I thought by then that I was safely over him. I was wrong.

It was November, and I was at an elegant evening fundraiser event at the Breakers in Palm Beach. I was with my friend Robert, a handsome funny man, an architect who graduated from East Winds Real Estate School with me. I was surrounded with affluent, beautiful, loving, generous, successful people who had just raised thousands of dollars for children. The music was enchanting and jazzy, and everyone was buzzed from the chilled champagne that fell into glasses like rain.

I was even flirting. I stood at the buffet table and looked at the mocha cake filled with whipped cream. As I turned to put the desert on my plate, I saw a handsome, well-dressed, tall man smoking a pipe, staring at me. I offered him some cake on a plate with a fork and my sweetest smile. He took it, and I rejoiced. Cute guy takes cake. Step one was complete. I was happy, and I felt that life was calm again. Suddenly, I was looking at the phone number on my ringing cell. I saw that it said "Johnny." Impulsively, I made the mistake of taking the call. I got up and left the table to go take the call in the rest room where I stood behind locked doors and said, "Hello".

"Where are you?" he cried, and I told him. I told him that I was with friends in Palm Beach, and he begged me to come by and see him. He spoke softly and told me it was okay, he understood, but he just wanted me to come by and say hello. So I did. I left an incredible party and broke a no violence order to go and see why this dangerous man was crying. It made no sense to me then, and it has never made sense to anyone who knows me.

As I drove across the Flagler Bridge, I passed the expensive yachts and the men who owned them, to subject myself to more suffering and punishment. I was heading to West Palm Beach in the middle of the night to meet with the poorest man I knew. It made no sense, yet in a somewhat hypnotic way, I up and left a party full of quality people, who lived semi-normal lives, for a face to face reunion with the one man I feared like he was the devil on earth.

I parked the car beside the cleaners and got out, and saw Johnny. He looked like an old man standing by the door, his pants half hanging off, his face smiling weakly. I suddenly felt all of the love and compassion, sorrow and tears coming. He opened his arms, and he closed them around me. He held me for so long. I started to cry, he started to cry, and he asked me to come in and meet his new cockatoo, Kasar, and I did. I was sitting there amongst the same, messy items, in piles again, that had grown in places that I had cleared. Again, I realized that he was lost, just as lost as the first time I met him.

"Baby, let me get you a drink." He got up and slowly walked to his fridge, still full of leftovers, meals and meals from takeout joints that he half ate and then stuffed in the back. He pulled out some scotch and he poured me a tall glass, and I drank it. I cried for nearly an hour, and he held me in his arms and rocked me, silently, and I realized how much I still loved him. Why was I here, why did I come back?

"Baby, can I come home with you tonight and just hold you in my arms?" he asked.

"Yes, Johnny," I said. For a moment all of the pain and sorrow in my heart was lifted, and the one who was hurting me so badly stopped hurting me. He was telling me how sorry he was, and how much he loved me. I thought for a moment that we could turn back time.

He could not drive because he had no gas in his car, and so we took mine. We drove home silently, and Johnny told me just one thing.

"I just wanted to show you how brave I am." Then, he fell asleep on my lap while I sang softly, caressing his hair, tears falling down my face. I was helpless in his presence. I took him into my home, into my shower, and I washed him for half an hour. I washed him everywhere, his hair, his back, his feet, his underarms and he was finally clean. I was so sad to see him so lost and alone, and I took him to my bed. He told me he was afraid. I asked him why, and he didn't answer. He made tender love to me and again I was somewhere I wanted to be, in his arms with him, alive with him, alone in the world with him. We fell asleep and in the morning, he woke me and looked into my eyes.

"I love only you," he told me.

I smiled and I began to cry. They were tears of joy because for a moment I wanted it all back. I wanted Johnny, his problems, his weaknesses, and his best attempt to show love. I wanted to believe that this was a miracle.

We dressed, and I drove him back to his dry cleaners. We walked in and he told me, excitedly, "Don't move, stay there, I'll be right back, just let me bring the dry cleaning to the plant, it won't be more than a minute, I promise."

He rushed out and I was left alone in the dark. A dreary place, blackness behind me, and I turned and saw the mess. The hoarded mess of his past, of the things that mattered to him, of the things he felt at home with, the mess he needed to feel secure. I wanted to run out and never come back.

I looked down at the counter, and I saw cutout ads from dating services. I realized he was looking for new women to be with, and it was too much. I got my purse and went outdoors and got into my car and drove straight to the airport. I heard the song, "What a Fool Believes" and I heard the phone ringing, and it was Johnny.

"Where are you? Why did you leave? Get back here, I need you, I love you, what is wrong with you?" He was in a panic.

"Johnny, I can't do this, I saw the dating stuff. I know what you are doing. I know you are hooking up with new women for money, I just can't handle it." My hands were shaking and sweaty on the soft tan Italian leather on the driver's wheel that I held onto for dear life. In reality, it was as though I wasn't there, because mentally there was no driver at the wheel. I was hiding up in the soft cumulus clouds that floated above me in the sky. I was softly moving across the sky blessed with sunlight, and only my mind was dark with sorrow.

"Baby I told you I would start to date if you didn't come back?"

"So that makes it right, that means you did nothing wrong." I thought about it. I thought about how Johnny always came out of any mental crash without a bruise. Only I was a total loss.

Another love song was playing, "You were the dream that saved my life, you were the reason I survived…" I listened to the words of the song and felt love, but as I heard his words, I felt fear. I was unable to think or move, like a deer that was blinded by headlights. I was driving away and I knew I was out of his reach, but inside me, his grip held on to my stomach and squeezed it like a cobra.

I said quietly into the phone, "Goodbye." I was still shaken when I parked my car at the airport in economy parking, and wandered in circles until I reached the bus stop. I sat there still numb from what had transpired. I actually spent the night with the man that I was terrified of and broke my own rules. Rule number one, stay away from the danger that is Johnny. Rule number two, don't forget rule number one. Rule number three, respect the danger.

I got into the plane, and I left Florida in a daze without even going home to the condo to get my stuff. I went through security clearance with only my purse. I boarded the plane like a zombie, aware that Florida would never mean the same to me. My simple dream of having a good marriage and a house on the beach and a dog, well that dream had died, and I was all alone again. I slept all the way home and woke up only when the plane landed and jarred me back into reality. What had I done?

I was alone with my sorrow and I was dealing with rebuilding my life and my future alone. I slept, I ate, I slept, I cried, I ate, I cried. Then, I could not sleep, and the panic attacks began. I could not find a comfortable place to be alive and breathe and feel. I could not live in my skin. My life became unmanageable. I was losing faith in my ability to survive. I spent my life helping others manage their problems until my own problems became overwhelming. I realized I needed help from the source of wisdom that was God. I attended AA and Narcotics Anonymous meetings, and I felt safe where others bared their souls and asked for help to live one day at a time, with help and love from above.

I started to feel the roots and shoots of self-love reappear ever so slowly, little tiny shoots, so green and sweet, and serene. I knew that the love I felt for Johnny was real, but he was not real. I knew I had done nothing wrong, nothing but fall in love with a man that was like the character your favorite actor played in romantic movie. The transition was as clear as is stepping out to the busy city street outside a quiet movie theatre. You felt something different when you listened to the movie sound track and watched the screen in the darkened comfort of the chair in the right row. It was very different from what you felt when you exited from a beautiful movie into real life as you walked out of the theatre into reality. You were able to go and see the movie over and over as much as you liked, especially if you preferred it to real life. My relationship with Johnny was like watching Lauren Bacall and Humphrey Bogart in their 'You Know How To Whistle' scene. Their chemistry was magnetic, their love mystique. So was ours, so mysterious was the feeling I had for the character that Johnny played in my life. Compared to who he turned out to be, a dangerous criminal, his false persona was romantic and memorable. I could search for the phantom Johnny forever, or like a good movie, I could just forget about him and move on to other movies. I had to stop trying to relive the good parts of the film, as the bad parts started to outnumber the good parts. This movie had to end and I could never watch it again.

Only, Johnny wasn't a character that you could forget easily. I felt lucky to be alive and I was ready to start over where I left off. I walked away from my dreams with Johnny. I realized I would never stop loving the man he said he was. I felt the person that I dreamed of, the person that I used to love, fading into non-existence, and I felt that I would never find him again because he never existed. I was sad beyond belief. I was sad and sorry, and mourning more than I ever did for my mother. I looked for signs of him everywhere, and there were none. He was in West Palm Beach and I was in Montreal. I realized that he had never been in my life in Montreal.

There was no evidence of him in my life; no pictures on the mantle, clothing, or shoes, none of the remnants that usually survive a broken marriage. I looked around and there was nothing in my office where I spent 15 hour days again. Even when I returned to Delray Beach to handle official legal matters, I looked around my condo and he had taken every remnant of his time with me. The only thing that reminded me of him was the tile floor that he laid, the floor I had to finish. Johnny left unfinished business everywhere. Now, apart from the mess he left in my life, it was as though he never existed. It was as though our marriage never happened. Our relationship was based on my dreams that he mirrored. It was my money that was used to fund his existence, my love that was supporting the warm place that I thought we occupied together. When our relationship ended, I knew that he would find another victim whose life he would mirror, to whom he would whisper the same lies.

Even though I tried to comfort myself with the thought that he lost me, that maybe he would miss me and everything that I was to him, I knew he was gone. When I thought of the sweet songs I softly sang to him while I caressed him, the way I would wash him down after his hard day at work and massage him till he fell asleep, I knew that his next victim could easily replace me. There would be another woman who would probably do similar things to show him how much she loved him. I was just one in a series of women who would find the pain that Johnny had waiting for them. Pain would cause some to spend years alone distrusting all men and all love, wishing they had never met him. Johnny was like the wrong message in a fortune cookie. You wanted to keep opening more until you got the right one, the fortune you were seeking. No matter how many times I tried my luck, I kept getting the same message: 'Run as fast as you can and don't look back'.

I was numbed by medication and would think half-truths and feel half-pains, never so intense as to feel real. It was all a daze for a year, until I felt safe enough to stop taking the Paxil and started trusting myself again. I was not the same girl I used to be, and the world would never know that girl's love and trust and happy smile again. The girl that would give everything to have true love, well, I have hidden that girl in the Louvre behind the Mona Lisa. She would never come out again and was just a memory.

CHAPTER TWENTY-TWO: SWITCHING GEARS

Just as I started to make progress and the healing appeared to be working, out of the blue, Moe Mason called. Moe, my dear friend who used to tell everyone I was his sister; my black brother, a real hip friend who danced all night and who dressed like a movie star was calling me. Even though he felt that my decision to leave Johnny was none of his business, he wanted to reach out to me. He was so happy to hear my voice, and when he realized what had happened he told me everything. He then told me he wanted me to see Johnny because he was heading downhill fast. Moe told me that Johnny was falling apart without me, that people were concerned about his state of mind.

I listened and my hands started shaking. I was looking out the window at the rain that was softly falling on the Florida palms outside my condo. I heard the pitter-patter and it was calming. I listened to Moe's voice which sounded so unreal, telling me how Johnny explained to him that he got my Jaguar put into his name to steal it from me and that next, he was going to take my condo and get that into his name. He told Moe that this was how he made his money. Moe told me about the whores and drugs and drinking and how Johnny couldn't get enough after I left him and stayed out of town. He told me that he wanted me to get tested because Johnny had been with very lowlife-looking girls who were obvious prostitutes and who looked sick. He reminded me that he had called me one night at three in the morning to warn me. I remembered not understanding what he was saying that night, because I did not want to believe it. He apologized over and over again for not telling me everything before. He told me I was like his sister and he asked me if I would forgive him for not telling me before. I told him I forgave him. I cried for hours because he told me that Johnny was now on drugs and trying to meet women on sex websites.

I called Johnny's family and begged them to intervene to save his soul and his life. No one cared, and I realized they had been through this before. Johnny had stolen his brother's identity and racked up a fortune in credit card debt, so they were not sympathetic at all. Johnny hurt them all so many times that they turned a deaf ear, and I was alone again with the pain of still loving the man who ruined my life. I began to hate myself for still caring about him. I was torn between protecting myself and protecting him. Then, I realized again that he did not love me, and I needed to stop mourning a one-sided unfulfilled wish for a happy ending love story. This ending would be one of imminent danger and certain trauma if I did not look for a way out of my saving-Johnny addiction.

It was a moment of weakness. I auto dialed his number by accident and did not hang up. I just needed to be sure he was still alive. Though it was against the law for me to do so, I had to know he was okay and I heard his voice. His voice was tired, lost, and lonely. He said he knew it was me, even though I said nothing and hung up, shaking at the sound of his voice. I was wary of saying anything at all to him because I could not send mixed messages. I could not break the restraining order because it would then appear as though I was not afraid for my life, and that Johnny was not a danger to me.

Two steps forward, a thousand steps back, and again the feeling of fear escalated. I started to have nightmares that I was married to Johnny again. These were dreams in which I had to start the whole process of leaving him from scratch. In my dreams, I would panic and jump out of bed because I needed to call my attorney. Worse, I would have dreams in which over and over again, I would hear the sound of him with Taneisha, having passionate sex. I wanted to die from the anguish that I felt. Johnny invaded my life, my dreams, and even came sneaking into my mind with intrusive thoughts.

How and when would this end? I decided not to succumb to my maternal instincts to protect and save

Johnny. I started the process of saving myself. I tried to tell myself that he was not a good husband who died in a car accident, not someone to mourn. If God could help women survive the loss of a good husband, surely I could survive the loss of a monster. I tried to find relief knowing I did not suffer a painful end like some victims of domestic violence. I tried to face that he was not ever going to be a friend. He was someone I could never let back into my life. Every day, I would have to resist wanting him. Like an alcoholic that has to stay away from booze, Johnny represented that one more drink could kill me.

One evening out of the blue, I decided to email Amy Simpson. She was his last long-time live in love, and I asked if she would accept to talk to me about her loans to Johnny. She was surprised to see Johnny's name in her email inbox. She gave me her phone number in Hobe Sound, Florida. It was there that she and Johnny had lived together. I called her immediately and heard a beautiful happy woman in her voice. She asked me if I was still with him, and I told her I wasn't but that I needed her help to fall out of love with Johnny. I told her about how difficult it was for me to leave him, our life, and our friends in West Palm Beach behind. She was very surprised to hear from me and offered her help. Her first piece of advice was chilling...

"Brigitte, there is only one way to put this. Run. Run like you are on fire. Run away as fast as you can." What followed was a moment of silence as though we were commemorating the death of our innocence.

She told me I was in grave danger. She said Johnny was evil and dangerous, and would destroy me if I stayed. She began to describe the life she lived with Johnny; how he left her with massive debt, and destroyed the companies and properties that she had bought at his insistence.

He failed to take care of the bills, and never gave her any of the income from the businesses or properties. He ruined the properties by not cleaning the pools, ignoring cockroach infestations, and leaving his hoarded junk all over them. He ruined them by sucking all of the cash flow out of them.

Johnny had also leased a coin Laundromat rent free for several months. It had 20 washing machines and 20 dryers, and was in a good location. He would drive around town picking up women who were walking with bags of laundry to a Laundromat. He would bring them to his on Broadway, where they would do their washing and drying, and then he would drive them home. It made no sense. He paid none of the bills and pocketed all of the cash that came from the business, leaving the owners with unpaid water and electricity bills. They quickly threw him out.

He chose to spend his nights without Amy, opting for the rooming house he bought with her money. The house was supposed to bring in a fortune for them, but in reality it was just a comfortable place he could stay with the hookers, whores, and drug dealers he rented all of the rooms to. It didn't matter that Amy was beautiful, intelligent, and worked hard to get deals for them that would bring in good cash. He wanted to be with junkies and drug addicts, not her.

He broke her heart, emptied her wallet, and left her to clean up his mess. She said that she could no longer feel any love for him at all. She was also in a new healthy relationship, and told me that I too would soon fall out of love with Johnny; once there was some distance between us after I realized the full impact he had on my life.

I knew I had to stop looking at my life through the rearview mirror. I knew I had to get a hold of the reality of my situation. I knew I had to take the reins in my life, and regain trust in myself. I knew I had to work with the facts, and not the fantasy of what could have been.

Amy agreed to meet. She knew I needed her advice. She was a good Italian girl from New Jersey; tough, smart, perky, and appeared not a day over fifty. In fact, she revealed she was seventy and still working hard to pay off the debts that Johnny left her with; a whopping two hundred thousand dollars' worth of mortgages and creditors that still called, seven years later, and a headache that just never seemed to go away.

She told me that in the beginning there was romance and sex, he bought her lingerie, and they danced all night at clubs. She was happy. Johnny was working hard and was the best rent collector in the world. Before long, his natural habits revealed themselves to her and she realized he was not the man he pretended to be. All he wanted was more and more money to buy new properties so that he could rent them out. Amy decided that enough was enough. None of the businesses were working, so she stopped giving him money. Johnny changed his attitude, never again sleeping in the house with her, and towards the end he wouldn't even come home. She had to evict him to have him remove all of the junk he hoarded in her yard when the code violation notices started arriving. Neighbors objected to the old cars, wood, and furniture that were strewn all over her lot. She kept receiving notices from credit agencies and demands to collect debts that Johnny had incurred while he lived at their home. Finally, the court judgment came through and he had to collect his junk when she successfully evicted him.

She understood my pain. She was kind and saved my life, becoming my BFFF, my best friend in Florida forever. She was always there to help me, either through long talks or emails, and even visits to my condo when my friends and family decided they had enough. I asked her how she got over him. She said she managed to stay away from him even though she was living in the same town and had integrated him into her life. She said she made it clear to him that all she wanted was her money. She told Johnny that if he came near her or tried to do anything to her, she would shoot him dead with her concealed weapon.

I continued my spiritual search for the truth about how this could happen to me. I wanted to find out how many others survived this wreck. Eventually, I emailed Ronnie Messier; his second wife in Indiana. We arranged to call each other and spoke for hours. She was very understanding and even humorous about him and told me that he was rotten to the core, dangerous and evil, and capable of murder. If I wanted them, she had all of the pieces of evidence that he left in her house. She had recordings of things he said that could convict him, and I was suddenly more afraid than ever of the man I had married.

She told me about her husband Mike, a retired policeman who was dying of cancer. He was the center of her life, and I listened to her describe their relationship. He was the first man she trusted after Johnny, seven years after she threw him out of her house and out of her life. When I first reached her, Mike was still alive and suffering, so I told her not to think of me. I said that I would meet her when she was over with the part of her life that required that Mike get her full attention. She told me that we were in the same boat; her husband that she loved was dying, and my love for my husband was dying. I felt so sad for both of us. I realized I had been mourning a man who did not deserve it at all.

One day I flew into Indianapolis to meet her, and she was one of the most remarkable women I had ever met. I was amazed at her beauty, inside and out, her selfless nature, her laughter and smile that she shared abundantly. She was a bundle of positive energy, fun, and the perfect wife. She owned half the town and had her own construction company, successfully renovating and leasing stores to retailers, and lofts to artists.

I remember her face as she told me the story of her brief marriage to Johnny as we sipped our wine, on a full moon lit night, on her terrace in Indiana. He met Ronnie when she was vulnerable; months after her brother had just lost his life when he drove his car into a trailer truck that was crossing the highway in front of him. He had been decapitated, dead on the spot. She was devastated and depressed, but decided to escape through her work.

Ronnie met Johnny at a construction show in Chicago. He flirted with her, told her how beautiful she was, and they began to date. In no time, Johnny was proposing repeatedly. She began accompanying him on visits to his buddies, scared of how criminal in nature these visits appeared. There were many financial transactions in hidden places, far from town, and many talks of aircrafts and speedboats that were stored out of sight in hangers away from creditors. There were shady looking men who looked like they were gang members on Harleys. They welcomed Johnny into their clubhouses and provided him with the kind of hospitality that made her nervous.

She found Johnny frightening but fascinating, and she started to fall in love with him big time. Ronnie hadn't noticed that the new guy Rick and his wife Alison, hired to work for them in the office, were too friendly until much later. There were double dates and fun times. She ignored the intimate nuances in the conversations between Johnny and Alison. She was too busy running the businesses and trying to figure out why the cash wasn't balancing.

Several months later, they married. It was a large wedding in a Catholic church, and they celebrated with friends and family. She had a dozen bridesmaids, a live band, and a party that no one would forget. Late one night, Ronnie was alone with Johnny and his father at her kitchen table after they had been drinking heavily. They started to reminisce and tell stories about warehouses and explosions, drugs and insurance money, and Ronnie wanted no part of it. She listened to their tales and realized she had married a mobster. She had made a terrible error in judgment. Johnny's grip was so very strong, and she began a spiral into hell.

Johnny concocted a plot to steal her corporate clients and bank accounts. He started a parallel business intended to take her suppliers and clients away. He made her put his name on all of her business bank accounts, and then came to her with checks to co-sign. He presented them at the bank and said he would rather take the cash out, as cash would give him a ten percent discount. When the suppliers started sending thirty-day late notices, he told her the checks must have been lost in the mail. She began to call her suppliers. Her payments were well over 30 days late. When she confronted him, he threatened to leave her. He then served her with a cease and desist order. He stopped her from communicating with her suppliers and clients after she tried to explain to them that she was still the owner of the business that she started; that she was the bonded one. She told them that she was the rightful owner of all the working capital he stole, but they were already working with Johnny. He laughed at her as she fell apart.

She filed for divorce two months into her marriage. The entire process cost her no less than four hundred thousand dollars. It took her ten years to repay everyone with interest and penalties, including legal fees for getting her business back on board, clearing her banking and credit problems, and restoring her good name. She was more than devastated and never recovered financially from Johnny's presence in her life. He tried to win her back, promised to get counseling, but she told him that if he ever came near her again, she would shoot him dead.

Ronnie, who said she was a white witch, wanted to cast a spell that night under the full moon… a spell that Johnny should die for what he did. I told her, "No, Ronnie, please, I still love him, and that would hurt me. Let's throw a spell to help him find wealth and maybe a woman who doesn't care if he fools around and then maybe we can all get of our money back." So she laughed and said okay, and we did.

We spent the evening talking about her life since Johnny, and what strength and drive it took to fix the many messes that he had made in her life. She played cassette tapes for me that revealed conversations that were evidence against Johnny in which he discussed things he had done. One of the tapes even featured what she thought was a gunshot. She gave them to me and said, "These will come in handy one day. Don't use them until you know it's safe. Don't give them to the wrong person, there are no other copies." She hugged me and I left on the next flight. I thought about Ronnie on the flight and how unfair it was that she still had to work at seventy years old. Her last words to me that day were "If you like men with no teeth and no money then I'll take you to downtown Indianapolis, there are plenty of them there for you to choose from!"

She laughed and I waved goodbye at the airport. She was the perfect American woman, the perfect wife and friend. I could not understand why Johnny tried to destroy her.

I planned on giving the tapes to the FBI. I played one of them for my therapist. We heard an argument between Johnny and a woman.

"I am so tired of all of this arguing. I'm leaving. You'll never know how much I love you." Johnny said, sadly and softly. Then there was the sound of a single gunshot. The tape ended.

"Remember, this is the only copy. Don't lose it." Ronnie looked at me in the eyes. "Stay safe."

Ronnie had given me the tape so that I would recognize the danger I was in. Even after hearing the tape over and over, I still suffered from the delusion that I loved Johnny. I was in more danger than anyone thought.

CHAPTER TWENTY-THREE:
BACK TO REALITY

That Christmas my daughter Pamela and I flew to the Cayman Islands to be as far away from civilization as possible. I was miserable and the only thing that could make me stop crying was the prospect of snorkeling every day.

We flew first to Grand Cayman, then to Little Cayman and then finally to Cayman Brac, an isolated island in the middle of the Caribbean. The ocean was crystal clear, with beautiful coral everywhere and a breeze that was sweeter than sugar cane. We stayed at the Alexander Hotel and made quick friends with the bartender Jose who made sure we felt at home. Fresh fish, barbecued meats, and dishes that surpassed any resort I had stayed at before were part of the menu at the bar. We ate dinner every night under the stars. We snorkeled every day and spent our evenings at the bar of the hotel, next to the pool, meeting the locals and the other guests. It was quiet and private, and I relaxed. At night, I would look at the endless stars in the sky, brilliant as diamonds in the sky. I thought about Johnny and wondered whose arms he was in on this holy Christmas night. I cried myself to sleep every night.

We wanted to spend New Years in Miami so we prepared our luggage to be able to leave early in the morning and decided to spend our last evening at a karaoke bar down the road. We enjoyed the music and the singers who attempted to channel Frank Sinatra and Diana Ross. Some sang better than others, but we were all drinking just a little so we enjoyed every note. I remembered how I had met Johnny on such a night in a karaoke bar in Delray Beach. I was up next to sing 'What The World Needs Now' by Dionne Warwick when I heard my daughter screaming.

"Mom, help!" She echoed into the night.

I jumped up, ran to the parking lot and saw her being thrown onto a car by a man as he separated her from her friend Jose, the bartender from the hotel. Suddenly this strange man was jumping on Jose and punching him and slammed his head into the gravel. I stood there watching as three men tried one at a time to pull him off and they failed. They were thrown off and rolling on the ground, clutching their stomachs. Two other men just made a gesture of backing off and I felt that this young man who had been so good to us was going to die.

"Give me a cigarette Pamela!" I screamed at her and grabbed the lit cigarette, bent over and put it out on the attacker's neck. He did not notice. I realized he was high on something that made him feel no pain, and that the only way I could save Jose who was now out cold was to use leverage. I used my right hand to grab the collar of the T-shirt that this crazed man was wearing. Then, while he was still punching Jose who by this time did not react, I grabbed the bottom of his t-shirt with my left hand and turned the hands in opposite directions and formed a tourniquet. I took a very deep breath, spread my legs to steady myself, made a very strong move as though I was lifting weights and I hauled him off in one shot, throwing him off onto the parking lot floor. He stood up and looked at me, surprised that a woman could do this and humiliate him. He started to lunge for me and I said,

"Come on motherfucker, come on! Let's go! Right now, try me!" I looked at the guy and used the anger boiling inside me at Johnny and I was sure that I could hurt him badly.

My daughter jumped between us yelling "No mom, run!" So I did. I turned around and grabbed Pamela by the arm and I laughed nervously as we ran all the way to the car.

Pamela said to me, "Mom, you are so crazy, what if you got hurt?"

I laughed and said, "Honey, it was the other guy that you had to worry about, not me. I was pretending it was Johnny and used every ounce of anger that I had buried inside me to pull that fucker off."

My adrenaline was pounding and I suddenly realized that I had the strength of my grandfather inside of me, a biological talent that came in quite handy that night.

We filed a police report with the only cop in town. He was a lanky twenty-two year old and the police station had only one gun under lock and key in the safe. The Cayman Islands use British law and use batons to fight criminals. I wanted to get off the island as quickly as I could. We didn't sleep that night.

We left for the airport before dawn and had a drink at the bar for breakfast. Half of the people at the Karaoke Bar from the night before were sitting at departures and recognized me. Suddenly, the island's famous 'Captain' who was with us at the bar on our last night walked over and said "I saw what your mother did yesterday and she saved Jose's life. You should be very proud of her." We thanked him for his kind remarks and took two flights back to the mainland, with a story to tell about our quiet relaxing vacation in Cayman Brac.

When we returned to the condo in Delray Beach, it was still New Years Eve so we had dinner at the Breakers and toasted to the year 2012. I secretly prayed that the New Year would bring me strength and perseverance. I sat there and saw women with husbands and huge diamond rings and was pulled back into the dream that Johnny had promised would come true. Pamela saw me thinking, knew exactly what I was feeling and told me that I needed to get rid of the ring.

Two days later, we returned to the pawn shop where Johnny had bought the ring. The manager looked at the ring and asked for the receipt which I gave him. Johnny's name was on the receipt.

"Mr. Sorella will have to consent to this return and I need his permission to give you the money." He stared at me straight-faced and I lost it.

"You mean that I need the permission of a triple felon con artist that came here with my money and bought this ring for me in order to get my cash back?" I fumed at this poor man who kindly repeated to me that without Johnny's permission, he could not give me the money.

Okay. I took a deep breath and dialed Johnny's number and he answered.

"Hey baby, what's up?" I sighed at his greeting, the greeting he gave everyone who called him.

"Johnny, I am at the pawn shop trying to return the engagement ring you bought here and for some reason I need your permission. Can you come here please, and sign for the release I need?" I was shaking.

"Where are you?" He sounded as though he had just woken up.

"I am waiting for you at the pawn shop on Gateway. Please try to get here soon." I waited for him to reply, hoping there would be no argument.

"I'll be right there baby." He sighed softly.

I was standing at the counter looking at the watches when I felt him come in. He walked in the door and approached me at the counter and said,

"Hey baby, I'm here. How are you?" He looked into my eyes and I saw a tired man, a man that was old and weary.

"I am fine, thank you." I lied. I looked away from him at the man who stood there waiting for Johnny's signature.

"How was your Christmas, how is your business?" He continued to try to make small talk and smiled as though we were old friends as he leaned on the counter staring at me.

"Fine, Johnny, just fine." I mumbled.

He looked at Pamela, gave her a nod which she ignored, and turned back to me.

"Alright then, take care of yourself."

He looked at the man behind the counter and he said, "Give her the money."

As quickly as he came, he left... in my Jaguar.

I felt the blood drain out of my heart and nearly fainted. Every ounce of me wanted to run after him, to hold him, to pretend that nothing had gone wrong in our marriage and that he still loved me. What a wimp I was. So much therapy, a fortune spent to fix me and there I was, ready to cry. I was such a weakling, a real joke.

On our drive home, we entered a furniture store and Pamela picked a couch and two arm chairs for our living room. She also chose some framed artwork that made the condo cozy and welcoming. She had such good energy and was always finding ways to distract me from the mistake I had made with my life. We spent the rest of the week on the beach, shopping for bargains in the after Christmas sales and bonding like a mother and daughter should. She was truly a gift from God and gave me the will to live.

I arrived home in Canada that weekend to a mess. My finances were destroyed. I had no savings. My income taxes were due and unpaid. Unlike others who plan for this kind of day, I had no "Fuck You" money hidden anywhere, no liquid funds to bail me out. I had given all of the money I stored away for my quarterly tax deposits to Johnny for the property investments.

It was shortly after that the income tax agencies initiated procedures to seize 85% of my business income, seized my bank accounts, and left me with barely anything to live on. I had made an error when I did my income tax declaration and had pressed submit twice so they came looking for taxes on half a million dollar income, twice what I should have declared.

"Madam, it will take us a while to undo the seizures. We have never seen this before. Most times people declare half what they made, not twice their earnings." I told them the story about what Johnny had done to me and they decided to work faster to fix my mess.

In the meantime, I had to fire my secretary, double my workload, and stay at the office 18 hours a day trying to sort out the disaster that my life had become. I had two big cases that would pay off my taxes and more, and they occupied all of my waking hours. I began to work on finding my clients missing money so that I could invest it and recover my standard of living. I had no choice but to make money right now.

I began to realize that I could not possibly love Johnny anymore because he left me in a horrible mess, and he could care less after taking whatever I had that was not tied down. I reached another bottom. No one told me there were bounces. I was more determined than ever to stop him from ever hurting another woman again.

In February 2012, I made an appointment with West Palm Beach FBI for a meeting in which Amy and Ronnie would participate so that we could explain our cases to Eric. He worked at intake and agreed to meet all three of us. Ronnie, who had grown up in Florida in the Sarasota area, was happy to fly into Fort Lauderdale and stop off on the way back from a cruise with her family. I picked her up at the airport.

We spent the evening talking about her life after Mike. Her husband had finally succumbed to cancer. She told me how hard it was to live without him, without the love he brought into her life. It was the night before our meeting with the FBI so we called Amy and spoke for an hour over speaker phone. It was amazing to hear the stories flowing like lava about what Johnny did to them; how he destroyed their finances and broke their hearts without any conscience or regret. We agreed to meet up the next morning at the FBI offices on Flagler.

Ronnie wanted to help me take the photographs we needed of the license plates of the cars that Johnny had stolen from me, so we drove to West Palm Beach and parked about twenty feet away from his shop.

"Ronnie, you stay here while I get close enough to take a picture of the plate number. Don't be scared." I calmly said.

"Don't be scared? Of course, I'm scared. I haven't seen the asshole in twenty years!" Ronnie said under her breath.

"Why are you whispering?" We laughed and I got out of my old Land Rover and snuck up on my Jaguar sitting in front of the dry cleaners like it was born there.

I crept up behind it in the dark night and bent down with my head peeking around the side. I noticed Johnny was standing at his counter. He was wearing his "I am so intelligent" glasses, writing down something and then reading whatever had captured his complete attention.

I suddenly realized that my iPhone would flash when I took the photos, but I decided to do so anyhow, just as he turned away for a bit. Flash! Then he suddenly looked back as though he saw something, and stared out into the parking lot as I crouched silently. My heart beat a mile a minute and I felt as though it was speeding away from me, down the mall and over the horizon by the canal. Johnny almost caught me.

I waited a bit, and then urgently signaled for Ronnie to drive my Land Rover over to me. I was crouching behind the car and was terrified he would decide to get into it, back out of his parking spot, and run me over. I was so nervous that I started to laugh uncontrollably, and I motioned again and urged, "Ronnie, get your fucking ass over here!"

She motioned that she couldn't. She tried to press on the gas pedal of my old Discovery, but her foot did not reach the pedal because she was too short. I had to run to the car before Johnny saw me. Ronnie couldn't drive any closer to come and get me. She was in complete fear at the thought that Johnny would run outside and see her sitting there like it was 1986.

On the way out of the strip mall, we saw the Lincoln parked at the end of the parking lot and we took pictures of that license plate too. We laughed hysterically, worrying about what we did and the risk we took, all the way home. At least I had the license plates on camera so I could provide the info to the FBI to identify my car as stolen property. We got home, drank ourselves to sleep and woke up hung over and still laughing the next day. We had such camaraderie. It was amazing how she could make me happy at the saddest time of my life.

The next day we drove to the FBI offices on Flagler in West Palm Beach. We saw the clerk at the reception window.

"May I have your identification, please?" We handed over our drivers licenses. We passed through the metal detector and entered the waiting area. We sat down and took a deep breath, and looked at each other with a sign of relief. I watched as Ronnie and Amy looked at each other at their first meeting. They had spoken to each other before at my home on speakerphone, but when they saw each other, it was magical. They were almost carbon copies of each other. Both were dark-haired, shorter, buxom, and full of spitfire. What amazed me was that I was not at all jealous of either of them, nor was I worried about their feelings about Johnny or their past experiences with him. There was no competition about which one of us he had loved more because we had all been his victims. Only I had any vestige of love in my heart for him.

After waiting an hour, we were taken into a room by Eric at intake, and we showed him our data. Ronnie and Amy brought dozens of files and gave Eric evidence of thousands of dollars stolen from them by Johnny.

"This man stole my business, my clients, all of my money and destroyed my reputation and made me afraid for my children's safety." Ronnie spoke first and appeared relieved to finally get to disclose what happened to her to the FBI. It took her half an hour to explain all of the details and then it was Amy's turn. Amy went over documents showing that she reported his crimes to the local police and they refused to consider any charges, claiming she had made voluntary gifts to him. She also appeared relieved to finally talk to a higher authority about how Johnny had borrowed money, never intending to pay it back. She explained how he told her that he chose women who were just a little older, a little fatter, and a little desperate for love. She told them how she had met him and how in one night he had her under his spell. She explained how she had to evict him to get him out of her property. She showed that she was still getting collection letters in his name.

Then I showed him my evidence. I explained how Johnny had conned me into believing that he was a Certified Remodeler. I gave him copies of the correspondence from the various women that he was contacting online to repeat the same offence, over and over. There he was online claiming to be looking for love and a business partner, claiming to make over $100,000.00 a year, claiming to be a one woman man who wanted to meet the last love of his life to spend the rest of his life with in marital bliss. Every document was the same. Every document repeated the same phrases and declarations and it was clear that Johnny had a system and was fixated on profiting enormously from the use of wire and internet to commit fraud against vulnerable women who were just looking for a date that could lead to love. Johnny had a predilection for rich, sick old ladies.

After discussing our cases with him for over two hours, he came to the conclusion that I was the only one with a case. Ronnie's case was prescribed and so was Amy's. So I agreed to work with Eric and intake by sending them the necessary evidence that they needed to have him arrested. Amy and Ronnie and I had left there feeling confident that the FBI would do something to stop Johnny who was showing interest in out of state and Canadian women online that made it a federal offense.

Later that day, Amy, Ronnie and I had lunch together at Longboats on Singer Island. We had a wild meeting of the minds. I had the waitress take a picture of us with our arms wrapped over our shoulders. We looked beautiful and were smiling as though we had just won the lottery. Amy was so funny when we were eating and talking and suddenly she said with the cutest smile on her face,

"Looky, looky what do I have here?" She gave us a peak at her concealed weapon under her belt.

"I have told Johnny that if he ever comes near me, tries to hurt me in any way, he is dead." She gave us that New Jersey "don't mess with me" smile.

I told her to put it away before she got arrested and she continued to laugh that signature laugh, that New Jersey happy laugh that I loved. She always had the ability to be happy and make me smile despite the years that it took her to get over the damage that Johnny had caused to her life. We were so happy to finally break bread and to know we had not been the only ones to think that what happened to us was a nightmare, a criminal recipe that Johnny had concocted to earn tax-free capital from women whom he thought had more than they needed or deserved. We speak often and have stayed close to this date.

As instructed, I provided further evidence to the FBI for the next six months. I would send them more and more evidence that would show that Johnny was sending hundreds of messages to women all over the US and Canada online and was conducting an enterprise through which he gained the confidence and trust of women he targeted on Internet dating websites. He targeted lonely, sexually-neglected, widowed women in possession of assets or money that he could steal. I showed them emails on my email account where he would tell 300 pound women that he could not wait to wake up beside their beautiful blue eyes, how he was looking for that one true last love of his life, how he was a one woman man and the lies about his past, about his credentials as a Certified Remodeler, false credentials that he used to gain the trust of women who would then lend him money to buy tools to renovate their homes and how over and over he got away with it.

I showed them how he told each woman tales in which he stated that he needed a partner in his successful laundry business and how he was a successful businessman who made over $100,000.00 a year. Whether she was in Alaska or Alberta or South Carolina, I counted 15 states in all, he told the same lies, just changing the names. In some, he would tell black women that he was black. I could see in their responses that they believed him and would become his next victims. They received enough proof to put him away for wire fraud. I placed myself at risk to submit evidence that I obtained by various means. I spent hours emailing everything to the private email address that Eric gave me for the FBI Intake Division in Miami. It was the most difficult thing I ever did in my life because it was a constant reminder that I had been victimized by a man who was a dangerous predator. I relived the initial trauma each time I was reminded that Johnny had lied. I realized over and over again that his words were just a formula he employed to convince me that he loved me and needed my understanding and compassion in order to make us happy for the rest of our lives. I remembered the first day I had to check our email to be certain that Johnny was not stealing my identity or obtaining credit in my name. It was then that I found his emails to hundreds of women. I couldn't help but feel that he did it on purpose. He never changed our email password and had to know I would be looking for my emails and see what he was doing. He wanted me to hurt very badly and it worked.

I was sickened. I had to sort through dozens of emails that women sent back to him and I suffered heartache over and over as I read the exchanges that were made on the email address I had paid for, the email address he had used to send me love letters.

I chocked when I found one particular email that was significant. This woman was soft and gentle and caring, a widow who had just lost her mother and her husband. Her words to Johnny were sincere and loving. All he wrote back to her was a short message. "I hope I live up to your expectations."

I knew this was going to be Johnny's next victim. I took the time to notify the FBI that I was certain that this woman loved him enough to do exactly as I had done for him. I saw myself in her. I knew there was very little time left to save her life. I sent them a warning and described the urgency in the case. It involved a woman whose husband had just died. They had been happily married for forty years. I was right and later was too late when Tonia became a near statistic who almost died at the hands of a three time felon that the FBI refused to arrest.

The FBI told me that I would not know whether they were acting on the case as the matter was confidential. They said that they did not risk their cases by discussing the progress with the victims. They told me that if they would still take my calls it was a good sign. I believed them. Over the months, I saw that Johnny was surfing for women out of state, heading North, first through Georgia, then the Carolinas, then to Canada. The emails he was sending to women in Canada scared me. I watched my back all the time wherever I was, especially out in public and even in my office where you would think I could relax.

My office was in a high security building and you needed to unlock five locks before you could sit in my executive chair at my executive desk. The office building was next to a famous synagogue in an area in which there was the highest concentration of wealth in Canada, the area in which I worked and resided. The first door into the building where the list of office occupants showed my name was also restricted by a Medeco lock. The second door three feet further, was a door that was the entrance into the lobby and the elevators and it also had a Medeco lock. Then I had a private, locked second floor elevator key and the front door to the general office had been secured with another Medeco lock and alarm system. My private office also had a strong lock. I felt safe there so I spent sixteen-hour days working like crazy to make money to pay all of the taxes and bills that Johnny refused to acknowledge existed. The greatest danger was my walk home at two a.m. after my eyes couldn't stay open anymore. I lived one block from my office. I usually made it home in two minutes, walking in the night, the street so quiet, only an isolated taxi going by. I kept looking back to see that no one was there. I did not feel secure at home with a fire escape window by my bath. I was never able to enjoy a good night's sleep there and spent hours pacing the floor, wanting to end my life.

I continued for months to spend hours monitoring Johnny's behavior online in our email account and I submitted the data I found. I spent much of my time, hours and hours, looking for ongoing proof in every way I could. I talked to our friends and his family who still wanted nothing to do with him and they kept me informed on his whereabouts, his visits, and I felt that what I was doing was important. I felt that I was doing the right thing. I knew that what I had lived through and survived by a bare thread and Johnny's crimes could only be prevented if I spoke out and got someone in law enforcement to listen.

I should have known better. Amy had tried to get local law enforcement to pay attention. She had gone to the media, lawyers, anyone who would listen. They told her to go home and tough it out. They told her that her donations to Johnny were consensual, and they made her feel like she was insane because she seemed to be the only one to think she had been victimized by a criminal. There were many other women who had tried to get him arrested and failed.

Although I was afraid and I knew that my actions put me at risk, I felt that God was watching. He would not let anyone harm me. Johnny was again subject to a second no contact restraining order after his last conversation with me. He started by begging me to come back and ended with threatening to set me up with drugs in my car that would send me to prison for life.

"Johnny, I need my money. I want my Jag back," I said in the last call I made to him begging him to pay me back.

"Baby, I want a lot of things back, too. I want my wife back." His words tore me apart.

"Johnny, I don't want to talk about that, I just need my money, please," I repeated. "Johnny, do I need to go legal on you? Do I need a police escort to come and get my Jag?" I could hear that regular, deep breathing that meant he was thinking.

"Baby, you come near the Jag and I will have someone plant drugs on you and your car and you will be busted and I will have witnesses and you will go to prison for life."

I could almost see his face, the look on it that would have scared me had I been with him, but now I wasn't just scared. I was desperate and broke too. He knew how much I traveled and loved to travel whether for business or pleasure. He hit the button that he knew would scare me. My anger built up inside of me when

I realized he was trying to get me arrested and thrown into prison. I took him seriously and I told him that his threats would be reported to the police.

"Johnny, I'm calling the police. You will not threaten me or set me up. You will not get away with intimidating me any longer. These words you just said will come back to haunt you."

I was able to restore the no contact restraining order, but I was not able to restore my peace of mind. I never did go get my Jag that I loved. I lived for months, afraid of him planting drugs in my house, on my car, in my luggage, on my person, so much so that I had nightmares of getting busted and him laughing at me in court.

Despite my depression and fear of him, I felt that my efforts would at least protect other women from the same situation. If the FBI acted on the file quickly enough and arrested him for using the internet and a phone for committing financial crimes of larceny and fraud against women, maybe it would be worth all of the pain that this effort caused me.

My reality would change immediately when, after six months, I would call the FBI offices in West Palm Beach to discuss the file. I asked for the complaint division. I needed to know when to stop gathering evidence. I was told to contact the Miami office. I spoke to someone in Miami, a male agent, who told me I could not have an appointment and could only present myself in person and take my place in line. I explained to him that I had an open file in West Palm Beach. He said there was no file opened in my name. I told him that the file was in the name of Johnny Sorrella. I said that, for six months, I had been sending proof by email to Captain America, which was the code email name at intake in Miami for my files. I said that the intake office in West Palm Beach had accepted to open my file in the presence of two other victims. I repeated that was already a file and I needed to discuss the progress since I had to ask for a second restraining order. I was told that I would not get an appointment. I felt that I was getting run down from the way the FBI was ignoring my rights. I was told to unblock my caller ID and to call back. I did.

"Hello Melissa," the agent replied.

"I am not Melissa, I am Brigitte." I was frustrated and it showed in my voice.

"I don't know why I am calling you Melissa," he laughed.

My whole body was shaking, my hands trembling and I told him I needed to have an appointment and again he told me to come and wait in line if I wanted to bring in evidence.

"I have emailed the contents of tons of files, and apparently there is no file, so I need an appointment if I am to bring it all to you. Please guarantee that I can meet with an agent who can reopen the file that I opened in West Palm Beach so this evidence will go into the right file."

He told me just to show up and he emphasized how I wouldn't get any special treatment before he hung up.

I dialed the number again and asked to speak to his supervisor. I got the same man on the line and this time he was furious! "Ma'am if you don't stop calling I will have you arrested for tying up the FBI line!" His ugly words thundered in my head.

I hung up, and I called the Sheriffs and the West Palm Beach Police and both referred me to FBI Internal Affairs. I called FBI Internal Affairs, and I was told to write to them, and I did. I officially filed a complaint based on the FBI's refusal to process my complaint against Johnny. I also reported their intimidation and threats. All of this was a process that began to make me feel diminished. I fell apart, crying, sobbing, and feeling that Johnny had all of the power. The light in my sense of justice was slowly getting dimmer, and I went to bed for several days, crying, feeling re-victimized, alone, unable to eat, sleep or find a place in my head where this abuse made sense.

I wanted to kill myself, to end the cycle of injustice that was spinning in my head. I felt that the FBI was male-dominated, sexist, biased, and unreliable. I felt that their agents who told me I had a case had betrayed my trust. It was wrong of them to ask me to give them proof that somehow wound up in a cesspool with their word that their jurisdiction covered the crimes of my situation with Johnny. I finally received an official response on official letterhead that stated that no employee had broken any law or done anything wrong. They completely ignored my complaint against Johnny.

The words *just kill yourself* became an unwanted mantra in my head as though that would solve everything. I was at a dead-end. It was the bottom. I thought that I had hit bottom. There was nowhere to go but up. I prayed for strength and enlightenment and guidance. I tried to sleep for a couple of hours and as soon as I could face the morning light, I got up, showered, felt reinvigorated and decided to get back into the ring. I wasn't going down that easy.

CHAPTER TWENTY-FOUR: RISKY BUSINESS

There cannot be a happy ending where there is no truth. I got a call from the FBI. The gentleman speaking to me was kind, soft-spoken and genuinely sounded as though he genuinely cared about what I had been through because of the miscommunication. Nevertheless, the FBI decided to close the case because there was no conclusive proof that any criminal named Johnny Sorella had committed a crime. I told them that they didn't look at the evidence. It made no sense that without even looking at the evidence they based their decision on the withholding of my evidence and how that in itself was obstruction of justice. They decided that Johnny had done nothing wrong and so obviously all of the documentation that I gave them about Johnny's other identity and the number of crimes associated with it was never looked at. They claimed to have one page in their file when in the presence of Amy Simpson and

Ronnie Messier; enough evidence was handed over with which to wallpaper the White House.

What did I expect? By now, Johnny was a triple, maybe four time felon. Mr. WitSec boy was able to hide behind every police uniform, every motorcycle cop shirt that he whitewashed. He had that cop uniform kind of immunity, one that was so frightfully incredible. When cop uniforms came in with questionable things in their pockets, they were safe with Johnny. He knew their professional and personal secrets. Cops would spend time with him at the dry cleaner chatting about criminals, crime and the law. Johnny was obsessed with reading the Palm Beach Post and the Sun Sentinel to see who was arrested, who was in court for what and who was found guilty and sent away to the pen.

Once he tried on a full motorcycle officer's uniform and looked at himself in the mirror and said sarcastically, "Do you love this look or what, baby?" Johnny wasn't a cop, but he knew the right ones. That was why Johnny got away with everything. I knew how dangerous it was to blow the whistle on him.

The FBI had told me that they had no budget. Budget cuts? No excuse. I could not believe that. I wanted to go all the way to the top, to Headquarters in Washington. I wouldn't stop until someone stopped him.

I wanted Johnny to admit what he did and so when they suggested it, I finally agreed with the FBI, at their request, to wear a wire.

"Are you prepared to wear a wire?" The man sounded like he was someone who knew I could put Johnny away.

"Yes, I am. I have had so many offers to take him down, to hurt him, and kill him. All I want is justice. I want him to acknowledge all of the crimes that he has committed against women." I was so afraid to tell them everything, so afraid they were in on Johnny's attempts to discredit me.

"I want to deal with you rather than deal with the Mob." I couldn't believe what was coming out of my mouth. Strange men had come into the dry cleaners and said that they were looking for Johnny.

"They asked me where they could find Johnny. They told me that I looked like a nice lady. They told me that if I just said the word, he would be taken care of, disappear." I waited for the agent to reply. He said nothing. I told him that I was afraid of how many people hated Johnny.

"So many people want him dead but I just want justice, not vengeance." I waited for them to say something, but there was only another long silence. I knew they were taping our conversation. I believed that vengeance would be up to God.

Then I made the mistake of asking them an obvious question.

"Why can't you get a federal agent on the payroll to do this undercover sting? Why use me? Evidence would have to be accurately gathered, the chain of evidence preserved to serve as official proof in court?"

I asked. "Why me? Why not an agent, someone covered by workman's compensation if Johnny decides to use physical force?" There was no reply.

Johnny would see me coming a mile away. He would know exactly why I was there asking questions about other women and about how he conned them out of not so small fortunes. I was still so afraid of him and of the power he had over me. I would melt in his presence and it wouldn't work.

"Then the deal is off." He replied. I had said the wrong thing and I felt betrayed, played with, treated like a fool.

If Johnny did his crimes using a gun instead of his penis, he would have been in jail the first time he pulled his financial predator gig. Was Ronnie Messier, his second wife one of many victims? His first wife was out of the picture after he went to jail during their marriage. I wondered what he had done to her finances. Johnny had no relationship with his daughter so I could not reach back further than Ronnie. She was of enormous help in my search for the rhyme and reason behind Johnny's history of using women for their money and leaving them penniless and destroyed. Still, nothing was going to stop him, not even all of the victims that over the decades had asked for his arrest.

In November 2012, after spending a fortune on investigations, the FBI, revealed that an inappropriate and risky relationship existed between a General Petraeus and Paula Broadwell. How much money did they spend on the case of a four-star general, a human whose poor judgment and misplaced belief in his invincibility resulted in self-sabotage? Cyber stalking evidence and explicit emails exposed the ultra extra marital affair. Security clearances to places, people and events were canceled for many people who shouldn't have had it in the first place. Why would a general engage in conduct unbecoming and put himself into a situation that exposed him to the risk of blackmail? His life then became a messy, open book on the front page of every newspaper in the world. He was the lead story on evening news for months.

Eventually the general needed to go, and he did resign. So a marital affair that could have been settled discretely with little expense to the public became an expensive public circus for no reason. Did the general do any time? Was this matter a crime? If not, then why were enormous sums of money spent to wash that dirty laundry in public? No wonder my little dilemma so bored the FBI. They had the biggest fish in the pond caught in flagrante delicto. If I had my way he would be ordered to pay back the government for the cost of hours of investigation into his inexplicable decision to go libido rogue. Wasn't this just a floozie, a flaky biographer who convinced him to forget his duty to America, at least while he had a hard on? So many decent, respectable men served in the military, army and navy and had a difficult time getting benefits from Veteran's Affairs, but there were millions to humiliate and expose an important, weak military man's seduction by a hussy.

The money spent on proving a general's philandering should have been there to allow the FBI to look closely at the process that was Johnny's enterprise. He wasn't the only one who had seduced women, stole their money and businesses and let the blame fall on those who were kind enough to fall for the con. There were many men who were committing the same crime.The victims of this type of crime were mothers and sisters and daughters and cousins. These were good American women. These were elderly citizens that deserved protection. Men like Johnny were robbing them and no one was going to stop them. No one dared. In Johnny's case, there were too many secrets he knew about law enforcement. Secrets that he held in his back pocket. So the FBI decided that this notorious informant was not covered in their budget. He would forever get away with his crimes against women. Over and over, I was told there was no budget to ensure that the case would be accepted as having enough evidence to win in court, and they would not proceed otherwise. No wonder, after at least fifty calls and countless emails, I was told that if I did not stop tying up FBI telephone lines, I would be arrested. I was a nuisance. The FBI would not do a thing to help us.

Instead of going away with my tail between my legs, I decided that I had to go to the West Palm Beach Police and the Sherriff's offices to try to deal with the matter on a local level and I again had a horrible experience. I entered the reception area on Gun Club Road, an area filled with people making their reports to the police, an area that also served as an interview facility. I asked the officer in charge for a private space where I could discuss the facts supporting my complaint in private, confidentially. He told me that there was no such private area available because they were in full renovations.

I began to tell the intake officer how I had gone from the station on Atlantic to the station on Congress where I was again sent to his station on Gun Club Road and I told him that I was tired of being sent from location to location. He stated that the officers should have taken my statement on Congress and that I should go back. I told him that I did not want to involve myself in human resources and jurisdictional disputes. He still refused to accept to take my complaint, so I asked him to call internal affairs so I could report him.

"Officer, I am a former deputy mayor of a large city. I worked with law enforcement for years. Not only are you refusing to take my statement, you are doing so in an unacceptable, public manner. You are forcing me, in this noisy crowded room to repeatedly say the name of the person I am accusing of committing an extremely serious crime, and all of this in full public view. How is it legal to discuss these crimes and name names within earshot of the public? The suspects have not yet been charged, it has not yet been proven guilty, nor have the police decided that the complaint is even going to be accepted as a case yet his name is heard by everyone here?"

My eyes were wide open as I realized that I was being drowned out by a quartet of cops in civilian clothes standing beside me, laughing loudly and discussing barbecues and beer and the weekend while I attempted to report a violent crime. This day was not going to be an easy one. I had been a victim of a serious crime by a three-time felon who was a career criminal, one who stalked senior women online to date-rape them and to steal their money and assets. I was not there to play games or to report a simple break-in with a stolen stereo that insurance could replace with a simple police report! I knew that I began to approach the crazy-lady syndrome. I tried not to appear like just another obsessed groupie that Johnny had neglected.

"Do you mind? I am trying to report a crime, and it is difficult to hear myself think with you talking so loud about non business matters?" I sat there and waited for the officers to disperse.

One of them approached me and said, "Are you threatening me?" He stood there big and tall, rigidly hinting that I should watch my mouth.

I stood up, pulled down my skirt and approached him and said, "I am a tax-paying citizen claiming a service that is of urgent public security importance. I am asking you again to go and talk somewhere else, the lunchroom or outside and stop trying to intimidate me."

They all looked at me and laughed, and I turned to the officer who was taking my complaint. I said, "I would like to file two complaints with Internal Affairs." They got the message and walked away.

He looked at me and sighed and called Internal Affairs and down came a simple, small matronly-looking woman who handed me two forms to fill out, and I did. I gave them back to her, and she left to go upstairs and to make photocopies. She came back down and gave the copies to me, and she kept the originals. I looked at them and stopped her as she walked away.

"These are not signed and dated by you and they aren't receivable because there is no proof that I delivered them to you."

She looked at me and said, "They are initialed here at the top."

"Please sign them where you should sign them and date them and then recopy them so we both have a copy of the originals correctly signified." I asked her with my exhausted voice.

My old deputy mayor blood was still flowing through my brain even years after I left politics. She sensed the anger that was behind my insistence that she follow correct procedures in order to register my complaint properly with the appropriate person in her office. These papers were evidence that could serve as proof of obstruction of justice if my complaints were not taken seriously. I was a deflated balloon of fear, grief and anger that was beginning to flutter to the floor with no more energy to fight. I took the papers back from her and thanked her and saw a look of sympathy on her face. I knew she had to work in a hostile environment that had tried to trip me up. I didn't have any patience for bad cops.

I went back through the general area on the way out of the station and as I was leaving, out of nowhere, a stranger, another angel with a message, a handsome young man came up to me and stated that I was right and very strong to do what I did. He said that he had seen everything, and he admired my actions. I thanked him and walked away to my car, and the tears began to flow, flooding my emotions with pain and sorrow that displaced my courage, and I sat in my car and thought about why they were protecting Johnny.

Suddenly, it all made sense. How stupid had I been not to figure it out earlier. Johnny had been committing these crimes for years without consequence. Johnny must be feeding the police info on drug dealers and their deals. He was providing them with easy arrests.

As deputy mayor, I worked on a similar case in Canada. The police had ignored the abuse of young girls forced into prostitution for years. Jack Midley had been keeping them locked in small closets, burning holes on their breasts, telling them no man would ever want them. The law protected juveniles, but these minors had been abducted from reform school by a police informant. These minors were ignored, treated as runaways, because they had been arrested as juveniles, and accused of selling their bodies for money. It took me months to acquire a million and a half dollar budget for a six-month undercover operation to do the investigation. Only then was it proven that my claim that these girls were victims and not criminals. These girls were not teenage runaways, they were young, misled, innocent girls being systematically sexually abused and forced into prostitution by a man who the police received several small leads from on a weekly basis.

When their parents told me how the police would not help them save their daughters, I went into full force legal combat mode. I mobilized an undercover operation and quietly asked for and obtained authorization to work with an experienced team of undercover vice cops to expose the corruption. After they arrested Jack, charged him, tried him and found him guilty he received a prison term as a dangerous offender. He got twenty-six-to-life and the news hit the front pages all across the country. He became our criminal celebrity. My name was disclosed in the media, while the same cops who had initially ignored the complaints were now getting in line to steal my thunder. The exposure was not something I courted, and I asked the newspapers to stop including my name in their myriad of long articles and news report series. They were using this case to sell loads of newspapers. I was afraid of repercussions. I had successfully exposed how cops worked with informants to benefit each other while victims were left to their own devices.

One day a police officer came to my home to take my report for vandalism to my car. He told me he knew who I was.

"You're Johnny's wife. I remember you from West Palm Beach." He said.

"I'm Gary." He smiled with such an honest face I could hardly believe he was a cop. He told me that no matter when I called or why I called, within one half hour Johnny's people cancelled the file. He told me that nothing would ever result in Johnny's arrest. He said he didn't know who called or who they worked for. He said that Johnny was untouchable. I was grateful to know that I didn't imagine that Johnny had a status that gave him immunity. At least I wasn't completely nuts.

We began to chat about his job and the risks that law enforcement officials faced in Florida. They had a rule. Unless it was worth giving their life for a call, they were careful about the risk. They were faced with so much crime every day that they had to prioritize those that were most urgent. They lived in a climate of danger that could result in an ambush at a simple traffic stop.

I told him that their violent crime rate held a large number of vendetta settlements. Citizens failed to have their day in court and if there was no occasion for a fair hearing, justice was nowhere to be found. If pleas for justice were ignored and law enforcement did nothing to arrest criminals that was when street justice took over. Victims demanded it. Individuals decided to make their own justice. Enemies died when matters remained unsettled. Criminals and victims alike reacted negatively when the justice system failed to satisfy them in court. Alongside liberal gun laws, it was a recipe for disaster when people settled their grievances without formal procedures.

I hated corruption in public office and mostly I did not tolerate it when crooked cops served corruption every day to the public like hot pizza. Good cops deserved better partners and a better, safer work environment.

Until we paid cops an adequate salary for the risks they faced every day, especially in West Palm Beach, corruption would reign and rule the justice system.

I wondered how many cops had post-traumatic stress disorder? Did they ever get used to seeing people who were dead, wounded or scarred? How many victims had they seen just in the wrong place, at the wrong time? Justice found its own level on the deserted, dangerous streets that corruption in West Palm Beach had created. Blood-filled, deserted streets had a heavy blanket of fear that floated on them at night. The West Palm Beach that I knew and loved was left unprotected and left to its own devices. I wanted so badly to fix it, to protect those lovely people who had treated me so kindly, who accepted me as one of their own. I accused the West Palm Beach Police and Sheriff's departments of prosecutorial misconduct, and there was no going back on my position anymore. Mothers formed lobby groups when their children were murdered and tried to educate the population and force prevention on anyone who would listen. I met women who lost their sons to violent crime. Many black young men found themselves involved in lifestyles that guaranteed them time in federal prison. The papers reported that a teenage African American boy who stole a gold necklace from his grandmother was arrested, but Johnny who stole hundreds of thousands of tax free money from men and women remained untouchable.

My knowledge of the politics of law enforcement and my ever-present streak of idealism was not welcome here. It did not help me in my struggle to expose Johnny because the authorities already knew all about him and they feared exposure for their role in his life. Johnny had enjoyed police protection for years and now my life was at risk. It was at risk for shedding light on the corruption that infested the West Palm Beach police, sheriffs and FBI agents. All of these powerful men made me feel crazy and they made me feel like I deserved what I got because of the way they treated me. I was just a stupid woman who had sex with Johnny, married him, and was just a scorned little wife who had no credibility. So I was told to go to civil court to collect the money and to the domestic violence court for a restraining order, and to stop bothering them about the disorganized-organized criminal that was Johnny Sorella.

Good old Johnny, the only guy I thought I ever loved. Yes, I was sick, I had a wicked case of PTSD after loving the man that Johnny pretended to be, and I was desperately trying to stop him from hurting even one more woman.

CHAPTER TWENTY-FIVE: THE FIGHT OF A LIFETIME

As time passed, the FBI continued denying my complaints, and the law enforcement individuals and departments that fueled my anger triggered the survivor instincts from my childhood.

Just as my entire family had refused to believe me when I was a little girl, I was again being told that my rights were nonexistent, my complaints unreceivable. I remembered as a child how I had called each and every one of my aunts to beg them to let me come live with them. Jim, my six-foot-three, two hundred and eighty pound grandfather wore size thirteen shoes. He once killed a man with his bare hands, this giant pig was abusing me and no one cared.

In fact, they told me I had imagined things. He would fondle me at three years old then give me a quarter and tell me to go to the candy store and get whatever I wanted. And then I was a beautiful little five-year-old girl, then a six-year-old starting school and then a seven-year-old getting ready for her first communion, and by that time I gave up believing anyone cared. I remained a virgin, but in my heart and soul, I felt that I was damaged goods and I would never know the purity and glow that came with childhood innocence.

Why? Why me? Why this? Why hadn't any grownups come to save me? No one cared and so I shut up about it. I lived in shame. I swore one day I would get out of this dark old house that was so clean because my grandmother spent all day, every day, scrubbing the floors until they were so clean that a priest could serve the holy host on them. My grandmother who went to mass twice a day, who prayed all day and all night could not find a way to protect me? Why was everyone so holier than thou while I was used every day like a toy? Why did I feel so old and so lost with no one to protect me?

It wasn't until I was eleven and starting to develop into a woman that I understood that I did not have to accept the abuse. One day my grandfather leered at me as he opened the bathroom door to stare at me while I sat there.

"I will kill you if you ever touch me again. I will have my friends kill you for five dollars and give me change." My grandfather never looked at me in the eyes again.

When I was seventeen, he had a heart attack and lay there in the hallway of our house. He squirming for breath, turning in pain, looking at me as I stood there staring at him, dialing 911, watching him turning blue, watching his blue lips turn so much darker than his dark blue eyes. He writhed in pain, with tears flowing, pain that rolled up into his lids. It was only after he stopped moving that I had started to give him mouth-to-mouth and CPR and saved his life.

I rode in the ambulance with him and watched as he broke the restraints that held him down. He sat up and screamed so loud that he sounded like a lion, as in the times in my childhood when he would look for me, and I would hide. He would make the sound of a lion and so I would run to the other end of the house again and hide. I was trying not to let him find me because although it felt okay when he found me and tickled me in my private area, something about it felt wrong. He would not stop until he made that funny sound that meant I could get up and leave. Sometimes I looked for him and asked for him to tickle me and so he told me it was our secret. I was never to tell anyone or he would die. In the ambulance, after I saved his life, I thought, Die you fucking pig, die.

When he finally did die, he left me all of his real estate. Still, my experience as a pedophile's victim would leave permanent scars. Even though that money paid for my entire college and university education and two years of psychoanalysis with the best psychoanalyst, I would forever be vulnerable to exploitation by men. Deep down inside I always felt that I was worthless, a whore, no matter how innocent I actually was.

Early in my adulthood, I decided I wanted to live a normal life and so I sought out treatment. I was given an appointment with a very important psychoanalyst who agreed to take me on. There were black stretch limos that I would see let rich women off at Dr. Patrick Mahoney's in Outremont, a very high class neighborhood with multimillion dollar mansions. I would take the bus or taxi depending on how miserable I was that day. Sometimes on a sunny day I would walk and think to myself, who lived in those huge houses, who had that kind of money? Many days I would arrive hours early and just sit and cry until it was time for my appointment. I felt it was a safe place to feel the real emotions that threatened to overwhelm me at any time. I never knew when it would happen, my hands shaking so badly I had to find a bathroom to hide in until the feelings subsided. I had panic disorder and hysterical neurosis, or whatever label they tried to use to explain how I began to tremble for no reason. I would wake up so often in the middle of the night convinced I was dying or dead.

All the while I worked and studied and tried to look normal and I tried desperately to have healthy relationships, but fat chance. I realized one day that I was on my own again trying to prove what Johnny had done to me. I didn't know where to start. I had to find all of the pieces of the puzzle and then I had to put them all together to find the sense of it all. I needed to prove that I was not delusional, that this truly happened and that I was a non-consenting victim of a financial predator. I did not give him the total of sixty-two thousand dollars voluntarily. Johnny took it, supposedly, to buy real estate for us. Johnny said he would invest in Laundromats, buy homes to renovate, and then remodel a home for us. He made everything sound perfect, that our love would continue forever. We would live happily ever after. Life would be beautiful. Johnny based his stories on the fairy tale movies he made me watch every Sunday morning. Only this love that he had to give was more like a horror movie with a terrible ending.

Near the end of my marriage, I lived in total fear that he would commit banking, credit card or investment fraud with my personal information. After I left Johnny, I worried even more. I called Vegas weekly to push for the annulment that finally came through in February 2012, on the grounds I had requested. I had sworn that I was on prescription tranquilizers and I could not make a clear decision about marriage. I wanted to take the blame publicly, on the record, so as not to enrage Johnny any further. In my heart I knew the truth. I was conned by an experienced manipulator, a certified psychopath, and I could not let go of the crime that ruined my already fragile life.

I then decided to contact more women that I knew had been involved with him beyond the whores who gave him blow jobs on Dixie highway, and I found them. Many of the women whom I spoke with were professionals, respected, successful, beautiful and loving women who each in their own way had given him so much opportunity, and he had destroyed them, one at a time, in the same way, with his same cold heart. Many wished to remain anonymous because they were married at the time or married now to good men, but they wanted me to expose Johnny so that others would not suffer the way they did.

I did not want to try to be the one to legislate morality, control sexuality, or force love on anyone. I could only try to document how it was not our hearts that Johnny intended to steal. It was love that Johnny used as a weapon. He would seduce and rip off women from the Chamber of Commerce, the attorneys who represented him, the tellers at the bank. Anyone was fair game. He'd offer to remodel their homes and the minute he got them in bed, he would get them to give him a credit card to pay for the construction supplies that he claimed he needed and then he would run the card to its limit without ever delivering a single nail to their home. No, all he delivered was a good screwing.

As he stole millions of dollars from vulnerable, lonely, sexually-starved, vulnerable, elderly and appreciative women, he pretended to love them. He proposed to them and made them believe they were special. These were not women who agreed to pay for sex. Yet he claimed that was the deal from the beginning. They would never see their money or Johnny again. I remembered the day I told him I was never coming back.

"You're going to have to pay for sex now Brigitte. No man will ever give you sex like I did for free." I shuddered as I heard those words because I realized that I had been played by a gigolo. Johnny was still a professional whore who turned the tables and extracted money from women for sex. What women had done to men for ages was now being done to them. Now it was women who were paying a fortune for sex disguised as love and marriage. The thought of paying for sex disgusted me and the entire experience with Johnny made me realize that I was getting old. I was old, so old and tired of gender politics. I wondered what they called us. Men were Johns, so were we Johnettes? How disgusting to think I ever slept with this repulsive pig. If I wanted to pay for sex, wouldn't I have picked a young, sexy dancer or model? I certainly wouldn't screw an old pimp. Johnny's propensity to commit fraud was inbred. He specialized in violence and intimidation, often bullying women into giving him money by threatening to leave them. He also excelled in killing the spirit and soul of those women that he ran over as he ran away with their money.

We were naive older women, suckered into fraud business deals, just waiting victims for crimes like Johnny's. His crimes were facilitated by the fraudulent credentials he put on his business card. I contacted The National Association of the Remodeling Industry. They gave individuals their certified remodeler's designation, and they confirmed to me that he never had certification. He was neither an active nor inactive member of the association. They wrote to him informing him to stop using their credentials without authorization. Johnny told them where to go. He continued to use the CR credentials to help him commit acts of crime against the public. Johnny had a target group, one composed mostly of senior and elderly women in Canada and the USA. The letters and phone calls from NARI did not stop him.

Soon after I became his wife, I had gotten him a passport so that we could travel the world. Now he could use it to go anywhere that did not have a reciprocity agreement with our government. There were many countries where he could hide, but Johnny would never leave Palm Beach County. It had become his territory, where he had learned where to hide, and when to latch onto another woman to defend him, swear by his love.

There were many women that would swear that he was a righteous man who needed God. Shortly after I left him, I heard that Johnny found the black churches in West Palm Beach and began to go to mass on Sundays. This was a community of good hard working honest God-fearing, good women who went to these churches dressed in their finest dresses and suits.

The jewelry they wore often belied their difficult circumstances. Many were single mothers trying to raise boys and have them survive past high school graduation. Many of their sons were already in jail for a crime they didn't commit or found guilty of something they did that sent them to prison for life. These women had the hardest job in the world. I remembered the dignity with which they treated their Sunday best, bringing their laundry in so they could wear a different suit or dress every week. They were beautiful in their hats and purses that matched their shoes.

These women viewed Johnny differently. He was nowhere near the kind of men in their community who hurt them and stole their money. Johnny came into their lives like a soft morning rain. They had no idea what he would do to them just to get their money. They were not prepared for his secret weapon. The men in their community were incorrigible wanderers who never went down on them, so to speak, and they began to receive Johnny into their homes on the down low. Word spread of Johnny's talent and many satisfied customers wanted more.

Many of them were Johnny's existing clients who had at one time come in to find me, his new wife, at the dry cleaners. Some of them had shouted at him that they deserved to know that he had married, especially since he married a white woman. A small few felt differently about me. Most of them were very polite to me and congratulated me. I figured out who he slept with by their reaction to my presence at the dry cleaners.

There were many different reactions to Johnny's charming psychopathy and they all seemed to contain the same message. I want my money back.

Taneisha was an addict, an ex prostitute who had fallen to bad times after trying to go straight and trying to become a beautician. Her face was badly damaged after a beating in the street. She said she couldn't find honest work. Johnny told me that she came to us trying to go straight and learn a trade. Soon she became envious of me and hated my status and what she perceived as great wealth. She took my hard-earned cash as though it was hers. She was able to saddle my horse, so to speak, and began acting as though she thought herself to be superior to me. She also had a great time driving my Jag. In fairy tales, we waited for the prince to ride in on a white horse and save the princess. In this case, the white horse was mine and Johnny stole it from me and rode it like it was his and never gave it back. Oh, how it hurt me to find out that he wrote in his dating profile that he had a Jag and how great his new woman would look driving it. Maybe that was his intention. It made no difference. I lost a car that I really loved. Sure it was old but it was a classic. It was the same model and color driven by the Queen of England.

Then there was Monique, a beautiful, successful businesswoman with a very powerful personality. I never had proof of their relationship, and her laundry sat in the cleaners forever so she was not a regular customer. She was furious when she met me.

"You don't think this deserves a special announcement in the paper? Johnny Sorella is now a married man?" She screamed at Johnny that she deserved to know that there was now a wife in the picture. After she calmed down, she even offered, in her own noble way, to get us a wedding gift. I couldn't figure her out.

The saddest case was the handsome and pious Miss Asia Bird. When she got wind of my marriage to Johnny, showed up looking for him and stood as a sentry at the counter in the front entrance and wouldn't talk to me. She looked right through me like I was a ghost until he walked in.

This dignified, proud, seventy-year-old black woman dressed like royalty. She had lent Johnny twenty thousand dollars, which he had never paid back. When he got back to the cleaners that day she gave him a speech full of preaches. She let him know that he was to move his large flatbed trailer from her backyard, off of her private property. Yet later on she was the first one to take him in after I left him. She cooked for him and begged for him to stay with her. Johnny had no interest in her anymore, not after he took all of the money she had.

That day he had pulled her away into the parking lot to explain that I was just a business partner from Canada who married him for citizenship. Oh my God. I saw her eyes light up with hope as he led her back to her car. He came back to me and said that she was crazy and that there would be many more like her, women who wanted to be with him and would make all sorts of claims. I needed to understand that he couldn't stop women from wanting him.

I had wanted to throw up. I was sick to my stomach. I knew a lovesick woman when I saw one. He told me she was a jilted wannabe lover who just wanted him to sit next to her in church as though they were lovers, and he refused. After we split up, he confessed to me that he had attempted to have sex with her, but she was unable to and so he performed his opera on her and that was enough to get her fixated on him forever.

I soon realized that like those women whose heart Johnny had broken, I had entered Johnny's world, where you had to play by Johnny's rules. There was no way out no matter how hard I tried to wake up from the nightmare of having been his wife. It became a double shot of hell on earth full of memories of repeated infidelities that he had claimed were just business meetings or networking.

Even in the beginning when I was in the car with him delivering laundry, he would stay up there at a client's apartment for 45 minutes. He would come back with a bag of dirty laundry or dry cleaning, smelling like sex, drowned over with a shot of cognac.

In the end, after I had tried to muster the courage to leave so many times, I sunk into a depression so deep that it would take a team of rescue firefighters to get me out. There I was drowning in the mental and emotional sinkhole that my marriage had created. It sucked in all of my self-respect and my drive, to the point that I began to want to sleep all day. I stopped eating anything and I began to drink to numb the pain. I would wake up in the morning and cry at the sound of a bird singing as it touched what was left of my heartstrings. I cried for my loss, for the realization that the gift that was Johnny was truly just a rotten carcass of lies.

In the end, his excuses and lies had become so stupid that they were hysterically funny actually becoming a source of the only laughter I had in my life. But nothing was funny about Johnny's exploitation of women. When the dance of danger became serious, my survival instincts kicked in. Luckily, Johnny had never drugged me again after the first time. In fact, he refused to allow me to use any drugs, not even pot and he forbade anyone from giving me any. I remembered though, how he insisted that I smoke the occasional puff of pot at the homes of drug dealers whose dry cleaning he picked up. While I played with their pit bulls, he would watch me, slowly, carefully. I realized later that it was to have people witness me smoking marijuana. I wasn't worried and I found that so stupid because, in fact, I had declared the occasional marijuana joint smoked on my life insurance policy. I was a child of the sixties, an old hippie who still supported the legalization of marijuana at least for medical purposes. He was always busy planning traps for me.

I had several life insurance policies, and he so desperately tried to find out one thing from me. Who was the beneficiary? I never told him the value of the policies, and feared he would arrange to end my life for the money he could get. He never found out that he was not my beneficiary. I left that out too.

For some reason, he required that I be pure. I had to know everything he had been through and still I was to believe that he had a pure heart. On one uniquely terrifying and most memorable evening after shopping for groceries at midnight, sitting in the Jag in front of my condo, he made me listen for more than an hour while the ice cream melted in our groceries.

He told me stories about working with his father to build hidden compartments in houses, invisible places in which organized crime hid weapons, drugs and cash and I started to shake in fear. He spoke about his time in prison, about solitary confinement, about his special friend, about how he helped others pursue their education. He told me how he had been the first graduate of a bachelor's degree program while in prison and how he helped his inmate friend prepare for an interview for a primetime news program. Throughout all of the incredible tales of his pain and suffering in jail, he never did portray himself in any way as the villain. In all of his stories, he was a good guy who could do nothing wrong and so I became the good guy's wife. In no time, I felt the frightening dissonance in our relationship which would nearly be the death of me.

CHAPTER TWENTY-SIX: LESSONS LEARNED

One day, Johnny had told me that Patty, one of his previous lovers had named him as the beneficiary on her life insurance policy. He told me he was coming into money when his parents died and that it was okay to trust him with loans for his business expansion plan. It was always about other people's money. He never had gotten a check from Patty's estate. So after we broke up, I contacted her. She was shocked when I told her he claimed he would receive one hundred thousand dollars when she died of cancer. Actually, her cancer was slow and she managed it. Still she was shocked even more when I told her that he claimed she was already dead according to her best friend who called him to tell him so.

In fact, she was very much alive and eventually she became a close friend of mine. As a retired social worker, she became instrumental in my recovery. We had long detailed and painful conversations about

Johnny's attempts to get her money. After exhausting her limited funds, he obtained more by capitalizing her remaining two year paid up lease on a beautiful condo that her former boyfriend gave her. That gave her twenty thousand dollars cash and it was his for the taking. The money ran out after two years. He then asked her to contact an old lover and solicit an invitation to visit him out of state. He told her she should ask him for a ten thousand dollar loan for old time's sake.

I listened carefully and told her, "Patty, he was turning you out, transporting you interstate for the purpose of prostitution, a federal offence."

I told her how I gained an understanding of Johnny's mental methods by reading up on pimps and how they controlled their stable of women by withholding love if the money was not coming in, then showing immense approval when it was. She was amazed at the thought that he tried to make money with a woman her age that way. Patty was also 70 years old. "Johnny can turn anyone or anything into money. Patty, he's like a magician. He thinks he is Aladdin." She was disgusted at the idea of what Johnny had tried to make her do. She was more disgusted with herself for not having seen it in progress. She hated the message I was giving her because this kind of discussion was not part of her mental repartee. She sat there quiet and numb.

Patty had also tried to report him to law enforcement, especially after he threw her against the wall one night when she refused to heat up his dinner at 2 a.m. when he wandered into their apartment hungry and high on something. They refused to consider her complaint, told her to go home, that he would be okay in the morning. It was only after she had nothing left to give him that he threw her out onto the street and she was homeless. He told her that he was keeping her car because he needed it to deliver his laundry and dry cleaning. He told her to call a friend or her son to come and get her. Her friends had warned her family about the dangerous man Patty was involved with. They told her son that his mother would wind up dead in the trunk of her car one day. Luckily one friend was there with her on the day she approached Johnny to take her car back. This woman was a brave friend who managed to force Johnny to give Patty her car back, throwing all of Johnny's junk onto the street, unafraid as he watched her with a look of surprise all over his face. Patty was safe again, out of his reach. Patty's family refused to speak with her for years. Patty paid a high price for a low ride with a felon.

I was in a bigger trap, one that law enforcement helped Johnny build, and one that could also be used against me. They could also set me up, and I knew I had to move fast, get better, get stronger, and prepare for the battle that was coming.

I was stuck in a no-man's land. I lost my self-respect and dignity because no matter how much I tried, I lived in fear of Johnny. I could not sleep because I worried that I would find him naked in the middle of the night at the end of my bed again. I put piles of chairs and suitcases in front of my front doors at home so that if anyone broke in, I would wake up. I set marble slabs on my back patio doors so no one could enter. I still slept with my eyes half open and my hearing became so hypersensitive that I could almost hear a fly shit.

The fear that he could steal my identity kept me watching our old email address, so as to be sure he was not applying for credit cards in my name. I had to cancel numerous purchases that he was making in my name on my cards. It kept me living half a life, wasting the other, watching to be sure he never came back for anything more that he felt entitled to.

Johnny knew I loved to wear expensive jewelry that Paul had showered on me and so I stopped wearing any. I started to wear scarves to cover my neck and never took off my sunglasses in public. I began to resemble Audrey Hepburn because I would always sneak out in disguise. In reality, most of the time the fear of Johnny coming back or wanting me back kept me scared to run into him so I stayed hidden in my home when I was in Delray Beach, alone with only my memories of his promise to protect me against all harm.

I became sensitive to any perceived threat and all attempts to enter my property or come near me. I started to get to know everything about my neighbors. The macho, under age Colombian who lived illegally downstairs was sorry he ever threatened me and scratched my car because I reported his every act of intimidation. I took different exits to leave anywhere, drove different ways to get to the bank or the mall. Even at the grocery store I watched out for anyone following me. When I drove, if a car was too near or took my path behind me, I pulled over till they passed. I was fried. My sanity was hanging by a thin thread. I thought of suicide every day. It was not a life. It was hell and Johnny was the devil on earth. I eventually thought there would never be any light at any end of any tunnel. I verified my life insurance policies. I started to write my last letter to my friends and family, telling them I could not find any way out of what had become a world of pain, remorse and hopelessness.

Then one day I saw the light. I decided that I had to write a book to warn women about the Romeo crimes that had become the perfect way for men and even women to steal money tax free with no consequence. I needed to try to validate what I had lived through, or my experience would be worthless.

For the next year, I actively used a blog that women in my situation posted on and shared the emotions and pain and obtained solace by openly declaring in a safe place what it felt like to survive a traumatic bond with a psychopath. If I could help anyone who was looking for love to recognize, avoid or survive a traumatic love bond with a narcissistic financial predator, I would. If I could give a compassionate understanding of the dangerous emotional journey that one takes to reach an island of safety after loving a psychopath, I would.

I did what a responsible person should do. I shared the truth about a shameful and taboo subject: women who are tempted by seduction into letting the wrong man into their lives. There were no statistics or figures about the numbers involved because most people would choose to go it alone, ashamed of their sexual mistakes, their choice of lover, the chances they took. They had placed a priority on the wrong person, someone they wanted in their lives, more than they wanted their family or friends. Most victims refused to believe that a spell that had been cast over them by an evil frog that they tried to reform into a prince. Some women committed suicide and never left a note and no one ever found out how they could not accept the loss of their fortune, their family estate, down to the last penny.

In life, as it is said in French, "Il faut profiter de notre passage dans la vie des autres." That was to say, one must use every experience in one's life, every passage in another's life, as a way to learn about life. If a negative experience could teach me to avoid repeating the pain, then in a Pavlovian manner, I have accomplished something, and I have taken a step in the right direction on the path to survival. Leaving Johnny taught me that I could not change someone. I could only change the way I thought about them. Then it was up to me to decide to remove myself from the situation and deprive him of my love, my support, my company. Oh and yes, my money. He had no idea what he left on the table. He really had no idea what I was worth, or how strong I was. The fragile woman he left behind was of no concern to him. I truly believe that he thought he had destroyed me and that nothing was left of me with which to come after him. There had been very few Kumbaya moments with Johnny while I was with him and even fewer now.

There was no reason to expect that the same pain that was destroying me would somehow magically turn into pleasure unless I turned into a masochist, which I would not, so goodbye was the right answer. Sometimes you think that there is no hope. Without hope, all life on earth can feel worthless, a wondering and belly-button analyzing of a situation that won't change. There was no hope for Johnny. If something is broken in two, there is a chance that it can be fixed, but Johnny was broken into millions of little pieces of himself. I could cry all I wanted, and I still do. I cry because I wish he were the man he said he was, the man I thought he was. But in reality, he was what he was, operating out of his brain stem, doing whatever he had to in order to survive.

It is everyone's choice to make. Do I change to fit the person I love? Do I give up a little piece of myself to each relationship in order to make it work? Or do I stay true to myself? Life is like a bicycle wheel. Unless I stay true to who I am, and what I want, then the ride will be wobbly and dangerous.

Through Johnny, I learned to respect the danger, listen, hear and see the signs of imminent harm. Once upon a time, I thought he was the one. In fact, he was. He was the one who would change me forever and ever. He was the one I would never forget. Did I wish that I never met him? No. I wouldn't trade a moment of my life with him. There are good moments I will always remember. Despite our traumatic bond and maybe because of it, I experienced a trust I had never known I could feel. If only I had not trusted the wrong person, if only I knew the price I would pay for ignoring my feelings in order to trust a man who could have taken my life. The good times were good, very good, and the bad times were awful. But I did survive so I could tell the story. There are many women who don't and won't. Laci Peterson, Dorothy Stratton, and so many more lost their lives without warning. They were loved by family and friends and they who didn't see it coming. They were women who trusted too much, too long.

I got away in time to salvage what little was left of my dignity and it's been slowly coming back. If the roots of anyone's dignity were strong, mine were. I always knew that I belonged in a place and time where life would be good to me, and now here I was ready to let in the love. First there was self-love, then, other love. But I had to learn to let go of people who wanted what I had, but who gave little in return. I had to let go of those who resented me for what I was and those who wanted to tear me down in order to have a shorter climb to reach my level of success in life.

I knew now that there was no shortcut to becoming whole. I was a work in progress, and if I slipped and fell, or if I was tripped, I still had to do the work of standing back up. I had to get back up by myself because my family was often too dysfunctional, harmful, and poisonous to my mental and emotional health. Born alone to die alone, we are all destined to live our own personal karma, but in this life, what was in between the beginning and the end was up to me. Somewhere in the middle I found myself and was never going to be alone again. Solitude could be good solitude and I was becoming better company.

So my goal became to wake up one day at a time, and dance all the way to my grave, even if I was the only one left at the ball.

CHAPTER TWENTY-SEVEN: SQUARE ONE

On a beautiful day in Delray Beach, more than two years since I had let Johnny into my life, I thought of him again. I had perfected my golf drive to over one hundred and fifty yards and I broke a hundred in my golf game. I was sitting quietly by the television watching the news when I decided to call Johnny about the money he owed me. My daughter was desperately in need of financial help, so it was time again to try to reach out and try to make some kind of effort to collect. I looked online for his name and number, and I found his business line and dialed, and he answered surprised.

"How are you?" I said. He told me he was great, and I was already saying that I needed to speak to him about the loans that I made him, and his mood changed.

"Things are really not going well here, and everyone is struggling at this time of the year."

I mentioned that he needed to be making money with his new partner Tonia Bailey. He suddenly asked me how I knew about her, and I told him that he was listed in her email address on their business website.

"Well, that didn' work out, and probably you could help me with my rights, to get what I am supposed to get because I did some work and then she stopped payin' me and locked me out of my business."

I was amazed again at his ability to turn everything into an opportunity for himself. I then said, "Johnny, I need my money so can you even give me a partial payment or can we come to an agreement?" I ignored that he always made it all about him and I steered the conversation back to me.

Then the conversation deteriorated, and he began to berate me because I was responsible for going and ruining his relationship with his parents whom he had not seen for over a year. He yelled that I had poisoned his family against him because I was telling his cousin Cassidy everything that he did. I realized nothing had changed, and Johnny was still blaming the world for his problems.

"You've ruined my life Brigitte, I hate you, you fuckin' bitch; you better not......."

I just hung up.

My hands were shaking and I needed a good shot so I poured myself a scotch on the rocks and downed it and felt the smooth burning. My nerves were calming down and I decided to be proactive. I called Tonia Bailey to try my luck with her. I dialed the listed business number and I left a message. Then I dialed 411 and good old AT&T gave me her current home number. I was nervous, and then this voice that sounded wounded answered. I thought quickly because it could not possibly have been her.

"May I speak to Tonia Bailey, please?"

"Who is calling?" she moaned slowly.

"My name is Brigitte Knowles. I am Johnny Sorella's former wife."

There was an awful pregnant pause and then there was a deep breath, another slow moan and then a final quick sigh, "Please don't do this, please don't play games with me."

I took command of my voice and said, "This is really his ex-wife and I need to speak to you about him."

"But I don't know anything about you," she pleaded.

"Well, ask away!" I tried to lighten the mood, but she started to cry.

"You cannot be calling me to help him, he has destroyed me." And then she began to sob. "That man assaulted me, I have a bad heart and my husband and mother had just died. I had just recovered from surgery when he came into my life. He took my money and made me put his name on my house deed because he told me that he needed protection in case my children who hated me threw him out. They thought he had no rights and so I did it and now he's gone. He stole my business and everything he could pawn."

I felt sick to my stomach as I began to recognize my own pain in her voice. "Please, tell me everything."

And I made myself comfortable because I knew this would be a long call, one I never thought I would need to make.

It began when she met Johnny online. She had lost her husband Thomas after a joyous marriage of forty years. She was alone and lonely, and her son and daughter were far away. After her heart surgery, which no one thought she would survive, she lost weight, so much weight that she had skin hanging, and she was self-conscious, but she was alive and more beautiful than ever and she felt that life was again going to be a beautiful gift. She came home to a house that her children had visited in her absence and removed their preferred objects from, so when she also found out they had also chosen her coffin, she felt so confused and alone.

She yearned for companionship and reached out online to a dating website that serviced older singles. She found a decent-looking man who wanted to meet her since they had both grown up in West Virginia. They met, and things moved so fast, and before she knew it he had moved into her home and began to wear her dead husband's clothes and sleep on his side of the bed, in Thomas's underpants after brushing his teeth with Thomas's electric toothbrush.

She was so happy and she was convinced that God sent him into her life, a gift for her to help her live again after losing her husband with whom she ran a successful decorating business. She had gone bankrupt after his death because she knew nothing about his accounting and nothing about the business. Her talents were limited to the art of decorating, and she lost the cash flow that was usually coming in, so the business folded along with her contact with the outside world. When Johnny began to take over, she almost welcomed it, not for a moment worrying about what he would take. She was only concerned with what he gave her: affection, companionship and passionate sex.

Tonia worked a bit to help him, and gave him ideas about redecorating his dry cleaning business that was in a hole. She met his employee Rhonda Todella and wondered about her health since she appeared to have open sores and cuts all over her body. She always looked as though she was going to pass out.

"Rhonda cuts herself because she is crazy. Pay no attention to her, she just washes my clothes and handles the cash, I am helping to rehabilitate her," Johnny lied as he carefully avoided revealing that Rhonda was his junkie lover heroin connection, and they were both shooting up heroin every day, all day, together in the needle's rapture. Rhonda brought her dog and cat to compete with Johnny's cockatiel that was jealous and bit everyone but Johnny.

It started slowly: he would ask Tonia for small loans until payday when his clients would come in and pay for their dry cleaning. But there were few paydays. South Florida, especially West Palm Beach, was in a slow downward spiral of financial depression that was taking forever to end. There were no jobs, so that meant no clients. Johnny had to hustle, to cold-call and even flirt with every woman who passed in the strip mall in order to flaunt his services and his goods. These included picking up and dropping off the laundry, as well as servicing his client's sexual needs. It was well known that Johnny was a male prostitute, and he had been arrested for soliciting a female cop. Tonia had no idea about any of that since she came from a sheltered background, so she never suspected anything.

It was a heavenly moneymoon. Johnny and Tonia spent weekends at her home while Rhonda ran the laundry store, allowing Johnny to work his magic and seduce Tonia's money into his pocket. She gladly loaned him the monies and felt that he was good for it because he convinced her that he also worked as a certified remodeler on the side. He claimed he made a small fortune by building storage and remodeling kitchens and tiling floors and redoing bathrooms for the last three decades. He had her under his spell and little did she know that she would never see that money again.

They leased a new business unit together, and she gave Johnny the money to buy the equipment and the material he needed to prepare the unit for their new decorating company. However, as time went on, she noticed that there was nothing being built despite the hours he would spend there. She continued to devote herself to him and worshiped the air he breathed, the ground he walked on. She introduced him to all of her family and she was surprised when no one liked him, and, in fact, they all expressed shock at his demeanor.

Even in Thomas's clothes, he was so far from the gentleman that Thomas had been. But he mesmerized Tonia who saw him as her romantic savior, a man sent from heaven to bring her back to the living.

She was so deep into Johnny it would take the teamsters to get her out. Johnny knew about her heart condition and he acted as though he would be there at every turn of the page of her recovery to speed her back onto his dance floor. Like John Travolta, he made her feel like a teenager again as he jived her into a frenzied trance. Despite her bad back, she would let him lead her as though she was on star search, so thrilled to be in a man's arms again. Only Johnny was leading her when they were off the dance floor too. It was too late to tell her anything. He told everyone in her family that he would love her and take care of her forever, and so everyone understood when Tonia put his name as co-owner of her beautiful half-million dollar home.

Johnny began to slack off in the bedroom and told her he was tired because of the drive from West Palm Beach to Port St. Lucie that was an hour each way, so he began to sleep at the dry cleaners or so he said.

Rhonda had just got out of rehab and had lost her house. Johnny had counseled her not to pay her mortgage, and he told her that she would qualify for a modification. After all that, she never did get one, she was homeless. She slept in the dry cleaners with Johnny. He had not paid his water or his light bill, so they had to steal water from the other businesses at the mall by turning on their outdoor faucets in the back.

They filled up their containers with water and dragged in more water every time they had to do a wash. They used a large pail for a toilet and that same pail was used for the clothing that had to be washed. After they had done their business, they emptied it into the canal behind the mall. The public health risk was worse than Ebola. The bacteria that remained on the clothing when it was dry could cause infection. Clients had no idea that the clothing they sent in for hand washing would cost them much more than they paid for and fluff and fold was not what they were getting.

Rhonda would spend hours cutting herself with razor blades and locking herself in the bathroom so Johnny had no choice but to improvise and his dignity, whatever dignity he ever had, fell by the wayside.

It was the day before Christmas Eve. "Baby, I will be going home to see my parents for Christmas. Rhonda will be driving up with me because she is visiting her family in North Carolina which is on the way up. I need you to look after the business for me. Can you water the plants, feed the cat, dog and bird? Can you open and close the store, and of course run it while I am gone?" Johnny wasn't at all shy to ask Tonia for anything he wanted anytime any place.

"Of course honey, I want you to see your family for Christmas. I can't go with you because I can't take the long drive so you go ahead. You know I love you and I will be thinking of you while you're gone." Tonia hung up the phone and went to bed and dreamt of her sweetheart all night long.

Johnny had told Tonia the next morning before he left. "You are my world Tonia so take good care of yourself until I come home to you. I am leaving tonight and I will be back in time to take you in my arms and give you all my love."

"Johnny, I have a gift for you and a card, open it tomorrow on Christmas morning and know that I love you," Tonia smiled. She kissed him on the lips and watched as he walked away. He turned and waved, and he was gone.

The next morning, Christmas day, Tonia went to the dry cleaners as promised and walked in. She turned on the lights and went to the counter and was surprised to see her card there, already opened. She picked it up, and something about it was different.

When she gave him her hand-written love note it said, "To Johnny with love, your darling Tonia."

Johnny's scratched out Tonia's name and his handwriting wrote over it, "To Rhonda with love, your darling Johnny S."

Tonia gasped for breath and nearly fainted as she held the counter and tried to get her balance. As her heart tried to stop beating, she reached for her pills, and she started to cry, a cry that came from the bottom of her soul. It was over, as quickly as it had begun. She knew immediately that she had been taken. She thought of days and nights full of "I love you's" and "We'll be together forevers' and she knew it was all a plot to get her money and her house and her business.

She knew she had made the biggest mistake of her life, and she thought she was going to die, the pain was so sharp, so deep, so strong, just like Johnny's arms around her, just like his love for her, and then she fell. She hit her head, and she lay there until her Yorkie puppy Jessie licked the side of her face. Tonia opened her eyes and saw him licking her tears, looking at her with his "let's go out and play" eyes. Jessie was too young to know that she was crying, only that he was thirsty and wanted to go out and run around and chase the birds. She got up, feeling heavier and older and sadder than she had ever felt before and she knew what she had to do and so she called him.

"Johnny I found the card, how could you do this to me, how could you break my heart and hurt me when all I have ever done is love you with all of my heart? I am not staying here, I am going home now, and I am never going to see you again, and I will take everything back. Everything I ever gave you." Tonia wept and waited for Johnny to say something, anything. She wanted him to explain to her that she was wrong, he loved her and it was just a joke.

Johnny was so high that he didn't care and he didn't want to. Rhonda had given him her twenty-three thousand dollar disability check, and she and he had scored from his old contacts in Martinstown, West Virginia where his parents lived. They were old, in their eighties, and they did not know what Johnny was on, nor did they want to. They listened as he told them that he was going to marry Rhonda. Rhonda sat there deaf, quiet as a church mouse; picking at her sores and feeling velvet grow in her veins.

Any thoughts of Tonia and her heartache were of no consequence to Johnny and Rhonda. They were in another place where the soft pulsing sound of their heartbeats kept them in a slow dance in their heads. Nothing mattered and nothing would spoil their rush. They felt the honey-soft feeling of time slowly passing them by. All the while, they heard each other breathing as they lay on a bed and didn't move for hours.

The world outside them did not exist, no one could reach them as they soared inside of their beating hearts, slowly feeling the velvet insides of their arteries as their blood sang for them and then they slept. Very late the next day, Boxing Day, Johnny woke Rhonda.

"Git in the car, we fucked up, Tonia won't open the store and we need to get back."

He rushed their goodbyes, and they sped back to Florida where the reality of their ways was waiting for them. He still had a shoebox full of drugs left in the car, and he wasn't going to feel any pain for a while. It wasn't until New Years' day that they walked into Tonia's Decor holding hands, and Tonia's mouth dropped.

"You need to leave now Johnny or I will call the police," she said as she looked at him straight in the eyes.

"You knock yourself out Tonia, I ain't goin' anywhere. This lease is in my name, too." He walked up to her and stared her down and said, "You leave."

He turned and took Rhonda into his arms and started to kiss her everywhere, her lips, her neck, putting his hands all over her, caressing her with his lips and his fingers, taking her breasts out and tasting them like they were candy.

All the while he watched Tonia's face, her heart pounding, her eyes tearing. All the while he waited for her heart to fail, knowing this could kill her, knowing he wanted her dead. She told him to leave and she called the police, and they came and told Tonia he had every right to be there. He told them she was a jilted lover and that she was getting crazy, that she was off her meds. The police officer told her she should leave and go home, and so she did. She drove home, crying all the way.

The next day, back she came thinking she needed to pick up some things that she felt were valuable. Johnny walked in, telling her he would be back and that she had better get her things out of there. She had sewing machines and decorating tools that she did not want to leave there. It was getting late, and she wanted to take the time to close up properly.

She called her son Jim and begged and pleaded for him to come to the store. He was angry that she had given Johnny the business when he had wanted to take it over after his father's death, but he loved his mother enough and still came. When he entered he walked around and was shocked at the mess. Johnny had been depositing his junk everywhere in the warehouse, distracting Tonia at the office. Then by claiming that he would rearrange her precious things, he counted on her confusion when he continuously displaced and moved things from right to left, from left to right. Johnny was also busy stealing her valuables from her home right in front of the neighbors' eyes while Tonia worked at the office.

Jim walked around, and he noticed wiring going into the attic and so he got a ladder and went up there. He came back down, and his face was white. Johnny had been building a secret apartment above the office. Johnny used it to stay overnight with Rhonda. They would shoot up drugs and pass out. The floor above their heads was filled with discarded needles and empty food containers. Tonia's son pointed at the hidden room that Johnny had constructed above the office rafters. Finally Tonia understood that Johnny had been building a home sweet home for his lover Rhonda and her son. There was a king-sized bed for Rhonda and him and a twin bed for her son who had just gotten out of jail.

Finally Johnny arrived with Rhonda. He stood there telling Jim that he and Tonia had never been in any romantic relationship.

"Your mother is sick and she needed sexual therapy. She is off her meds and she is dangerous." Jim glared with venom in his eyes at Johnny. It wasn't enough that he was fighting cancer. This animal before him had attended family dinners with cousins and aunts and uncles. Johnny had publicly declared his passionate love for Tonia in front of everyone. This vulture had told him that he loved him like a father loves a son. This festering, evil snake was trying to tell Jim that everyone had imagined Johnny's presentation of his absolute devotion to Tonia. Tonia was a dear, loving, gentle, lonely-hearted, nearly seventy-year-old woman who had just lost her husband and mother, an angel who had never known evil. It was despicable.

Tonia told her son to take the truck with her stuff home, she would handle this herself, and she told Rhonda to get in the car. Johnny stood there alone with her in the empty store and they said nothing until Johnny pushed her and told her to get out. He grabbed her hand and twisted it until the pain became unbearable and her fingers snapped broken and she cried out, and he pushed her again, and she fell hard on her side.

"You are never going to take anything away from me you crazy bitch," he stared at her and said.

He pushed her out the front door and locked it with the key and removed the key and so she ran to the backdoor and entered and saw him and tried to grab her keys from him, but he pushed her down again. This time he took her keys and cell phone and left her there on the floor and locked her in from the outside in the back. Tonia was trapped. She suddenly realized she could not get out, and her heart medication was in her purse. She knew she had to calm down. She measured her breath, saving her gasps, holding her arm, which was turning blue. A bulge was beginning to protrude at her elbow. Her back hurt so badly. Her back that she couldn't be sure about on a good day was out. She could not move an inch. She lay there on the floor and waited. Surely someone would come to her rescue.

Hours passed, and she thought of how her world had changed. She stared at the rafters and wanted to go upstairs. She wanted so badly to see the nest that Johnny had built for himself and Rhonda, but she was in too much pain even to lift a finger. She passed out and floated in a dreamlike state, where she begged Thomas, her deceased husband, to forgive her. She cried out for his arms to hold her just one more time. She wanted to die, to be back with the man she had loved for 40 years. He was the father of her children, a man who treated her as a princess.

The sun was rising. There was a slight sign of a warm glow in the sky when Tonia heard the door open. She saw Johnny walk in, walk to the end of the warehouse slowly looking for her. She was sitting on the floor behind and beside the door he had come in through. As he turned and walked back silently, he saw her, and his face changed. He concentrated, slowly observing her. He came closer, slowing like a panther, studying her, looking to see if there was any sign of life. As Johnny bent over and pushed his foot forward to touch her, he waited for her to move. He stood over her as she lay there with her eyes closed. He bent down further on one knee and nudged her and said, "Tonia, baby, wake up. Are you okay?"

She opened her eyes and saw a look of disappointment in his eyes as clear as holy water. He fell to both knees and said, "Tonia forgive me and let's go home. I'll take care of you baby, it will never happen again."

Tonia looked at him, kicked him in the balls and said, "It's over, get out of this place and don't ever come back, or I'll call the police. You mean nothing to me, do you hear me, nothing!'

He laughed as he got up and turned to her with his icy stare, "I will never give up my things. That's it, I'm getting a restraining order against you, you crazy bitch."

He dropped her purse and cell phone and all of her keys on the floor beside her and walked away. Tonia breathed deeply and prayed to God to let her live long enough to put him behind bars. She knew he had tried to kill her, and she knew there was no turning back. She had survived a murder attempt, a calculated, cold, definite attempt on her life, and she swore never to let anyone near her heart ever again, and she begged Thomas for forgiveness and thanked God for her life. He left and slammed the door behind him, and she called the landlord who came quickly and changed the locks and promised to put the lease back in her name.

She managed to get to her car and drive home with swollen, broken, painfully limp fingers and fought to get to her home where her medication was, her priority being to take her meds and calm down and decide how to proceed against Johnny.

Her cell phone rang as she was driving and she couldn't answer. It was the police that were responding to a call from her daughter for a safety check as her mother who usually called her every night did not do so and did not answer her cell phone or her home phone. Tonia ignored the phone, arrived home and got into her comfortable bed that received her with welcoming arms. She cried herself to sleep for the first time in months; her body shivered in her sorrow and drowned any joy that was ever alive in her spirit. She nearly died that night without her heart medication, and she realized Johnny wanted her dead, and then her house became his and Rhonda's happily ever after. Tonia wanted to throw up.

The next day her son drove her to the police station, and she filed for a restraining order. She looked in the mirror at the police station as she washed her hands, aching. She realized when they took pictures of her injuries that this was not a dream; it was a nightmare in broad daylight. The truth came out, and the police told her to get a no contact restraining order. She felt she had lost any hope in life of ever trusting any man ever again. She picked herself up and stood tall, walked out of the police station into the rest of her life.

CHAPTER TWENTY-EIGHT: THE BIGGER PICTURE

Tonia and I spent hours talking about Johnny, just as I had with Amy and Ronnie, about the way he was untouchable because there was no criminal law covering intra-couple financial crime. When I met Tonia, she looked magnificent and she had a new haircut and beautiful makeup that defined her new image that matched the snappy outfit she had on. Her survival instincts were in high gear, and she was stronger and smarter than ever. She was dating again and she had met a new man who cared for her and she was happy.

She had good news. Her ex-daughter in law who was a sheriff had spent time with her going over the facts, and she offered to take the case to her contacts in law enforcement, people she felt would care. How was it that everything was referred to civil court, and no law enforcement agency wanted to do the paperwork that would report this vicious man who turned women's lives into horror stories full of filth, destruction, robbery, rape and drugging, mental torture and attempted murder?

I spoke to this lady cop for three hours and told her about the failure of any law enforcement department to arrest Johnny. There was little hope of seeing justice.

"Donna, they were probably using him as an informant, as they had done with a case I had worked on in my public security work." I told her how I had busted Adam, a dangerous felon, by coordinating an undercover operation with Vice and Child Protection Services. I had granted them a one and a half million dollar budget that I got from my dear friend and colleague Trudy Solomon. Trudy was a fellow politician whom I loved dearly. She had worked with me on commissions, committees for municipal and urban politics. I told her that particular key drug cases prevailed in this situation where law enforcement saw us as a minor interference in their jurisdiction. Women's victimization was strategically filed under domestic violence. A "Go home, and don't distract us from our serious drug cases" message was clearly sent and heard. Message received loud and clear. I told her I was certain that Johnny was untouchable. She told me to trust her. She told me to wait and see.

It was vital to inform and educate the public about this kind of crime. I had turned down the suggestion by the Attorney General's office for an advocacy project. I had run a tedious Child Support Enforcement Legislative Reform Project that took a decade of my life and reduced legal aid, social welfare and social housing costs by millions. I did not have the ambition, time or energy to do it again. This was an important societal problem, but someone else would have to carry this ball. I was done. I had lost my will to survive and was living one day at a time, finances already in the grave that Johnny dug for me.

When children forget you, when you lose a close loved one, when your husband ignores you and leaves you for a newer model, or when you live alone and survive any life crisis, you are vulnerable. It is at this very time that you can become these human vultures' target. But the FBI tended to want to be heroes in larger battles. So I had to stop thinking that they could do anything about our plight.

While others argued for same-sex rights and others tried to demolish what women had worked on for decades, we were victimized for wanting love, companionship and sex. Our class of victim was ignored. We were just collateral damage in a battlefield where we were not strong soldiers. We were just the cost of doing business, the Pinto element in a world where aging women were dispensable. Added to the climate of undoing alimony for life for women by the right-wing conservatives in America, there was a disregard for single older women. Any stupid woman who dared to stop knitting comforters and who wanted to dance instead, deserved what she got.

The baby-boomer woman was not worth protecting, and a new kind of victim was losing ground in a war against aging. There was a serious attack on a woman's economy via her anatomy. Seduce and rob became the new hit and run.

The contrast was palpable, and Palm Beach County was the center of a change of fortune for those women who used to matter to their families and society. The women who used to raise fortunes for charity were now the brunt of resentment for wanting to live their lives in passion and love. They wanted to find a man to care for and who cared for them. We started to go back into the closet and we accepted that today's youth had abandoned us, and the government was starting to wear out our rights to a safe and sustainable retirement.

There was a new uncivil war beginning in which seniors had to do battle on too many fronts. Then it was said that this had also been happening to men for years. It was time that the government looked at the cost of caring for the aged after their monies were stolen. It was the start of the decline of the empire that once was America. A society must be judged on how it treats its elderly, those that built their country, those that made the history that declared that this society was a safe place to live in.

What happened to our place in a world that was changing so fast? There was no way to get off the dangerous roller coaster ride that our lives had become. We played the sport of life at our own risk so we had to take it or leave it. Sue in civil court or shut up. I had to reflect on what this issue had done to my life and where I was going. How much more time could I spend trying to fix this societal error? Why were we leaving our parents to their own devices, when it was clear that our elderly mothers were being victimized by professionals who knew their crimes would fall between the cracks of law enforcement? It was the easiest crime: pretend to love a single senior woman, steal her money and get away with intentional fraud.

God has a plan, and He doesn't make mistakes.

I learned the bottom is different for everyone.

I hit my bottom and I learned that there are some things against which I am powerless. I learned that lightning can strike twice if you don't learn the lesson a mistake was sent to teach you. I had become a person for whom only money mattered. I had given my soul to making money and to becoming successful. After reaching the height of the kingdom of charity work, I became someone who burnt out, who was angry with God and angry at the world, because two people who had stolen my life's work ruined my plans to live at the Ritz and drive a Maybach. God made me visit hell on earth. I had to learn about the devil's work here and I had to learn how to solve the dilemma of a loving God who let my mother die. How could He do this to me?

Yet that same God and His angels surrounded me when I almost lost my soul. I was a tired soldier in God's war against evil. The devil wanted to destroy the love I had for God, the trust I felt in Him even after my mother died. The closer I got to being ready to stop loving God, the more the devil tried to convince me that I was not loved by God.

Meeting Johnny was looking the devil straight in the eye because Johnny had sold his soul to the devil and the devil was living in him. I should have known from the start that Johnny was a very sick and dangerous man. Johnny was a desperate hoarder. He suffered from what is called Disposaphobia. He would not leave his things even if they were dirty and useless and old and destroyed and worthless. He found his comfort in the familiar, and the older and junkier things remained valuable to him. He wanted to destroy everything and anything. Love, new things, valuable relationships, good friendships, nothing was safe. Everything was fair game. Just when Johnny was surrounded by filth and ugliness did he feel at home, safe, familiar, and sound, amongst the whores and the prostitutes and drug addicts, those that no one loved or needed? He felt power and control over them because they were below him.

If only I had known then what I know now, I could have walked the other way when I first met him. It took me eighteen months, physically and emotionally, to leave Johnny, and I did it cold turkey. You cannot rewrite the ending. These kind of men don't stop until they get what they want and if there is no more of that supply that you were providing, whether it was money or adulation or whatever the fuel was that the predator was able to refine from you, if there is nothing left for them to feed on, they leave for new supply from new prey. There is no love or emotion or sorrow or regret on their part if they are truly in a predator-prey relationship with you. And no amount of therapy or professional help will rescue or heal them. They had a psychic break with humanity long before you came on the scene.

Run.

Run as fast as you can and don't look back.

Hold your therapist's hand along the way because it is a bumpy ride back to reality. There is no truth in the dream that men like Johnny weave. Break the spell before it is too late. Yes, there is such a thing as too late. It is usually too late when they kill you or when you kill yourself. You must learn to know what love is not. It is not painful, it does not make you suffer, and it does not put you down or kick you when you are already down. Love is good energy that makes you stronger and makes you love yourself even more, not hate yourself. Someone who loves you does not pretend to love you in order to steal all of your money. Learn the lesson, pay the price, grow and know that this too shall pass.

One day I will cry because I won't hear from Johnny anymore and that will really hurt because it will signal the end of the chance to rewrite the ending.

I lived one day at a time. I began by putting one foot in front of the other and started from zero, but I started. Walk away in the right direction. Look for a safe harbor. Be alone until you have healed. Try not to look back. Do anything but go back. That is not an option. That road leads to inevitable harm and imminent danger. There are many women in the news, beautiful mothers, wives, lovers, who were killed by their significant others. Why and how is often no mystery? The truth is that women die, are dying and have died because they took too long to leave. Like frogs on a slowly heated frying pan, they are lulled. Instead of jumping at the first sign of heat, they stay and wait and suddenly they fall asleep and die. Don't allow yourself to slowly live in hell on earth. It will only get worse, not better.

True psychopaths don't change. Even if Johnny's psychopathy was undiagnosed, I knew he would always be what he is. God help us all find peace with ourselves because the hardest part is forgiving yourself for having allowed that evil person into your life, betraying yourself by closing your eyes when you should have looked closer.

There is no price to pay for love, you can't buy it, you can't find it, just stay still and it will come to you. Be yourself, love yourself and allow yourself the time to heal. Pray for strength and guidance and reach out to others here in this sisterhood of women who know better. I could never let this happen to me again. Wisdom is like a medal on your heart. You cannot ever let anyone like this near you again. That is the first promise you have to make to yourself. The rest will follow.

I had been mind-fucked. I am educated, experienced, but I was no match for someone who had been doing this all of his life. I had never heard of anything like this before and now I know. When he told me I needed to come back and claim my husband, I know now that was just manipulation.

One day at a conference in Washington, I tried my engagement ring on, months after I annulled my marriage, months after the last time I saw Johnny again. I call it "my marriage" because he was never married to me or at least he didn't act like it. I was married, he was not, I guess. He magically called right then at a dinner party in front of my therapist. I thought, this is magic, we belong together. NO, my therapists told me, no, don't call him. But I did anyhow, and he said, "I was just trying to get you off of my favorites." I was devastated. So I was the sick one. He was just the evil one. Yes, there are two realities: what you wish it could be and what it never will be. You will never have a normal relationship with this kind of man. It cannot be repeated enough times, RUN.

Johnny was just an old pimp and whore who thought he would never get old, never stop turning women on, never lose his charm. I sat there in the middle of the night wondering whom he was holding in his arms. I yearned to forget his name, forget his smile, or forget how good I felt in his bear hug. Had I known this could happen to me would I have never gone out with him? Had someone told me this man was a dangerous psychopathic financial predator, I would have easily not looked at him twice.

All I can think of is that God wanted me to learn a lesson. I learned that the devil lives in West Palm Beach and that any woman who loves him well knows how close she came to death, how close she came to losing God. When I was afraid or angry around him, I felt the need to prepare to defend myself. I know I could have killed him in self-defense if he tried to kill me, and then I would not have wanted to live because he would be dead. To this day I know that when and if I hear that he is dead, I will cry because I don't think I can ever stop loving him. The thought that Johnny can continue to affect my heart, mind and soul makes me sick. My thoughts were intrusive thoughts about him, about his voice, his lips. When would I stop caring? When would he become just someone that I used to know? That is when I realized I was still in the relationship, but he was not and he never was.

Somewhere out there millions of women who loved the wrong man share my plight. In French we say, "Le naturel revient au gallop": If you chase away the natural in someone, it will come back with a gallop. Men who are violent need help. Violence is multi faceted. It is psycho-economic, physical, emotional and mental harm that can result in irreversible damage to your finances, your body, your heart and your mind. If no one has ever stood up for you, then be the first to do so. Stand up for what you could be if you could love yourself enough to get away from the man who makes you suffer. Life is hard enough without their attacks. Find self-love and then you will understand that love feels good in every way. Buy a puppy, take yoga, volunteer in a children's hospital and give your love to someone who will appreciate it. Don't throw it away on someone who will use it to steal your soul.

I told my close friend Tee-Jay, who operated a charity for the homeless, how I regretted that I would never see the Johnny I loved again because he did not exist. There was once upon a time a Johnny that made me feel that I was beautiful, worth loving, worth holding, worth making love to, worth laughing with, worth dancing with. That Johnny did exist for me, and she said that if I wanted him, that God would be sure to have him there waiting for me when I died, and so that soothed me. So I let Johnny go back into the cave that was his life. I knew I would not be able to save him from his destiny.

God does not make mistakes. He has a path for everyone and a plan for me, and I had to trust that this too would pass, and a mistake became a lesson in love. Love is giving, not taking, love is letting go of something and hoping that God will take care of it. I asked Johnny's family to pray for him, for me and I told them that he was out of everyone's reach now and that it was only a matter of time before he got arrested again.

As luck would have it, if and when Johnny is busted again, he will probably have enough information to give law enforcement on the network of criminals he is involved with. If he had the facts and evidence that the FBI needed, he would be able to buy his way out again.

There was a drug organization that was operating out of an organization that he had become involved with that surely was going to be busted. I felt I knew the ending before anyone else did. He would give them details that he had hoarded about everyone he knew and everyone he met that had any drug dealings in West

Palm Beach. He would create the organogram or flow chart with names and dates and details that would buy him a one-way ticket out of West Palm Beach. Where he would go and what his new WITSEC name would be was anyone's guess. I wondered if I would hear his voice one day on the phone. I still do.

As for me, was it possible that the FBI did me a favor? They erased all of the data that would make anyone believe that their ex-witness had gone rogue. There should have been a file with hundreds of pages of emailed proof and testimony and evidence that Johnny, Johnny S, aka Randolph, aka James Delaney Pierce, aka Sonny, was responsible for stealing millions from innocent women over the past thirty years by posing as an innocent gigolo. Well, every single piece of paper in the file disappeared. Nothing remained about his involvement with organized crime, his informant status. If only one page sat in their file, it was probably a picture of me with the word "potential menace" and "neutralized" with a big X across my face. Nothing would be left that would indicate that there was any truth to the bureau's role in a campaign to discredit me.

CHAPTER TWENTY-NINE: EPILOGUE

It is New Years Eve 2013 transforming into 2014, another year gone, out with the old, in with the new. I am more than sober, longing for some fine champagne, thinking about cold Crystal, bubbling in my antique flutes. I am deciding without the comfort of wishful thinking, about what I want the rest of my life to be like. I am debating with fate, what I keep, what I let go of. The heavy heart that holds on so tightly to what could have been had been replaced with a lighter heart, one that knows what can be, what can become of what was and be a better version of what could have been. I cannot dwell any longer on what was right and what went wrong. As I think about this year, I remember that it was a busy year, for one case there was a thirty five thousand dollar check just like old times. I thought less and less about Johnny, less and less about what I thought had been good times. I had let go of what I thought would never change, what I could never fix, what wanted to stay broken. Sometimes in life we meet people that masquerade as someone that will bring us joy and happiness without end. We want to hear what we need to hear so we listen selectively to what we like and ignore the truth because the truth is one big stop sign that we can't pretend we didn't see. So we close our eyes, we close our ears, we close our minds and surf on the fantasy of what we know will never be.

I finally understood that my unmet childhood needs would never be met and that I had to live my life as a broken adult with unmet needs. I knew that even broken people survive if they are not broken in the wrong place. So often I wanted to rethink and review what my life with Johnny could have been but I couldn't go there. I did not want to dwell on things from the past even when dwelling used to be my only comfort. Sitting and staring at my past as though it was alive when in reality there was nothing I could do to change it as it stormed away from that moment when I thought time stood still. As my life moved on, sometimes I stood there thinking that if I was fast enough I could run backwards and fix what didn't work, adjust what was not in the right place at the right time, the kind of childlike fantasy thinking that got me into trouble in the first place. Sometimes I wanted just to be on a runaway train, heading away from Johnny.

So I would never have a mother and father who were happily married and loved me more than anything in the world. I would never have a brother and sister whom I could play with and giggle with about the way our puppy stole our toys. It just wasn't going to turn out that way no matter how many times I fantasized about who my father was. He had been a father not in name, only in skin. One day when I was six, I told everyone he was a fireman who drove a big fire truck and saved lives and the next day I told everyone he was a policeman afraid of no one. I internalized this entire fantasy rescue thinking because it made reality so much less painful. All that pain had never gone away, it sat inside me and required that I feed it more and more until it choked me like an elephant sitting on my knees looking at me and saying what's next? What shall we pretend today?

I had safely survived all of these years being the best girl, good girl. I was the one you could count on no matter what you needed. I was the one that proved to you that the world was a good world. I wanted to believe that there was no evil. All of my life, I took a slight detour around the corner to Imagination Avenue, down the street from Pretend Circle. It had worked for so long, deferring to others, proving my worth and performing a well meaning act of resilience covered with butter cream frosting. But now, I was turning 60 and could no longer act as though I was a victim of anything. I had to start wearing the big girl shoes, my mirror told me so. I didn't recognize myself as I looked into the mirror and saw a tired lady whose smile is weary, whose heart is no longer on her sleeve, whose mind has put out a no vacancy sign. There was no longer room to maneuver anything in my reality. I had become what I always feared. I was a lonely, isolated, single older woman. I felt that no one needed me and no one cared.

One day months earlier I awoke in the middle of the night and heard a woman screaming on the street outside of my apartment. She was shouting and crying the way a woman does who is being harmed. I threw on my jogging pants and t-shirt and ran downstairs out the door, across to the other side of the street where I found a middle aged woman, lying on the sidewalk. Tears flowed and words hardly spoken dripping down her face with mangled meaning.

"He threw me out of the taxi, he hurt me, and he told me to get out. I fell on my back, it hurts, please help me." She moaned and writhed in pain. I leaned over her and tried to help her, but she didn't respond to me, it was as though I wasn't there. She looked right through me, and I suddenly thought that she was in some form of dementia. I asked her where she lived and there was no response. Whatever words she mumbled were partly nonsense as she repeated that it hurt and that she did not want to live, to let her die, to go away and let her die, alone, without meaning. I knew the language. It was broken English. I did not know what to do, other than call the police and have them take her where it was that they took someone in this condition.

I saw something that scared me. She was a woman alone, crying in the street, harmed by a man, frightened of her fate. The police came and took her away and I was left alone sitting on a bench in the street. Silence sat heavily beside me and I wondered how she got that way. After a few minutes, I went back to my apartment back into my still warm bed and fell asleep.

I never thought about it again until I was in a similar state of fear. Now I understand what fuels our crazy, what reaches our mad, irreversibly mad mind and tears it apart until it is just little pieces of the past, nonsense that finally takes over without our permission.

That feeling made me afraid to go on living alone without love, without someone who cared about me and wanted to share my life, hold me in the night and make me know I was not alone without love. There was more than just the bag lady syndrome to fear. Living longer than your money, being broke and hungry and homeless was worse if you had no one to love and no one who loved you. It was the lonely old spinster lady syndrome. We all knew one, an old aunt that we couldn't argue with at Christmas dinner because she was one clown short of a circus with her crazy outfits and stupid ideas about her importance in a world that no longer cared about her. It was the fear of being irrelevant, unimportant, the need to belong somehow.

So Johnny saw that dim light of self love that could guide him into where it hurt, where I was weak, where I was unable to say no. I finally admitted to myself that there was no romance in what happened to me, there was only injury by force, a broken life that he made me want to end when he did what psychopaths do. Johnny would tell you that he could dance on a dime and you would believe him. His lies had cleverly ended the dream and made my life a nightmare that I could not exit, not until I had paid for every moment of pleasure, every glimpse of a dream come true. I was three years post Johnny now. I had to learn to walk alone no matter how far there was to go to get to my real life, the stage of life I had been avoiding.

These moments were not a rehearsal, not a play, they were real. There was no way to dim the lights to make me look better. My life before Johnny would never come back and pick me up and brush off the dirt off my soul. His forsaken soul had covered me in shame. There was no energy to think of anything but survival. I worked. I fixed what I could and asked God to fix the rest. There were parts of me that I thought even He could not replace, parts of me the devil stole that I would never get back. So I gave up on believing that I could change the ending, make myself happy again. I just wanted to survive and so I became a Survivor of Attempted Murder by a Narcissist Psychopath, like Jane in chapter 4 of the last self help book I read. Day by day, however slow, my progress made me grateful to be alive. I began to smell the pure sweetness of the air after the rain, see the rainbow as a sign that better days were coming, waiting ahead for me around the corner if I could just hold on.

Then one day Suzie brought it all back, just like that the danger was there again as though it was the day I left Johnny. It was January 2014. I was sitting in her condo in Delray Beach, waiting for her to get ready for the short drive to Ocean Avenue, corner Atlantic. We were heading for a carefree day at the beach. It was a beautiful warm day with a breeze that made your hair dance in the wind. We got ready to drive there in her antique Jag, top down, smiles ready for the looks that came our way every time we drove in it. Navy blue canvas removable top panels on a sleek, low white body, it had a V12 engine, with the sexiest purr a car could ever make. For years it led us to the adventure, places and people just like a beloved companion.

Suddenly Suzie looked at me and said, "You should get Johnny to sign that paper for a tax deduction for everything he stole from you. You know he said he would. You need the money. Just do it, just call him. Here's the phone, I'll dial his number."

I looked at her and said "No way, I can't go there. Please don't do that, you have no idea what will happen, Suzie. Johnny is a dangerous man in a dangerous world that I can't go back to not even for a minute, not even for a second, not ever."

She stared at me and smiled that smile that means she didn't hear a word, "I'll call him, I'll meet him, I am not afraid of anybody."

Before you knew it she had him on the phone and was laughing hello, smiling as though it was an old friend, saying "Ok, I will meet you in half an hour." I sat there and a cold chill gathered in my spine as I felt that old feeling. "Give me the paper, I know you can print it up, use my computer. Let's go I will get you your signature and it will be finished, fini, done."

I said no a thousand times, but it was no use. So I went to the computer and logged in and was looking for the form when the door slammed shut. I heard Suzie's car start and she drove away. I ran to the window and Suzie was gone.

The phone rang and I answered it not thinking and the voice said "Hello" and I sank sitting down on the edge of the chair and it was him. Johnny.

He said, "Hello, who's this?"

I said." It's Brigitte". I should have hung up.

"Why are you callin' me, Brigitte? What are you doin' callin' me Brigitte?"

I sat there deaf mute, frozen unto myself, terrorized by the voice that could reach into my guts and make my insides turn upside, down and inside out. I felt as though someone had hit me in the gut with a sucker punch, the kind you get when you aren't looking, the kind you can't fight back from.

"I didn't call you," said a tiny little girl inside me.

"You need ta stop callin' me, if yer not comin' back where you belong. You either need to claim yer husband, git back where yer supposed to be. If not, then you need to stay away from me Brigitte, or you'll come to a bad end." He held my mind at gunpoint with those words that reminded me of the danger that was Johnny.

"Johnny don't threaten me, I will call the police." I spoke slowly as though they were the first words I ever said in my life.

"I'm not afraid of you anymore." I blurted.

There was a silence between us that made me recall the day he had me on my knees, picking up all of the things that I had in my purse. It was a flashback to a moment in which he seemed so big and tall and dangerous and I felt so small and vulnerable. I could just imagine what he looked like, thinking, as a robot that needed to search the data bank of what to do next. I heard the process that was Johnny wondering if it was worth it to engage in more drama with me. Would he get anything valuable out of it?

"Baby, you know that every woman I have ever been with has been better off after bein' with me, I've always left them better off, always..." He waited for my response, holding his breath until I spoke.

"Really Johnny, you know that for a fact? Am I am better off since being with you and having my money stolen, having you cheat on me, having you plan to kill me? You told me you would take a bullet for me when really all you ever wanted was my money? But you took more than that Johnny; you took my heart and soul, my dreams, my life. Was Amy better off after you, was Ronnie, and was Tonia? Yes Johnny, I know all about you, what you really are. You are a dangerous psychopath, an old gigolo, a sick man with no heart, no soul, no conscience and I never want to hear your voice again."

A feeling came over me, a sense of partial closure. I hung up the phone and sat there so sick to my stomach, as though I was still there next to him as he decided what to do next. But it was over.

Suzie ran back into the condo. "I forgot the paper, what's wrong; you're white as a ghost, what happened." She stood there, half in half out, and I said "forget it

Suzie, don't you put yourself in danger, he just called
here looking for you and I answered, and he threatened
me and I just can't..."

"Oh, lala, stop it, give me the phone" and she dialed
back the last caller and it started.

"Allo, Johnny, please, can I speak to Johnny?' She
smiled at me with that funny face she makes when
there is a challenge. Suddenly that look was gone and
she frowned and said, "Who are you and why are you
answering Johnny's phone? Give me Johnny; I have
to meet with him so give him the phone. Oh, you are
so classy, Johnny found himself a real classy girl. Get
off the phone and give Johnny the phone. Are you
threatening me? Don't you threaten me? No, Brigitte
will not speak with you." The phone went dead. Suzie
looked at me in shock.

"My God, these people are crazy, threatening me,
saying I won't last the day. I want to go to the police,
to the FBI; I want to make a complaint, right now. You
cannot threaten people like that." She stared at me and
I felt as though I was watching a movie. I knew the
beginning and I knew the end. For someone who wasn't
afraid of anyone, her face sure looked white, drained of
blood, wondering what hit her.

She insisted that she wanted to report the woman.
I was sure it was Rhonda. I had no intention of ever
seeing her face to face. I wanted nothing to do with
crazy Rhonda with the cuts all over her body. Still, I
drove Suzie to the police station and then to the FBI.
I watched as she filed a complaint. I watched as the

Sheriff and then the FBI told her the same thing they told me. "Just send the information to this number and we will look into it." Here we go again, the same guy, same smile, same chair, same table and the same door. I took a deep breath, held back my tears and I looked into Eric, the FBI agent's eyes. It took all of my energy to say what I had to say.

"I already spent six months of my life sending you everything, risking my life, showing you who Johnny's next victim would be and it happened and you did nothing. He almost killed a woman and he's out there without anybody stopping him, so what's different now? This man is a four time felon with two identities, one a Witness Protection Identity with its own Social Security Number, with hundreds of violations, dozens of arrests. You want me to go back over everything he has done for the last 30 years for you again?" I knew that this office had a bottomless pit into which these papers would fall, never to be seen again.

"C'mon Suzie, let's go" as I closed the door behind us and took back our ID's.

I told her, "Suzie, I love you, but you need to let this go. I need to let this go. There is no justice for us here. Give it to God and walk away. It's too dangerous to start over and start giving them all the same info, hoping they do something. They don't care, they never will. There are guns and there are bullets and there are the holes made with them and that is justice here. No one cares, so let it be. No matter what Johnny does, no one will ever arrest him. He is invisible, untouchable, a rat, an informant with no soul and nothing will ever happen to him, so let it go. Please, go on with your life, I know I have gone on with mine. I can't go back there and I never will."

When does one go from victim to survivor? I still stood on the corner of I *love him so much I can't live without him* and *I would die for him*. I needed to cross the street to the other side. That intersection was my way out to the other side of my life, the life I wanted to live now. Yes, I was ashamed that, as a professional in the world of finance, educated and experienced, at an age that labeled me as worldly, the lonely girl inside me had given Johnny the PIN number to my precious life accounts. I gave him my heart, trusted him with loans, given him cash to put down payments on houses, and all I had to show for it was a pile of credit and tax debts with interest compounding like a bad migraine.

But here I was again, knocking on the wrong door at the wrong time in the wrong place. The FBI was not going to change anything that they were doing. They had no interest in this kind of crime. Neither did the Marshall's office that was responsible for WitSec members. I was just going to get angrier and angrier and it was only damaging me. The agents and cops went home to their families and played with their dogs and kids and thought nothing of leaving me hanging out to dry. It was just a job to them but to me it was my life. My final attempt to get justice was to re-contact the US Federal Marshals Service and they told me to send the facts in by mail and that they would read the information and get back to me in six to eight weeks. Three months later I called back to find out they had no file and they were just a call centre and had no information at all on file regarding my complaint. I was not surprised. I finally called them again and they stated that they would neither confirm nor deny knowing who he was, what he was or where he was. They stated that they did not provide immunity to anyone.

Part of the anger of the citizens of the United States of America was the injustice in the justice system. There was none. The only way to get justice was to hope that a vigilante or angry husband, son or brother would decide that Johnny was going to stop harming women. Although I knew it would happen one day, that he would hurt the wrong woman, it hurt to think that all of the women who were his victims would never know what Johnny's justice would be. Every woman was left with no closure, no realization of any justice. This applied to many crimes. Many Americans were tired of waiting for justice.

Enough was enough. I knew what I had to do. I knew how to do it. It was just a matter of time. Everything is just a matter of time. I had everything to lose if I kept going on the path of most resistance. I had done everything I could do. Life was too short for this to go on and on. Although I had promised God I would one day take care of someone whom no one else wanted, Johnny was beyond my reach. Nothing I could do would make him stop what he was doing. Now I was going to let go and let God do the rest. I had the opportunity to walk away and I was taking it. I had to let it be.

Sometimes letting go of the smallest thing was so hard to do. Holding a half full glass for a couple of minutes was okay, holding on to it for an hour would be difficult, but holding it for a day was impossible. I had been holding on to this pain for three years and it was dragging me down, so low, so heavy, so full of sorrow. It was time. It was time to admit that I had to live with the consequences and no one could live my life for me. What happened to me had started to become what I was and so I had to move on. I took the paper with IC3.gov written on it and I knew I had to let it go. I crunched it up into a ball and threw it in the gutter along with the hate and sorrow I had held onto for so long.

Tomorrow was another day. I was not going to waste it on the past. The future was in the sunshine, the warm ocean breeze on Flagler Drive, the wind blowing through my hair as we drove away. A song was playing about how someone we used to love becomes just someone we used to know. I understood the message. It made me realize that Johnny wasn't someone I wanted in my life. I didn't need his drama. I wanted him to be just someone that I used to know. The song ran through my mind over and over again. Yes, that was what I wanted to think, that he was far away and long ago.

Was I free of Johnny? No. I will never be. Like alcohol to an alcoholic, I would have done anything for just a sip of him and still could. Johnny is my disease, a disease that can debilitate me on any day, strike me at any time. With what I knew that day about the system that protected him and the lawless phenomenon that was Romeo Fraud, I was able to bring my mind back to the truth. My truth was not Johnny's truth. I had to separate the illusion that was Johnny from my fight for justice, a fight that would make me confront and fight the attachment I had to him every single day. As long as I tried to get Johnny to face the consequences of the crimes he had committed against me and other women, I was stuck in his life and it had sucked all of my energy out of me trying to make his life legal. So it was time to choose. It was his world or mine. Johnny had used my ideals against me, using my compassion to get his way.

I had to decide once and for all and I did.

I made a vow that day never to go back to the police or the FBI or any law enforcement agency about Johnny ever again. This time it would be my justice that would come from my world that would settle this once and for all. They say that revenge was a plate best served cold and maybe one day I would get mine. But for now I made a promise to abandon my fight for justice. One day he would face the ultimate justice, a justice that I had no control over, a justice that would one day be the death of him. He had made too many enemies, broken too many lives.

My decision to let go of the madness made me feel free.

I was free.

I was finally free.

Although I had big deals in the making, waiting to pay me hundreds of thousands of dollars just like old times, my cash flow was hurting and I had no choice but to sell my condo in Delray Beach. It held only bad memories now, and when I went there, I had a hard time getting over the memory of what I thought were the good times with Johnny. The only thing that could get me over it was to move on, find a new place to visit and it couldn't be here in Florida anymore. My deals with Johnny had ruined my business plan to buy and refinish and sell cheap condos to Snowbirds so I decided to move on and never look back. Johnny was slowing down in the past and I was speeding away from him. I sped away until he was just a small dot in the tunnel of my past, a miniscule black dot that I could hardly see.

Shortly after, I packed my belongings after I sold my condo and was leaving Florida for good. It was the best thing I could do to forget everything that happened to me. As I packed the fragile objects in the kitchen, I saw a familiar face in a story written by a reporter. On the front page of the newspaper that I was using, I saw a picture of a very sad black woman sitting in a wheelchair with her leg cut off at the knee. Her lower leg and foot were missing. It was Taneisha. I remembered how she and Johnny had laughed at me and called me bowlegged. I remember how she robbed me of time with my husband, taking his sexual desires and feeding them while I worked like a dog to pay the bills and her salary. I sat there reading the article, thinking how unlucky she was. I read that Taneisha had gotten sick, had surgery on her leg and caught MRSA. Her life was a mess, and she wanted a less violent place to raise her son so she had left Riviera Beach and was now in West Palm Beach. She was asking for public donations and living on welfare, saying that she had no money for Christmas presents for her son.

Somewhere in the back of my mind and heart, I felt that I had to be grateful to her and thank her one day. Somehow I wanted to believe that she was like an angel that God sent me that day to get me away from Johnny. For a minute, I thought of sending her some money to help her and maybe someday I would, but right then and there I just wondered whose son it was and I threw the paper in the garbage.

I packed my suitcases in the car and sent the moving truck with all that I wanted to keep. Then I came back upstairs to do a final walk through of the condo and as I left, I turned back and looked inside at the place I once called home, a place where I had fallen in love with Johnny and I felt a heavy sorrow that was so dark in my heart. It took all of my strength, but I walked away and closed the door forever, closed the door on Johnny, on all of the dreams that would never come true.

I made my way to the airport and told myself there were other places to see, other beaches to snorkel, other adventures waiting for me if I just left the past behind. So I had come to the end of my saga with Johnny. I prayed that I would never see him again as my plane climbed into the blue sky. I hoped that I would never have to think about him or the danger he had brought into my life ever again.

AFTERMATH

Out of evil can come good. The only feelings that I had left for Johnny had been magnified tenfold by the danger that escorted them out of my heart. I had ignored the instinctive knowledge that he was not what he presented himself to be so I paid the ultimate price. While my heart was open in compassion, Johnny put his foot in the door and presented me with a complete package of love, sex, companionship and dreams that would finally come true. It was all lies. I had never before known true evil. After Johnny, I learned to believe in it. In the experience of romantic intimacy, I had let a con artist into my life. I was not by far the only victim of his game of survival. It made it somewhat easier to understand that this was the way that Johnny survived since his prison years. He was never able to vote, carry a gun, never again held a decent job so he stole from women to survive.

The crime represented here does not get detected by border inspection. It is global. Through the internet of the new world, access is provided to any criminal whose intention is to harm you, steal your money, break your heart and leave you penniless. Every lonely grandmother, every saddened mother and innocent daughter are available online, posting their pictures, habits and travel plans. How easy is it to set a trap, knowing ahead of time what your target likes to eat, wear, listen to, and travel to. A crime that dates back centuries is now facilitated through technology.

Johnny's entire world was out of compliance. He saw nothing wrong with finding new prey online and promising them the salvation of his love. He would post lies and profess adoring love to women who were as helpless as a fawn captured in the headlights of not one car, but stuck in a traffic jam of emotion and sensual revelation. Few women were a match for his darkness. There was no ritual that could heal Johnny. He was a fallen angel that fornicated his way to riches that did not belong to him. Everything he took from innocent women was stained with evil. I wondered how many souls he corrupted. How many young women did he convince to sell their bodies for him? Even if I had known the depths to which he would go to capture what he wanted, I did not have the power to reconcile his fate. I failed to make him stop serving the devil. I never knew that this kind of soul existed.

I failed in my commitment to love him for better or for worse, till death do I part. I had little comfort in the certainty that I was not the only woman unable to resist his strategy. I found more comfort knowing I had done everything humanly possible to stop him from delivering his soul to the devil when he died. So I let go. Part of me died when I did this. I lost my belief that God could fix everything anytime. Even when my mother died when I was only twelve, I still had faith that God had a purpose for me, a reason for leaving me alone in the world. I thought when I found Johnny, I was no longer alone. It was the opposite. Johnny had made me feel lonely even when he was with me because he wasn't really there for me. That is the worst kind of love. After Johnny, sometimes I have felt so alone that returning to his side seemed it would be a better fate than being in this state of separation from a destiny I had welcomed. That is the incredible power that loving a psychopath has over your life.

After Johnny's devastating departure from my life, I found solace in writing this book. I found peace in nature. Like a salmon swimming upstream to lay eggs in its birth place, I sought out my original purpose in my life. I returned to the place that I once called home. I worked relentlessly to regain the spiritual strength that had carried me so far in my life.

I regained access to my feelings. That led to renewed access to my intuition. That gave me a chance to trust myself again. With these baby steps came a better vision. I developed my perception of the energy that people carry into your life. I wanted only positive and pure energy.

I started my journey by renting an oceanfront cottage with a promise to myself to become self sufficient. I grew my own fruit and vegetables in a garden that overlooked the bluffs that graced the ocean. I watched the changes in the sky that sometimes matched my moods. It was an endless playground for whales and dolphins. I let a dog and cat adopt me and learned from them to trust my feelings again, become vulnerable to receiving love and affection again. My pets taught me that survival includes bonding with an energy that comes from surrounding yourself with positive interactions. I had met an new man, Kenneth, who was a retired army man who worked in counterintelligence. His honesty and devotion showed me what a good friend a true man could be. He led me out of the darkness into the sunlight with his kindess and friendship.

I was finally at peace with myself. The equilibrium I had lost had resumed somewhat and sometimes I woke up mornings just happy to be alive. The collateral damage was disappearing and over time I changed into a better person.

The last step was to forgive. I had to admit my failure to respect myself enough not to fool myself ever again. Once I forgave myself, I found the compassion to forgive Johnny. It was much easier to let go of him with both hands. There was no upside to continuing to love him. There was no purpose to remembering anything he said or did. I was a quantum leap away from ever believing in his voice ever again.

As I watch the sunset, I remember how close I came to losing my life. So it began to make sense that I close the door in my mind to that room in which I stored all of the facts, truths, evidence, pictures of my life with Johnny. I no longer needed the proof of that time so long ago when I nearly lost my future to a man who had no noble purpose whatsoever.

I burnt it all in a bonfire one night during a full moon. His cards with words of love that baited the need I had in me for another, the other, the missing half of my lonely soul. The crackling sounds in the burning of all of my worldly ties to him found their way up into night sky, laden with stars that made me feel so small. Our world was full of so much more than my suffering. I was healed.

There was no longer any evidence around me to remind me that once upon a time I thought I found my Prince Charming. I was a broken angel that learned to fly with one broken wing. I believed that I had fulfilled the promise I had made to God. I was safely in God's grace again.

The devil had finally lost his grip on my soul. I was free.